MW00356061

INCLUSIVE EDUCATION

STORIES OF SUCCESS AND HOPE IN A CANADIAN CONTEXT

INCLUSIVE EDUCATION

STORIES OF SUCCESS AND HOPE IN A CANADIAN CONTEXT

KIM CALDER STEGEMANN
Thompson Rivers University

ANGELA AUCOIN
Université de Moncton

Editorial Director: Claudine O'Donnell
Acquisitions Editor: Kimberley Veevers
Marketing Manager: Michelle Bish
Senior Program Manager: John Polanszky
Project Manager: Susan Johnson
Developmental Editor: Katherine Goodes
Production Services: Cenveo® Publishing Services
Permissions Project Manager: Shruti Jamadagni

Photo Permissions Research: iEnergizer Aptara Inc.
Text Permissions Research: iEnergizer Aptara Inc.
Interior Designer: iEnergizer Aptara Inc.
Cover Designer: Anthony Leung
Cover Image: Shutterstock
Vice-President, Cross Media and Publishing Services: Gary Bennett

Pearson Canada Inc., 26 Prince Andrew Place, Don Mills, Ontario M3C 2T8.

Copyright © 2018 Pearson Canada Inc. All rights reserved.

Printed in the United States of America. This publication is protected by copyright, and permission should be obtained from the publisher prior to any prohibited reproduction, storage in a retrieval system, or transmission in any form or by any means, electronic, mechanical, photocopying, recording, or otherwise. For information regarding permissions, request forms, and the appropriate contacts, please contact Pearson Canada's Rights and Permissions Department by visiting **www.pearsoncanada.ca/contact-information/permissions-requests.**

Attributions of third-party content appear on the appropriate page within the text.

PEARSON is an exclusive trademark owned by Pearson Canada Inc. or its affiliates in Canada and/or other countries.

Unless otherwise indicated herein, any third party trademarks that may appear in this work are the property of their respective owners and any references to third party trademarks, logos, or other trade dress are for demonstrative or descriptive purposes only. Such references are not intended to imply any sponsorship, endorsement, authorization, or promotion of Pearson Canada products by the owners of such marks, or any relationship between the owner and Pearson Canada or its affiliates, authors, licensees, or distributors.

If you purchased this book outside the United States or Canada, you should be aware that it has been imported without the approval of the publisher or the author.

978-0-13-418413-5

2   17

Library and Archives Canada Cataloguing in Publication

Stegemann, Kim J. Calder, 1960-, author
     Inclusive education : stories of success and hope in a Canadian context / Kim Calder Stegemann (Thompson Rivers University), Angela AuCoin (Université de Moncton).—First edition.

Includes bibliographical references and index.
ISBN 978-0-13-418413-5 (paperback)

     1. Inclusive education—Canada—Textbooks. I. AuCoin, Angela, 1968-, author II. Title.

LC1203.C3S74 2017   371.9'0460971   C2016-905782-8

Meet the Authors

Dr. Calder Stegemann is an associate professor at Thompson Rivers University teaching in the School of Education. She has been a general and special education teacher in both public and private settings, worked as a consultant for school districts, and provided professional development opportunities across western Canada. For the last 20 years she has been an instructor at Thompson Rivers University, sharing her expertise with both pre- and in-service teachers. She has taught and presented nationally and internationally. Her research interests include inclusive and special education, interventions for reading and math disabilities, teacher dispositions and teacher education admission procedures, and most recently, educational neuroscience. Her most recent publication is a co-authored module for the Pearson Teacher Education Series titled *Students at Risk in the Classroom*.

Dr. AuCoin is an associate professor at la Faculté des sciences de l'éducation de l'Université de Moncton. She began her career as a teacher. Her passion for inclusive education developed when she started working with students of different cognitive and physical abilities as a resource teacher in the Northwest Territories. In 2012, she co-authored with Gordon Porter (C.M., O.N. B) a report on inclusive education in New Brunswick, *Strengthening Inclusion, Strengthening Schools*. She has since worked province-wide with principals and resource teachers to implement the recommendations of their report. Her research interests deal with inclusive leadership, policies, and pedagogical strategies.

Case and Commentary Authors

CASE AUTHORS

Dr. Sheila Bennett is a professor at Brock University and works in the area of policy and practical issues in the field. She is the former chair in the Department of Teacher Education.

Kathy Howery is a PhD candidate at the University of Alberta and an educational consultant.

Dr. Jennifer Katz is an assistant professor at the University of British Columbia and the author of "Teaching to diversity: The three block model of universal design for learning" and "Resource teacher: A changing role in the three-block model of UDL."

Dr. Kimberly Maich is an associate professor at Brock University's Department of Teacher Education, affiliated with the Centre for Applied Disability Studies, and the chair of Social Science Research Ethics Board.

Sheri Mallabar is a postgraduate student at Brock University's Department of Teacher Education.

Sophie Pitre-Boudreau is a vice-principal in an elementary school of New Brunswick's district scolaire francophone du nord-est and a former student services inclusion coordinator for the Department of Education and Early Childhood Development.

Maureen Sabin is a retired special education coordinator at the Huron-Perth Catholic District School Board.

Dr. Steve Sider is an assistant professor at Wilfrid Laurier University and a board member of the Comparative and International Education Society of Canada.

Monique Somma is a PhD student in Educational Studies at Brock University.

Nan Stevens is a teacher educator in the School of Education at Thompson Rivers University and a doctoral student at the University of Calgary.

Gabrielle Vienneau is an elementary teacher in Moncton, New Brunswick and a former student at Université de Moncton.

COMMENTARY AUTHORS

Dr. Angela AuCoin, Université de Moncton

Dr. Sheila Bennett, Brock University

Dr. Kim Calder Stegemann, Thompson Rivers University

Denise Hook, University of Victoria

Dr. Nancy Hutchinson, Queen's University

Dr. Donna McGhie-Richmond, University of Victoria

Dr. Nadia Rousseau, Université du Québec à Trois-Rivières

Monique Somma, Brock University

Dr. Jacqueline Specht, University of Western Ontario

Dr. Gabrielle Young, Memorial University

I would like to dedicate this book to those people who light up my life every day—my husband Karl, my children Arthur, Stephanie, and Caitlin, and my mother Lou. Thank you for being my cheerleaders!

– Kim

I dedicate this book to Lauren, Marco, Leonardo, and Maximilian, whose stories inspire me to become a better educator.

– Angela

Thank you to all contributors and commentators who were kind enough to share their vision of inclusive education with us. Most importantly, we extend deep appreciation for all of the students who have blessed us with their presence in our classrooms. We have learned so much from you about acceptance and the beauty of the human experience.

– Kim and Angela

Brief Contents

Contents

Foreword

This book is needed to point public education to a place where inclusion is no longer considered a "critical area" of controversy in our schools. Let's hope this book, and others like it (along with much improved teacher education programs in our universities), will make this possible.

My teacher education program did not prepare me for the challenges of the diverse classroom that we find in today's schools. In the 1960s, special education was a minor "sideshow" of public education, not at all the "main attraction." It was about children and youth who were not seen in public school classrooms and who were served—if at all—on the periphery, in segregated schools and classrooms or in some cases, large, residential institutions. This included children with intellectual disabilities, physical disabilities, and multiple disabilities.

At the time, it was not uncommon for 50–75 percent of primary school students to fail to complete high school. My age cohort in a small rural high school in New Brunswick had 11 of 42 grade 6 students graduate six years later in 1964. They fell by the wayside for as many reasons as you might imagine: poverty, learning disabilities, behaviour challenges, inflexible and highly academic curriculum, rigid teaching practices, literacy problems, and more. These students had to make it in the regular school program or find the exit door and be gone!

It is no surprise that this system was considered a very "Darwinian" environment. Then things changed.

In Canada, the adoption of the *Charter of Rights and Freedoms* in 1982 and the coming into effect of the equality provisions in 1985 amounted to the bugle call for action. Educators were challenged to make schools work for most, if not all, children and youth. Many accepted this challenge and started to introduce changes and innovations. Things have not been the same since.

That is not to say equality—and inclusion—have been fully achieved in our schools. Far from it! However, the segregation game has been named for what it is: a failure to build a public education system with the commitment and capacity to serve ALL of our children.

Today, Ministries of Education in Canada are committed to equality and inclusion. Many would contend they have been less than vigorous in ensuring implementation of inclusion in local school districts. It certainly is a "work in progress," depending on the province/territory or region of the country you look at. However, I believe the tipping point has been reached and inclusion is a reality in increasing numbers of classrooms in every jurisdiction in Canada, from east to west and north to south.

That's why this book is so important. The stories and experiences found in these pages are what we need to set the stage for further progress. We need teacher education programs in our universities that prepare their graduates for the reality of today's classrooms.

And those classrooms are defined by **diversity**—diversity in the academic, social, cultural, and development needs of the students. That's a reality and it will not go away. This is not a temporary trend or experiment. It is the result of the fundamental commitment to equality and inclusion that the *Charter* brought to our communities in 1982. International undertakings, including the United Nations Convention on the Rights of Persons with Disabilities (Article 24), are another pillar of this new reality. I was privileged to attend the meeting of the General Assembly in New York when Canada, and dozens of other countries, signed the Convention in 2007.

Inclusive education is about removing barriers to school success for all of our children in their neighbourhood or community school. Inclusive education is not just a meshing of general and special education systems. It is about creating something new that meets the aspirations we have for 21st century public education.

A few final thoughts

Inclusive education is about the curriculum and support systems that make the public education classroom a place of learning and success for children and youth—*all of them.*

Teachers have one major responsibility: to think of their students in a positive way. Every child can learn and every student can be successful. When a student doesn't have the success considered appropriate, the teacher needs to consider and enact strategies to improve instruction through differentiated instructional methods, adjusted learning outcomes, utilization of alternative assessment approaches, and models like "Universal Design for Learning" and "Response to Intervention." These and other approaches will enhance and improve the success of both students and teachers.

While students may indeed have diverse needs, they must not be considered defective or deficient. None of them are exactly alike. They are all different, just as different as their teachers. We must respect and accommodate their differences.

While inclusion means that today's teachers have to meet a challenging mandate, it places a similar mandate on the school system itself. The supports provided by public education must reflect the needs of teachers as well as the students they serve. To put it simply, teachers need support.

Even the most experienced and proficient teacher will at times find a circumstance when the path forward is not clear. In a practical sense that means that general education teachers will receive the professional assistance of experienced and knowledgeable "support teachers" with whom they can actively collaborate to create solutions to instructional issues.

Teachers also need on-going professional learning opportunities and as important as anything else, they need time and opportunity to jointly plan and problem solve with other teachers in their school. Effective school systems invest in capacity building for their staff.

The inclusive school is one that can effectively support the success of both teachers and students. The stories and experiences shared in this book provide the context for meeting this challenge.

Gordon L. Porter, C.M., O.N.B.
Director of Inclusive Education Canada

Preface

Inclusive education is both an *ideal* and a *process*, and is consistent with the Canadian imperative of a multicultural and pluralistic society. Realizing this vision, however, is less straightforward. This text is intended to highlight how inclusion is *operationalized* for students with *various learning needs* in different educational jurisdictions across Canada. Much has been written about the problems and challenges associated with inclusive education; this text will take a different perspective. Rather than focusing on what is not working, each case study in this text will highlight how each member of the educational team works together to create a successful inclusive experience. All of the cases are of "real" students, families, administrators, and educators. As such, none are perfect examples of inclusive education. These cases do, however, demonstrate the types of beliefs, attitudes, knowledge, and skills that are required in order to optimize the learning experiences of all children, and in particular those with unique learning needs.

This text presents nine in-depth case studies of children, youth, and young adults who have unique learning needs. The cases are diverse in terms of age of the students, level of functioning, and geographical location. The topic grid at the beginning of each chapter identifies the key concepts or main attributes for that chapter. Each case is comprised of a brief introduction followed by the "voices" of various members of the educational team, including the students themselves (in some cases), peers, parents, general and special education teachers, teaching assistants, principals, counsellors, and therapists. Artifacts are presented whenever possible, including individual educational plans, psycho-educational reports, and student work. Each case study begins with learning outcomes and a Fast Facts box describing the exceptionality and its key characteristics, and provides questions to consider, definitions for key terms, and useful websites following the case. In cases where DSM-IV categories were used in original diagnosis and documents, we have also included the DSM-5 terms.

The first three chapters of the text lay the foundation for the case studies that follow. Chapter 1 provides an overview of inclusive education, discussing the definition (we are using the UNESCO 2005 definition), general purposes, and goals. This chapter also includes direct quotes from those who are impacted in different ways by the process of inclusive education—a young adult with an intellectual disability, a university professor, a high school teacher, an educational assistant, and a superintendent. Chapter 2 provides a brief history of special and inclusive education, focusing primarily on the Canadian and US contexts. In Chapter 3, we introduce two fundamental frameworks—universal design for learning (UDL) and response to intervention (RTI).

Each case study also includes a commentary by a Canadian leader in the field of educational inclusion. The commentator will highlight for the reader the critical aspects of the case that support the philosophy of inclusive education. He or she will also analyze the case using the two theoretical frameworks that are introduced in Chapter 3—UDL and RTI.

Chapter 13 provides a summary of the case studies, highlighting common themes, successful strategies, and/or issues in practice. The commentaries are also summarized and key concepts are identified. The final chapter of the text, Chapter 14, presents the authors' thoughts about future directions for the practice and research of educational inclusion.

This text will provide pre- and in-service educators with a glimpse into the inclusive educational experience of real children and youth from across Canada who have unique learning needs, providing hope and a path to enhanced educational opportunities in the future.

INSTRUCTOR'S MANUAL

An Instructor's Manual containing a variety of additional teaching resources is available for download from a password-protected section of Pearson Canada's online catalogue (catalogue.pearsoned.ca). Navigate to your book's catalogue page to view a list of those supplements that are available. See your local sales representative for details and access.

LEARNING SOLUTIONS MANAGERS

Pearson's Learning Solutions Managers work with faculty and campus course designers to ensure that Pearson technology products, assessment tools, and online course materials are tailored to meet your specific needs. This highly qualified team is dedicated to helping schools take full advantage of a wide range of educational resources, by assisting in the integration of a variety of instructional materials and media formats. Your local Pearson Education sales representative can provide you with more details on this service program.

Acknowledgments

We wish to thank the following reviewers who provided valuable feedback throughout the development of this book:

Carrie Dutkiwch, University of Regina

Tara Flanagan, McGill University

Jared French, University of Calgary

Sonja Grover, Lakehead University

Kathy Howery, University of Alberta

Linda Jones, Mohawk College

Nectaria Karagiozis, University of Ottawa

Breanna Lawrence, University of Victoria

Jacqueline Specht, Western University

Gregory R. Steeves, Crandall University

Angela Wilm, Lakeland College

Gabrielle Young, Memorial University of Newfoundland

David Young, St. Francis Xavier University

Chapter 1
Overview of Inclusive Education

Dr. Kim Calder Stegemann & Dr. Angela AuCoin

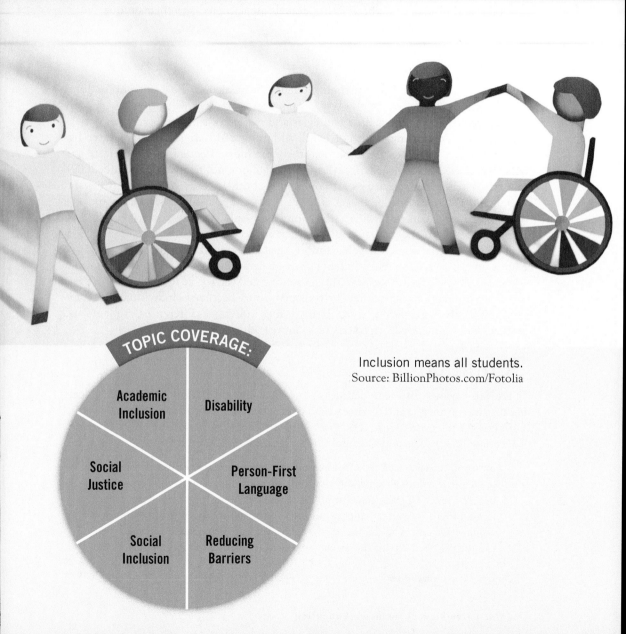

TOPIC COVERAGE:

- Academic Inclusion
- Disability
- Social Justice
- Person-First Language
- Social Inclusion
- Reducing Barriers

Inclusion means all students.
Source: BillionPhotos.com/Fotolia

The student will:

■ State the UNESCO definition of inclusive education

■ Explain the purpose of inclusive education for all members of the learning community

■ Describe how inclusive education relates to civil rights, and the creation of a fair and just society where all individuals are accepted and their unique strengths are celebrated

All educators want the best for their students, in particular those with exceptional learning needs. In the past, "the best" was often segregated settings with specially trained teachers using specialized strategies and materials. This approach was deficit-driven, however (Cochran-Smith & Dudley-Marling, 2012). In addition, research has proven that special education is not routinely the most effective way to educate students who have learning challenges (Porter, 2010; Zigmond, Kloo, & Volonino, 2009). In fact, based on their reviews of the literature, both Lindsay (2007) and Ruijs and Peetsma (2009) acknowledge that it is more beneficial for students with exceptional needs to be taught in the regular classroom. Not only do they perform better academically, research shows that they also have more friends and seem happier when included with other students. What's more, the latest research confirms that inclusive education is positive for ALL students both academically and socially (Prud'homme, Vienneau, Ramel, & Rousseau, 2011; Timmons & Wagner, 2010). Being social creatures, our interactions with others help shape who we become as individuals (Le Capitaine, 2012). By being part of a group that values individual differences, students and teachers will ultimately learn to co-create more inclusive societies.

Definition

There are various different definitions of inclusive education in Canada, largely because each province and territory has governance over education within its jurisdiction. For the purposes of this text, we are using the definition of the United Nations Educational, Scientific and Cultural Organization (UNESCO, 2005):

> Inclusion is seen as *a process* of addressing and responding to the diversity of needs of all learners through increasing participation in learning, cultures and communities, and reducing exclusion within and from education. It involves changes and modifications in content, approaches, structures and strategies, with a common vision which covers all children of the appropriate age range and a conviction that it is the responsibility of the regular system to educate all children. (p. 13)[*]

---

[*]From Guidelines for inclusion: Ensuring access to education for all. Published by UNESCO, © 2005.

Inclusion also means accessibility.
Source: Dan Race/Fotolia

We have chosen this definition for a number of reasons. First and foremost, we view inclusive education as a process and not a place. As we note in the opening paragraph, educators (and parents, too) want the best for their children, so that they will reach their fullest potential and grow up to be independent and healthy individuals, capable of contributing to society in their own unique way. The process is in finding better ways of meeting individual learner needs, which continually changes as we discover new technologies and create more equitable educational environments. Second, we believe that by reducing barriers to full participation in general education, we can reduce exclusion. That, too, takes creative problem solving, often initiating change within rigid school systems. Third, we believe that all children are capable of learning, and encourage parents and educators to hold high expectations for achievement of all students, whether disabled[1] or non-disabled (please see definition of **person-first language** below). It is the responsibility of the public school system to ensure these opportunities are available to all. Ultimately, by engaging in a process of inclusive education we hope to move towards a more just and compassionate society that includes and celebrates personal diversity.

Voices

Next, you will hear from five Canadians who are in some way involved in public education: a young adult with an intellectual disability, a university professor, a high school teacher, an educational assistant, and a superintendent. Each person provides a valuable perspective on the importance of providing inclusive educational experiences for all students.

---

[1] Disability is a contentious term, and though some prefer "challenged," we have included this wording in the text to parallel that used within the *Charter of Rights and Freedoms,* as well as other human rights regulations in Canada.

YOUNG ADULT MALE WITH A MILD INTELLECTUAL DISABILITY, URBAN NEW BRUNSWICK

"Classes need to be adapted so students with difficulties can be included. My years at the intermediate school were very difficult. I was pushed in the snow and left there. Some students shortened my crutches and left me alone to fix them. People made fun of me. Some asked if I wanted to smoke drugs with them. Others asked me at the age of 12 to have sex with them. It still hurts and I still struggle to get over it. In high school, things were different. My teachers took time to explain things to me. They taught me one thing at a time. I had friends.

To new teachers I would want to tell them to have patience and love us as we are. Even though we have special needs, nothing should prevent us from showing you how smart we are. We love to smile and we're always positive. It is not nice to be negative. We're always positive."

UNIVERSITY PROFESSOR, TROIS RIVIÈRES, QUÉBEC

"As a researcher, inclusive education represents countless occasions for me to work with different educational communities who strive to understand how their school can be transformed in a way that lets all students feel as though they belong, thus contributing to developing each student's full potential.

I associate numerous words to inclusive education: professional collaboration, creativity, unremitting reflection, gradual process of change, innovation, etc. Inclusion also speaks to me as a citizen. When I contribute to the development of the educational systems, I feel that I help establish societies that are more and more democratic, places where everyone has the possibility to become an important member of today's society."

HIGH SCHOOL TEACHER, ATLANTIC CANADA

"As a high school teacher, I believe that inclusion is the best way to teach students about courage, patience, compassion and perseverance. Inclusion brings about a win-win situation for everyone. The students who have greater challenges will have a better chance at improving if they can be among other students who can guide them or help them. Likewise, students have so much to gain by taking classes with others who don't give up or who remain positive in spite of their challenges. Inclusion helps us to recognize that we are all different and that it's our differences that add a little spice to our life. Wouldn't it be very boring if all our students talked the same, acted the same or had the same strengths? We have to stop seeing our students' differences in a negative light and start celebrating the fact that they are all unique individuals who deserve to learn together regardless of what they can or can't do."

NORTH SLAVEY EDUCATIONAL ASSISTANT, NORTHWEST TERRITORIES

"Inclusive Schooling is about everyone learning from everybody. I believe Inclusive Schooling has improved over time. We are moving in the right direction because acceptance and humility for each other and with each other, is the only way we can move forward for the wide range of students in our schools.

When I was a young child learning in a northern community, it was the hands on learning, opened minded teachers and the patience that helped me to see and experience. These things made me feel that school was a place for me and I had something to contribute. Not everyone has the same strengths. It is important for children to know that there is no judgment about their weaknesses. The most important message to a child of different races and abilities is to hear we all experience learning challenges and successes. Where I sit, when teachers enable support assistants and other staff to put ideas forward and be equal, valued members, students move forward."

SCHOOL SUPERINTENDENT, SOUTHERN ONTARIO

"As a superintendent of education, I believe that segregating students who have lagging skills is an issue of social justice. When any group of students is segregated, seen as the students in 'Room 109', identified by their disability first, not visible to peers and all staff in a school and not having access to all the opportunities that a school has to offer, such as extra-curricular activities, then there are inequitable social and academic outcomes which have lifelong implications for these learners and the broader community.

Inclusive education involves systemic change. The movement to an inclusive school system involves shifting the beliefs and practices of educators, support staff and peers. Principal leadership is an essential element in moving the change process forward with students, staff and families. It is not enough to move students from a segregated setting to a regular classroom. Students need to be included alongside their age-appropriate peers. All students need to be provided with rich learning opportunities by the classroom teacher. An inclusive education system recognizes that resources from the segregated model of service delivery need to be redistributed to support the staff within its schools.

Although we have made great progress related to student achievement in the province of Ontario, many students with developmental disabilities have not generally [been] represented in the provincial testing results. We need to look at students who have disabilities as capable learners. An inclusive school system sets high expectations for all learners and [provides] the necessary supports to ensure students and staff are successful.

An inclusive system offers a sense of belonging by moving the marginalized to the middle—creating a new normal—improving social and academic outcomes for all students."

SUMMARY

In the next chapters you will read about real students from across Canada. In each case, the educational environment was adjusted in some way in order to reduce barriers for participation. Some of these adjustments are physical, while others include teaching strategies or specialized technologies. Some of the cases are situated in rural settings, which can pose challenges for those students who require special community supports. However, you will note that we do not focus on the "place" as much as on how access and participation in general education has been adjusted to best meet the unique needs of each individual student. You will also notice that changes and adjustments are often ongoing, with programs being revised as the student grows and develops. It will become clear that the "process of inclusion is far more complex than simply placing students with disabilities in general education classrooms" (Ornelles, Cook, & Jenkins, 2007, p. 153).[†]

Whether you are preparing to become a teacher or you already are one, we hope that the cases presented in this book will provide you with a better understanding of both the philosophy and the practices associated with inclusive education. In today's classrooms, students and teachers across the country understand the importance for everyone to have access to quality education. Entire communities are working together to plan for effective learning to take place in high schools as well as in primary schools. But there is still a lot of work to be done! "Inclusive education is an unabashed announcement, a public and political declaration and celebration for difference… It requires continual proactive responsiveness to foster an inclusive educational culture" (Corbett & Slee, 2000, pp. 2–3). Together, let's make schools a better place for ALL students!

[†] From Middle School General Education Teachers' Perspectives on Including Students with Learning Disabilities by Cecily Ornelles, Lyssandra Cook and Amelia Jenkins from Journal of Learning Disabilities: A Multidisciplinary Journal 14(3):145-154, Published by Sagamore Publishing LLC, © 2007.

Key Terms

academic inclusion The purpose of including students with disabilities in the general education classroom is to increase academic achievement of all students.

person-first language It is often viewed as most appropriate to refer to individuals as people first, with the disability or challenge referenced second. For example, one would say "a child who has autism" versus "an autistic child."

social inclusion The purpose of including students with disabilities in the general education classroom is to enhance the social-emotional intelligence of all students and encourage the development of social networks between those with and without disabilities.

Questions to Consider

1. What is your definition of inclusive education? Is it directed solely at students with unique learning needs, or have you also included students from marginalized groups?

   _____

   _____

   _____

   _____

   _____

   _____

2. What do you think might be the social benefits (**social inclusion**) of including students with exceptional learning needs in the general education classroom? What might be the academic benefits (**academic inclusion**) for both students with and without disabilities?

_____

_____

_____

_____

_____

_____

3. Voices from individuals representing different interest groups were presented in this chapter. What message do they share?

_____

_____

_____

_____

_____

_____

4. If you had some physical or cognitive challenges, how would you prefer to be referred to? Why? Discuss how person-first language impacts our perceptions of individuals.

_____

_____

_____

_____

_____

_____

Useful Websites

Canadian Research Centre on Inclusive Education
www.inclusiveeducationresearch.ca

Exceptionality Education International
http://ir.lib.uwo.ca/eei

UNESCO on Inclusive Education
www.unesco.org/new/en/education/themes/strengthening-education-systems/inclusive-education

References

Cochran-Smith, M., & Dudley-Marling, C. (2012). Diversity in teacher education and special education: The issues that divide. *Journal of Teacher Education, 63*(4), 237–244.

Corbett, J., & Slee, R. (2000). An international conversation on inclusive education. In F. Armstrong, D. Armstrong, & L. Barton (Eds.), *Inclusive education: Policy, contexts and comparative perspectives* 1, 133–146. London, UK: David Fulton Publishing Ltd.

Le Capitaine, B. (2012). La socialization. In M. Mony & D. Malleval (Eds.), *Penser l'éducation avec la diversité. Étayer sa pratique professionnelle* (pp. 177–188). Lyon, France: Chronique Sociale.

Lindsay, G. (2007). Educational psychology and the effectiveness of inclusive education/mainstreaming. *British Journal of Educational Psychology, 77*, 1–24.

Ornelles, C., Cook, L., & Jenkins, A. (2007). Middle school general education teachers' perspectives on including students with learning disabilities. *Learning Disabilities, 14*(3), 145–154.

Porter, G. L. (2010). Making Canadian schools inclusive: A call to action. *Education Canada, 48*(2), 62–66.

Prud'homme, L., Vienneau, R., Ramel, S., & Rousseau, N. (2011). La légitimité de la diversité en éducation: réflexion sur l'inclusion. *Éducation et francophonie, 34*(2), 6–22.

Ruijs, N. M., & Peetsma, T. T. D. (2009). Effects of inclusion on students with and without special educational needs reviewed. *Educational Research Review, 4*(2), 67–79.

Timmons, V., & Wagner, M. (2010). *Inclusive education knowledge exchange initiative: An analysis of the Statistics Canada Participation and Activity Limitations survey, Final report.* Ottawa, ON: Canadian Council of Learning.

UNESCO. (2005). *Guidelines for inclusion: Ensuring access to education for all.* Paris, France: UNESCO. Retrieved from: http://unesdoc.unesco.org/images/0014/001402/140224e.pdf

Zigmond, N., Kloo, A., & Volonino, V. (2009). What, where, and how? Special education in the climate of full inclusion. *Exceptionality, 17*(4), 189–204.

Chapter 2
History of Inclusive Education

Dr. Angela AuCoin & Dr. Kim Calder Stegemann

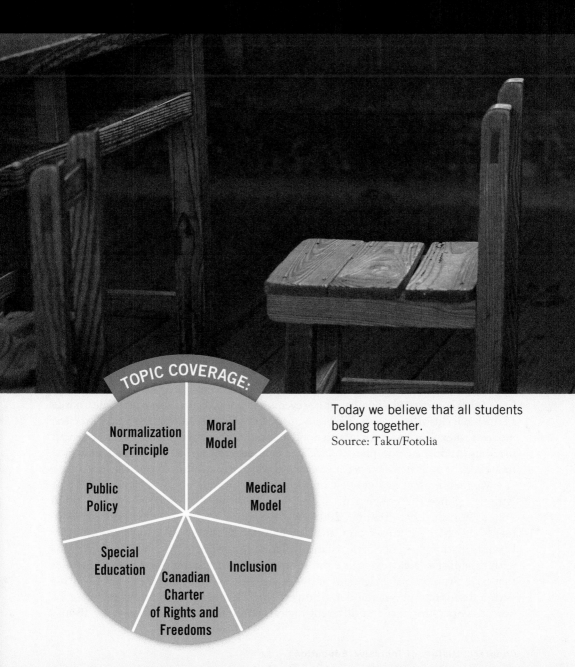

TOPIC COVERAGE:

- Normalization Principle
- Moral Model
- Public Policy
- Medical Model
- Special Education
- Inclusion
- Canadian Charter of Rights and Freedoms

Today we believe that all students belong together.
Source: Taku/Fotolia

The student will:

■ Understand the complex history of the treatment practiced on individuals with disabilities

■ Explain the contributions of community leaders, social advocates, and school personnel in the building of inclusive schools

■ Describe how history explains much of what is happening in today's society

Preamble

If inclusive education is becoming more common in Canadian schools, history shows that the road to get there has not been easy. Inclusive and special education has come a long way since the days of infanticide in the "Dark Ages." Historical accounts of societal perceptions and treatment of people with disabilities show progressive but overlapping tendencies (Winzer, 2006). Fortunately, most of the horrific measures that were practiced in the Middle Ages have long disappeared, but a careful examination of our current practices indicates that traces of former perceptions and attitudes still prevent disabled people from becoming an integral part of our society (De Grandmont, 2010; Mackelprang & Salsgiver, 2015). We think that a better understanding of these beliefs and behaviours will enable us to evaluate our own practices objectively, and progressively move towards actions that will invite individuals with disabilities to fully participate in our schools and communities.

There have been numerous significant events throughout history that have contributed to the development of special educational services for individuals with exceptional learning needs. Although influenced by international events and political movements, Canada has contributed a number of key events and public figures that have made Canada a leader in inclusive education. We begin this chapter by presenting the traditional societal models that explain how people with noticeable differences have been treated throughout the years (Middle Ages to present day). These models will provide us with a sociological framework to evaluate where we are today and what actions must now be taken.

We then present an overview of special education as it was developed in North America. Since the concept of special education was introduced in the United States (Winzer, 1990; Schlifer, 2005), we will discuss a few of those key developments that had an impact on Canadian schools. We then point out a number of key international events or legislation that have supported the rights of persons with disabilities. Next, we shine the spotlight specifically on Canadian milestones that have promoted the rights of individuals with exceptionalities. We follow this with a discussion about the definitions of inclusive education and a snapshot of how it is operationalized in different regions throughout Canada. Last, we discuss the current state of special and inclusive education, and how inclusive education is more than the overlap between special and general education.

Moral Model: Where Disabilities Result from Immorality or Sin

Early histories of people with any type of noticeable "difference" often portray disability in supernatural terms. The end of the Middle Ages, or the period also known as the Dark Ages in Western Europe, was the perfect setting for reformers who aspired to abolish all traces of perceived evil by focusing on any sign of physical or cognitive disability among their citizens (Munyi, 2012). In this model, disabled individuals were either thought to be possessed by the devil (De Grandmont, 2010), were considered the offspring of sinners, or were sinners themselves (Adams, Bell, & Griffin, 2007).

The Greek philosopher Plato recommended that the "deformed" be put away, far from public view (Munyi, 2012). In the 16th century, Christians such as Calvin and Luther believed that children born with disabilities were a manifestation of demonic powers and justified their physical and mental torture in order to exorcise their spirits. Between 1400 and 1700, more than 100 000 women were executed as witches. Today, we are aware that many had a form of mental illness or a disability (Adams, Bell, & Griffin, 2007). Although such actions were widespread, historical accounts show that more supportive measures also existed for the disabled. Where small communities were strictly governed by lords and churches, charitable duty included taking care of people with noticeable differences (Mackelprang & Salsgiver, 2015).

As European civilizations progressed through the Renaissance and later through the time of Enlightenment (18th century), there was a growing interest in building knowledge and refining society based on rational inquiry. While some still believed that supernatural powers and religious beliefs explained disability, the scientific community was gaining ground on trying to explain human differences.

Medical Model: Where Disabilities can be "Fixed"

In the early 1900s, when the bell curve and the normal distribution theory was applied to the human race, its founder, Adolphe Quetelet, succeeded in "presenting the average man as society's ideal" (Mackelprang & Salsgiver, 2015, p. 6),* and it was thought that anyone who was not considered average, or who seemed abnormal, needed "to be fixed." Charles Darwin's work on the social development of humanity led his supporters to believe that the human race could be perfected by eliminating groups of people that showed certain weaknesses or disabilities. This new philosophy of social Darwinism is said to have contributed to the eugenics movement responsible for the killing of 75 000 to 200 000 physically and mentally disabled individuals during the German

---

*From Disability: A Diversity Model Approach in Human Service Practice, 3e by Romel W Mackelprang and Richard O Salsgiver, published by Lyceum Books Inc., © 2015.

occupation of the Second World War (Mackelprang & Salsgiver, 2015). Gradually, in the 19th century, institutions arose which were designed to provide education for the deaf and blind. Later, the interest and care for other marginalized groups, such as the mentally disabled and mentally ill, lead to the growth of asylums.

Munyi (2012) reminds us that the traditional scientific and supernatural perceptions still influence how we think about disability. In other words, even though disabled people are now educated, in most cases they are still considered part of a group that needs "to be fixed." We will see that the influence of these models prevails in the earliest attempts to educate the disabled in North America.

The Dawn of Special Education in North America

Special education was first developed in the United States for economic, demographic, and social reasons (Winzer, 1990). As early as 1823, a state school was established in Kentucky for people who were deaf (Lipsky & Gartner, 1997). Quickly thereafter, various specialized schools and institutions were built across the nation to accommodate students from other marginalized groups. In the 1880s, special classes were introduced in Canada for struggling learners and immigrant children, but as was the case in the United States, individuals with severe handicaps were still being placed in institutions or excluded completely from society.

At the start of the 1900s, with growing immigration across North America, large numbers of children were being sent to school to be socialized and educated. Teachers needed to manage very large classes and were looking for ways to sort the students who could be educated in the regular classroom and those who could not. Two Frenchmen, Alfred Binet and Theophile Simon, provided the first formal instrument for assessing the intelligence of children (Winzer, 1990). When the Binet–Simon Scale was used by Henry Goddard with American children, he found at least 2 percent to be "mentally retarded." Segregated classes were thus opened in regular schools, or specialized institutions were built, for those who could not be taught in the regular stream.

Following the Second World War, families in North America were more affluent and had more time to focus on community development. With the advent of television in the 1950s, and the space race of the 1960s, there was a push, particularly in the United States, for all children and youth to develop to their greatest potential. The ability to publicize these efforts widely through television media helped to solidify special education. Parent associations were succeeding to establish schools for the education of their disabled children, but these were segregated and often held in church basements. These were times of great social change in North America, and a few key international events encouraged supporters of **special education** to pursue their efforts.

Key International Events

There are a number of social and political factors that have helped to establish and shape the rights of the disabled (Adams, Bell, & Griffin, 2007; Nesbit & Philpott, 2008). Vienneau (2002) identifies three as being the most influential in paving the way for **inclusive education**: the normalization principle, the civil rights movement, and policies and legislation.

NORMALIZATION PRINCIPLE

When the **normalization principle** was introduced in the Scandinavian countries by Niels Erik Bank-Mikkelsen and Bengt Nirje in the 1950s, it prompted a social movement that lasted for over twenty years (Vienneau, 2002). As a philosophical belief, it provided individuals with disabilities the hope of having access to surroundings, opportunities, and programs that were enjoyed by every other individual. As a guideline, it provided concrete suggestions on how to get there. In Canada, advocates such as the National Institution on the Mental Retardation in Toronto (today known as the Canadian Association for Community Living) eagerly adopted the concept. Winzer (1990) reminds us that the normalization principle will be actualized when everyone lives as respected and valued members of their cultural group, having access to all privileges and services.

CIVIL RIGHTS MOVEMENT

The African-American civil rights movement (1954–1968), whose goal was to end racial segregation and discrimination against black Americans, lent credence and focus on increased recognition and respect for human dignity for individuals with minority status because of colour, gender, ethnicity, language, or physical or cognitive ability (United States Department of Education, 1999). The landmark decision of the 1954 court case of *Brown vs. Board of Education* ruled that "separate is not equal" and became an important verdict that was used by supporters and parents of students with disabilities to organize activist rallies and seek alternative services. It succeeded in bringing forth the revision and abolition of exclusive policies and segregated schools across North America (Vienneau, 2002).

LEGISLATION

In 1975, Public Law (PL) 94-142 was passed in the United States. That significant piece of legislation ensured an appropriate and free education for all children, regardless of ability or disability status. It also ensured that children who were placed in special education settings would have an individual educational plan (IEP), that parents would be involved in the development of the educational plan, that the plan would be reviewed regularly, and that any needed assessments would be fair and culture free (Ballard, 1977). Today, the need to develop and implement the IEP is still considered an important part in the student's success, but note that it may be referred to differently in different jurisdictions. Over the years, a number of amendments have been made to the PL 94-142, which is now known as the *Individuals with Disabilities Education Act* (IDEA).

Accompanying these leading-edge pieces of legislation was the rationalization of the need for parallel and separate systems. There was a growing belief in mainstreaming and offering a continuum of services, with a focus on the least restrictive environment

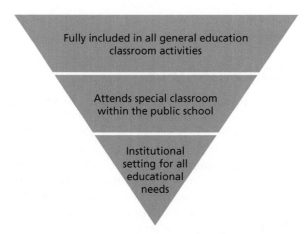

Figure 2.1 Former educational placement options

Source: Kim J. Calder Stegemann, A. Aucoin, *Inclusive Education: Stories of Success and Hope in a Canadian Context,* 1e, © 2018. Pearson Education, Inc., New York, NY.

(Goldstein, Freud, & Solnit, 1973). Figure 2.1 presents an example of the **Cascade Model**, which depicts the various educational placement options that were made available to the exceptional students. They start with the general education classroom being the least restrictive environment. Successive levels may include the general education classroom plus consultative assistance, then general education plus support in the Resource Room, to more restrictive settings such as full time segregated special education classrooms within a school, or to separate institutional settings.

The terms *mainstreaming* and *integration* are often used synonymously and typically refer to the bringing together of general and special education so that students from both settings and programs can learn, work, and play together. Winzer (1990) refers to mainstreaming as the educational parallel of the normalization principle. She explains that the basic goal of mainstreaming was to "provide free, appropriate education in the most suitable setting for exceptional children" (Winzer, 1990, p. 84).[†]

As early as 1984, Stainback and Stainback (1995) challenged the notion of having a dual system comprised of general and special education. Instead, they proposed the merging of the two systems in order to meet the needs of all students. This was probably the first step towards building inclusive schools as we know them today.

OTHER SIGNIFICANT EVENTS

Other significant international events that have influenced and promoted change stemmed from the work of the United Nations. The United Nations' International Year of Disabled Persons and the Convention on the Rights of Persons with Disabilities were spearheaded and supported by powerful worldwide organizations such as the United Nations Educational, Scientific and Cultural Organization (UNESCO), the United Nations Children's Fund (UNICEF), the Organization for Economic

---

[†] From Children with Exceptionalities: A Canadian Perspective, 2e. Published by Prentice-Hall Canada. © June 1990.

Co-operation and Development (OECD), and the World Bank. In 1994, there was a World Conference on Special Needs Education in Salamanca, Spain. This event, which was sponsored by UNESCO and the Ministry of Education and Science of Spain, led to what is called the Salamanca Accord, which is an agreement of intent signed by 92 governments worldwide (UNESCO, 1994). The countries that signed the accord agreed to work towards free and public education for ALL children within their respective countries, regardless of gender, ethnicity, or dis/ability.

Along with the world conference, came a focus on fiscal policies that support inclusive education. The focus was on cost-effective and efficient ways of educating all children, and avoiding restrictiveness of placements by eliminating fiscal incentives (Inclusion International, 2006; UNESCO, 1994). An OECD 1995 study found that "including children with disabilities in regular classrooms is 7 to 9 times less costly than maintaining a separate system" (p. 7).[‡] Unfortunately, the report also indicated that worldwide, 95 percent of children with disabilities were still <u>not</u> included in general education.

Canada as a Leader

Canada has become a leader in the rights of the disabled. Terry Fox and Rick Hansen are two key Canadian figures. In 1980, Terry Fox promoted awareness of the disabled with his Marathon of Hope. As an amputee, his goal was to run across Canada and raise money for cancer research. Rick Hansen further promoted the rights of the physically disabled with his Man in Motion World Tour, which culminated in 1988. Though both of these individuals were examples of the physically dis/abled, they represented the hopes and aspirations of individuals with different types of challenges.

CHARTER OF RIGHTS AND FREEDOMS

Canada is also recognized as a leader in political terms. In 1982, the *Canadian Charter of Rights and Freedoms* made Canada a clear leader by guaranteeing the rights of the disabled at a constitutional level; Canada was the first country worldwide to do so (Mackelprang & Salsgiver, 2015). In 1985, physical and mental ability was added to the Equality Rights (section 15 of the *Charter*), giving all Canadians, regardless of race, national or ethnic origin, colour, sex, age, and/or physical or mental ability, the right to be equal before the law. Although provincial and territorial legislation guides their respective educational systems, the *Charter* is considered the supreme law in Canada (Poirier, Goguen, & Leslie, 1988), thus uniting all Canadians on the issue of equality (section 32). This also applies to education.

PROVINCIAL AND TERRITORIAL SCHOOL POLICIES

In Canada, the rights of children with exceptionalities are protected through the *Canadian Charter of Rights and Freedoms*, provincial and territorial legislation, and other administrative policies (Poirier, Goguen, & Leslie, 1988). Since education is entirely governed by provincial and territorial policies, inclusion has developed at

---

[‡] From Better Education for All: When We're Included Too - A Global Report. Published by Inclusion International, © 2009.

no barrier migration life team
training love no disadvantage
motivation information joy of life
dialog solidarity integration
friends right of self-determination
Human rights
togetherness peace harmony
education satisfaction encouragement
social work inclusion community
dependable ideology acknowledgement
assistance esteem rights of man

Inclusive education is a human rights issue.
Source: wwwebmeister/Fotolia

different times and in different ways (Goguen, 1980; Winzer, 1990). As early as 1969, Nova Scotia guaranteed compulsory education for children with physical and mental disabilities (MacKay, 1989). In 1980, Ontario introduced Bill 82, a landmark decision governing special education (Edmunds & Young, 2007). But it is New Brunswick, with the passing of Bill 85 to address equality issues, that propelled Canada as an international leader (Porter & Richler, 1991; OCED, 1995). Bill 85 reads, in part:

> A school board shall place exceptional pupils such that they receive special educational programs and services in circumstances were exceptional pupils can participate with pupils who are not exceptional pupils within regular classroom settings to the extent that is considered practicable by the board having due regard for the education needs of all students (Province of New Brunswick, 1986).

While Canada can be proud to be a leader in inclusive education, there is still much to be done. Since each province and territory is in charge of its own education system, there is no clear definition or way of operationalizing inclusive education. This allows each region to create schools that are most appropriate for the unique cultures that they service. But the uniqueness can also mean irregularities. By 1980, only Saskatchewan, Manitoba, Québec, Newfoundland, and Ontario had adopted a policy guaranteeing the right to the "Least Restrictive Setting." It is difficult to identify a singular Canadian perspective when it comes to inclusive educational policies (Rousseau, 2013). Even though some provincial and territorial policies have existed since the 1960s, influential litigation in Canada has further shaped the inclusive education landscape to the present.

CANADIAN COURT DECISIONS

Section 15 (Equality Rights) of the *Charter of Rights and Freedoms* gave parents of children with disabilities the opportunity to question the legality of segregated educational programs. Both parents and advocates felt victorious in 1986 when Luke Elmwood, a student who had been labelled mentally handicapped since birth, was given the right to be integrated into the general education school program (*Elmwood vs. the Halifax County School Board*) (MacKay, 1989). A similar case followed closely in New Brunswick when Nathalie Robichaud, who had previously been placed in a segregated setting, gained the right in 1989 to receive her instruction in a general education classroom in a neighborhood school with non-disabled peers (Porter & Richler, 1991).

However, it was a different situation in 1997 when the final verdict was pronounced in the *Eaton vs. Brant County Board of Education* court case. While the Ontario Court of Appeals had previously stated that "unless the parents of a child who has been identified as exceptional by reason of a physical or mental disability consent to the placement of that child in a segregated environment, the school board must provide a placement that is least exclusionary from the mainstream and still reasonably capable of meeting the child's special needs" (Hutchinson, 2002, p. 16),[§] the Supreme Court of Canada overturned this ruling. At that moment, some parents felt betrayed by the court system. It took almost 30 years for them to feel victorious again when, in 2012, the Supreme Court of Canada handed down yet another landmark decision on disability rights. The Moore case (*Moore vs. British Colombia*) declared that schools and school districts have a duty to accommodate students by providing special education services to ensure that students with disabilities have access to the educational programs offered to all students (Council of Canadian with Disabilities, 2013).

The Impact of these Court Decisions

There have been a number of important impacts of the above court decisions. For example, following the Moore case, more parents realized that they could take school districts to court—and win! Some might say that parents are becoming more litigious, and school districts must prove undue hardship or be found guilty of discrimination. The result of the Eaton case is that teachers are viewed as professionals who have a strong voice in advocating for the most appropriate services for their students who have unique learning needs. Another important outcome, based on the Robichaud and Moore cases, is the need for educators to maintain accurate records that demonstrate the efficacy of their educational approaches. Ultimately, we hope that rulings such as those noted above will lead to the most effective and appropriate inclusive education for all of our students.

Difficult Times for Aboriginal Children

While Canada is considered by many to be a leader when it comes to championing equality rights, it has one very somber chapter in its history that must not be overlooked. In the 1880s, wanting to provide Aboriginal youth with the education that would help them integrate into Canadian society, the federal government along with Christian missionaries developed a system of residential schools. For

---

[§] From Eaton v. Brant County Board of Education, [1997] 1 S.C.R. 241.

most Aboriginal students, the experience proved to be more negative than positive (Miller, 2012). According to the Truth and Reconciliation Commission of Canada, at least 4000 Aboriginal children died, underfed and malnourished, while in residential schools. The students were particularly vulnerable to diseases such as tuberculosis and influenza (including the Spanish flu epidemic of 1918–19). By the 1940s, it was obvious that residential schools were ineffective, and growing protests by Aboriginal groups helped to prompt a change in policy.

In 1969, the system was taken over by the Department of Indian Affairs and the government decided to phase out the schools. Although no longer involved, the Catholic Church voiced its disapproval of the closures saying that segregated education was the best approach for Aboriginal children. On June 11, 2008, Prime Minister Stephen Harper, on behalf of the Government of Canada, offered an apology to all former students of Aboriginal residential schools in Canada. The apology openly recognized that the assimilation policy on which the schools were established was harmful and morally wrong. In Miller's (2012) words, "the apology recognized the profoundly damaging and lasting impact the schools had on Aboriginal culture, heritage and language and was one of the steps that the government has taken to forge a new relationship with Aboriginal peoples in Canada" (par. 14).

Inclusive Education in Today's Schools

Recent surveys (Timmons & Wagner, 2010; Canadian Council on Learning, 2009) have found that inclusive education has multiple benefits for disabled students, non-disabled students, teachers, school communities, and families. Before and since these surveys, much has been written about attitudes towards inclusion, pre- and in-service teacher education related to inclusive education, how to mentor inclusive practices, teaching models, inclusive practices in rural settings, and the overall effectiveness of inclusion. Findings that continually arise are summarized below:

- Many general education teachers agree with the philosophy of inclusive education, but they are concerned about their own lack of skill (Avramidis, Bayliss, & Burden, 2000; King & Edmunds, 2001; Philpott, Furey, & Penney, 2010), insufficient planning time (Marshall, Ralph, & Palmer, 2002), limited physical resources (Trump & Hange, 1996), insufficient support personnel (Mastropieri & Scruggs, 1997), and inadequate school leadership (Mastropieri & Scruggs, 1997; Philpott, Furey, & Penney, 2010; Waldron & Redd, 2011).

- Special education teachers see the benefit of inclusive education, but struggle with how to best support children with special learning needs in the general education classroom (Jordan & Stanovich, 2004). There is a need for established models for co-teaching (Gurgur & Uzuner, 2011; Ornelles, Cook, & Jenkins, 2007).

- Parents of children with special learning needs favour inclusive education, particularly in the primary and elementary grades (Garrick Duhaney & Salend, 2000; Leyser & Kirk, 2004; Rafferty, Boettcher, & Griffin, 2001). As these children become teenagers, parents express concern that life skills need to be the focus of their children's education (Garrick Duhaney & Salend, 2000).

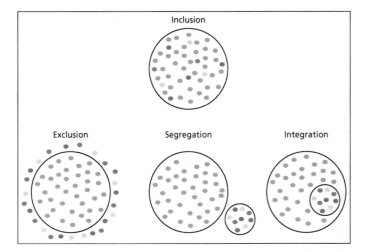

Graphic depiction of inclusion versus exclusion, segregation, and integration.

- School administrators support inclusive education, though some have concerns about the amount of time required of all staff in order to plan effectively (Graham & Spandagou, 2011; Irvine, Lupart, Loreman, & McGhie-Richmond, 2010). Some researchers have reported the concern of a lack of safety net when special education services are absorbed into the general education system (Friesen, Hickey, & Krauth, 2010; Pugach, 1995).

Indeed, public education is evolving and the distinctive line between general and special education is blurring (Ford, Pugach, & Otis-Wilborn, 2001; Fuchs, Fuchs, & Stecker, 2010; Wolfberg, LePage, & Cook, 2009). The way that we educate children, regardless of learning needs or abilities, continues to evolve. As educators, you can play a role in this evolution and development, keeping in mind the UNESCO description of inclusive education:

> "a process of addressing and responding to the diversity of needs of all learners through inclusive practices in learning, cultures and communities and reducing exclusion within and from education. It involves changes and modifications in content, approaches, structures and strategies, with a common vision which covers all children for the appropriate age range and a conviction that it is the responsibility of the regular system to educate all students" (UNESCO, 2005, p. 13).

For more information about inclusive education practices in Canada, please see:

Hutchinson, N., & Martin, A. K. (2011). *Inclusive classrooms in Ontario schools.* Toronto, ON: Pearson Canada.

Mackelprang, R. W., & Salsgiver, R. O. (2015). *Disability. A diversity approach in human service practice* (3rd ed.). Chicago, IL: Lyceum Books.

McLeskey, J. (2007). *Reflections on inclusion: Classic articles that shaped our thinking.* Arlington, VA: Council for Exceptional Children.

Vienneau, R. (2002). Pédagogie de l'inclusion: fondements, définition, défis et perspectives. *Éducation et francophonie, 30*(2), 257–286.

Key Terms

Cascade Model This service delivery model is a continuum of educational placements for students with exceptionalities, ranging from least to most restrictive. The goal is to educate students in the least restrictive and most productive environment possible.

inclusive education Educational inclusion is both a philosophy and process where all students attend, and are supported to learn in, their neighbourhood school in age-appropriate general education classes. All children, regardless of abilities or needs, contribute and participate in all aspects of life at school.

normalization principle Developed in the Scandinavian countries, the normalization principle sought to ensure that people with disabilities had access to everyday living conditions that were as close as possible to the typical ways of the greater society.

special education Special education programs incorporated specialized materials and approaches in order to meet the unique learning challenges of students whose needs could not be met in the general education classroom.

Questions to Consider

1. In what ways are traces from the moral and medical models still noticeable in how students with disabilities are being educated today?

    _____

    _____

    _____

    _____

    _____

    _____

2. How does an historical perspective influence the way you look at our current educational practices?

    _____

    _____

    _____

    _____

    _____

    _____

3. How does history permit us to progress?

_____

_____

_____

_____

_____

_____

4. What position does your local school district take on inclusive education?

_____

_____

_____

_____

_____

_____

5. How might initial teacher education better prepare new teachers for effective inclusive educational practices?

_____

_____

_____

_____

_____

_____

Useful Websites

Canadian Research Centre on Inclusive Education
www.inclusiveeducationresearch.ca

Alberta Education
https://education.alberta.ca

Ontario Ministry of Education
www.edu.gov.on.ca

References

Adams, M., Bell, L. A., & Griffin, P. (2007). *Teaching for diversity and social justice* (2nd ed.). New York, NY: Routeledge.

Avramidis, E., Bayliss, P., & Burden, R. (2000). A survey into mainstream teachers' attitudes towards the inclusion of children with special educational needs in the ordinary school in one local education authority. *Educational Psychology: An International Journal of Experimental Educational Psychology, 20*(2), 191–211.

Ballard, J. (1977). Education for All Handicapped Children Act of 1975. In F. J. Weintraub, A. Abeson, J. Ballard, & M. L. LaVor (Eds.), *Public policy and the education of exceptional children* (pp. 113–130). Reston, VA: The Council for Exceptional Children.

Canadian Council on Learning. (2009). *Does placement matter? Comparing the academic performance of students with special needs in inclusive and separate settings. Lessons in learning.* Retrieved from http://files.eric.ed.gov/fulltext/ED519296.pdf

Council of Canadians with Disabilities. (2013). *The Moore Case: Summary of key points.* Retrieved from http://www.ccdonline.ca/en/humanrights/litigation/Moore-Case-Key-Findings-9Nov2012

De Grandmont, N. (2010). Historique – Acceptation de la différence dans la société : Perspective historique et éléments réflexifs. In N. Rousseau (Ed.), *La pédagogie de l'inclusion scolaire. Piste d'action pour apprendre tous ensemble* (pp. 47–62). Québec, PQ: Presses de l'Université du Québec.

Edmunds, A. L., & Young, D. C. (2007). The evolution of special education policy in Ontario: 1968 to present. In T. G. Ryan (Ed.), *The reflexive special educator* (pp. 57–72). Calgary, AB: Detselig.

Ford, A., Pugach, M. C., & Otis-Wilborn, A. (2001). Preparing general educators to work well with students who have disabilities: What's reasonable at the preservice level? *Learning Disability Quarterly, 24,* 275–285.

Friesen, J., Hickey, R., & Krauth, B. (2010). Disabled peers and academic achievement. *Education Finance and Policy, 5*(3), 317–348.

Fuchs, D., Fuchs, L. S., & Stecker, P. M. (2010). The "blurring" of special education in a new continuum of general education placements and services. *Exceptional Children, 76*(3), 301–323.

Garrick Duhaney, L. M., & Salend, S. J. (2000). Parental perceptions of inclusive educational placements. *Remedial & Special Education, 21*(2), 121–129.

Goguen, L. (1980). Right to education for exceptional children in Canada: A growing national concern. In M. Csapo & L. Goguen (Eds.), *Special education across Canada: Issues and concerns for the '80s* (pp. 175–184). Vancouver, BC: Centre for Human Development and Research.

Goldstein, J., Freud, A., & Solnit, A. J. (1973). *Beyond the best interests of the child.* New York, NY: The Free Press.

Graham, L. J., & Spandagou, I. (2011). From vision to reality: views of primary school principals on inclusive education in New South Wales, Australia. *Disability & Society, 26* (2), 223–237.

Gurgur, H., & Uzuner, Y. (2011). Examining the implementation of two co-teaching models: Team teaching and station teaching. *International Journal of Inclusive Education, 15* (6), 589–610.

Hutchinson, N. L. (2002). *Inclusion of exceptional learners in Canadian schools. A practical handbook for teachers.* Scarborough, ON: Prentice Hall.

Inclusion International. (2006). *Hear our voices: A global report – People with an intellectual disability and their families speak out on poverty and exclusion.* London, UK: Author. Retrieved from http://inclusion-international.org/wp-content/uploads/2013/07/Hear-Our-Voices-with-Covers.pdf

Irvine, A., Lupart, J. L., Loreman, T., & McGhie-Richmond, D. (2010). Educational leadership to create authentic inclusive schools: The experience of principals in a Canadian rural school district. *Exceptionality Education International, 20*(2), 70–88.

Jordan, A., & Stanovich, P. (2004). The beliefs and practices of Canadian teachers about including students with special needs in their regular elementary classrooms. *Exceptionality Education Canada, 14*(2–3), 25–46.

King, W., & Edmunds, A. (2001). Teachers' perceived needs to become more effective inclusion practitioners: A single school study. *Exceptionality Education Canada, 11*(1), 3–23.

Leyser, Y., & Kirk, R. (2004). Evaluating inclusion: An examination of parent views and factors influencing their perspectives. *International Journal of Disability, Development and Education, 51*(3), 271–285.

Lipsky, D. K., & Gartner, A. (1997). *Inclusion and school reform. Transforming America's classrooms.* Baltimore, MD: Paul H. Brooks.

MacKay, A. W. (1989). The Elwood Case: Vindicating the educational rights for disabled. In M. Csapo & L. Goguen (Eds.), *Special education across Canada: Issues and concerns for the 90's* (pp. 149–158). Vancouver, BC: Center for Human Development and Research.

Mackelprang, R. W., & Salsgiver, R. O. (2015). *Disability. A diversity approach in human service practice* (3rd ed.). Chicago, IL: Lyceum Books.

Marshall, J., Ralph, S., & Palmer, S. (2002). "I wasn't trained to work with them": Mainstream teachers' attitudes to children with speech and language difficulties. *International Journal of Inclusive Education, 6*(3), 199–215.

Mastropieri, M. A., & Scruggs, T. E. (1997). What's special about special education? A cautious view towards full inclusion. *Educational Forum, 61*(3), 206–211.

Miller, J. R. (2012). Residential schools. *Canadian Encyclopedia. Historica Canada.* Retrieved from http://www.thecanadianencyclopedia.ca/en/article/residential-schools/

Munyi, C. W. (2012). Past and present perceptions towards disability: A historical perspective. *Disability Studies Quarterly, 32*(2). Retrieved from http://dsq-sds.org/article/view/3197/3068

Nesbit, W., & Philpott, D. (2008). The plight of individuals with cognitive disabilities: Social and educational facets of an arduous evolution. *The Morning Watch. Educational and Social Analysis, 36*(1–2), 1–21. Retrieved from http://www.mun.ca/educ/faculty/mwatch/Nesbet%20and%20Philpott%20The%20Plight%20of%20Individuals.pdf

Organisation for Economic Cooperation and Development (OECD). (1995). *Integrating students with special needs in mainstream schools.* Paris, FR: Authors.

Ornelles, C., Cook, L., & Jenkins, A. (2007). Middle school general education teachers' perspectives on including students with learning disabilities. *Learning Disabilities, 14*(3), 145–154.

Philpott, D. F., Furey, E., & Penney, S. C. (2010). Promoting leadership in the ongoing professional development of teachers: responding to globalization and inclusion. *Exceptionality Education International, 20*(2), 38–54.

Poirier, D., Goguen, L., & Leslie, P. (1988). *Educational rights of exceptional children in Canada. A national study of multi-level commitments.* Toronto, ON: Carswell.

Porter, G. L., & Richler, D. (1991). Changing special education practice: Law, advocacy and Innovation. In G. L. Porter & D. Richler (Eds.), *Changing Canadian schools. Perspectives on disability and inclusion* (pp. 9–33). Toronto, ON: The Roeher Institute.

Province of New Brunswick. (1986). Bill 85: An act to amend the Schools Act, Section 45(2)1, (1987).

Pugach, M. C. (1995). On the failure of imagination in inclusive schooling. *Journal of Special Education, 29*(2), 212–223.

Rafferty, Y., Boettcher, C., & Griffin, K. W. (2001). Benefits and risks of reverse inclusion for preschoolers with and without disabilities: Parents' perspectives. *Journal of Early Intervention, 24*(4), 266–286.

Rousseau, N. (2013). *Éducation inclusive au Canada: Analyse comparative.* Trois-Rivières, PQ: Université du Québec à Trois-Rivières.

Schlifer, C. (2005). The sociology of special education. *College Quarterly, 8*(1). Retrieved from www.collegequarterly.ca/2005-vol08-num01-winter/schlifer.html

Stainback, W., & Stainback, S. (1995). Contemplating inclusive education from a historical perspective. In R. A. Villa & J. S. Thousand (Eds.), *Creating and Inclusive School* (pp. 16–27). Alexandria, VA: Association for Supervision and Curriculum Development.

Timmons, V., & Wagner, M. (2010). *Inclusive education knowledge exchange initiative: An analysis of the Statistics Canada Participation and Activity Limitation Survey. Final report.* Retrieved from http://en.copian.ca/library/research/ccl/inclusive_edu_know/inclusive_edu_know.pdf

Trump, G. C., & Hange, J. E. (1996). *Teacher perceptions of and strategies for inclusion: A regional summary of focus group interview findings.* (ED397574) Retrieved from http://files.eric.ed.gov/fulltext/ED397574.pdf

United Nations Educational, Scientific and Cultural Organisation (UNESCO). (1994). *The Salamanca statement and framework for action on special needs education.* Paris, FR: Authors. Retrieved from http://unesdoc.unesco.org/images/0009/000984/098427eo.pdf

United Nations Educational, Scientific and Cultural Organisation (UNESCO). (2005). *Guidelines for inclusion: Ensuring access to education for all.* Paris, FR: Authors. Retrieved from http://unesdoc.unesco.org/images/0014/001402/140224e.pdf

United States Department of Education. (1999). *Impact of the civil rights laws.* Washington, DC: Office for Civil Rights. Retrieved from http://www2.ed.gov/about/offices/list/ocr/docs/impact.html

Vienneau, R. (2002). Pédagogie de l'inclusion: fondements, définition, défis et perspectives. *Éducation et francophonie, 30*(2), 257–286.

Waldron, L., & Redd, L. (2011). Providing a full circle of support to teachers in an inclusive elementary school. *Journal of Special Education Leadership, 24*(1), 59–61.

Winzer, M. (1990). *Children with exceptionalities. A Canadian perspective* (2nd ed.). Scarborough, ON: Prentice Hall.

Winzer, M. (2006). Confronting differences: An excursion through the history of special education. In L. Florian (Ed.), *The SAGE handbook of special education* (pp. 21–33). Thousand Oaks, CA: Sage Publishers.

Wolfberg, P., LePage, P., & Cook, E. (2009). Innovations in inclusive education: Two teacher preparation programs at the San Francisco State University. *International Journal of Whole Schooling, 5*(2), 16–36.

Chapter 3
Theoretical Frameworks: Universal Design for Learning and Response to Intervention

Dr. Kim Calder Stegemann & Dr. Angela AuCoin

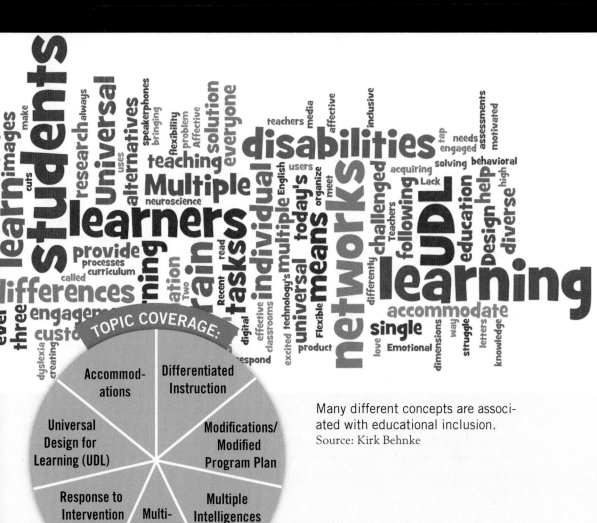

TOPIC COVERAGE:

- Accommodations
- Differentiated Instruction
- Universal Design for Learning (UDL)
- Modifications/ Modified Program Plan
- Response to Intervention (RTI)
- Multi-Tiered System of Supports
- Multiple Intelligences

Many different concepts are associated with educational inclusion.
Source: Kirk Behnke

The student will:

- State the components of universal design for learning/universal design for instruction and provide an example of each

- Explain how differentiation fits within the UDL framework

- Describe the response to intervention framework (three tiers) and explain the benefits and challenges of this model over traditional special education pullout practices

- Distinguish the practices of differentiation, accommodation, and modification

Inclusive education is deeply rooted in a philosophy of social justice, equal access to education, and the standard curriculum. As we saw in Chapter 2, however, there are different definitions and approaches to the operationalization of inclusive education, particularly across Canada where each province and territory has jurisdiction over education. Despite this, there are established frameworks that support the philosophy of inclusive education. We present two models, both of which incorporate research-based teaching strategies to effectively address the learning needs of exceptional learners: universal design for learning (UDL) and response to intervention (RTI). While there are other approaches to enacting principles of inclusive education, we have chosen these two because they are widely used and are contained within the policies of many jurisdictions, and both have a solid research base.

Universal Design for Learning (UDL)

The basic premise of UDL is to reduce barriers to learning that occur when students interact with the curriculum (Rose & Meyer, 2002). Universal design has its roots in architecture and was a movement with the purpose of creating buildings that were equally accessible by all individuals. For example, using a universal design approach, buildings would be created so that any individual, whether able-bodied, physically challenged, hearing-impaired, etc., would be able to easily enter the building through the front door. Ramps and other sorts of functional designs and technologies would be incorporated in order to achieve universal access. Meyer and Rose added other principles to the architectural concept of universal design for teaching and learning contexts.

At the core of UDL is a belief in the inherent value of all learners, acknowledging the richness of their diversity. Further, a foundational assumption of UDL is that difficulties in learning occur not because of deficits within the learner, but because of problems within the curriculum delivery. It is therefore incumbent upon the educator to make pedagogical adjustments so that all lessons are "accessible" to all students.

UDL is also referred to as UDI or universal design for instruction and means that the educator creates educational experiences that maximize learning for all students. The educator designs instruction (including materials, facilities, and strategies) that is appropriate and usable by all students, to the greatest extent possible. In this way, every lesson should appeal to a wide range of abilities, disabilities, ethnic backgrounds, language skills, and learning styles. The principles are based on what science has revealed about how learning takes place within the brain. Specifically, it addresses the recognition, strategic, and affective networks of the brain (CAST, 2015).

Rose and Meyer (2005) point to three specific ways to maximize the learning experience for all learners (see Figure 3.1). The first relates to the "what" of learning (recognition network) and means presenting information and content in different ways (representation). An example of this would be when a classroom teacher realizes that reading the explanations and instructions at the beginning of each chapter of the math textbook is not the most productive way of teaching a new concept for every student in the class. Rather, the teacher incorporates hands-on activities that serve to teach the concepts in a different way. The second way that a teacher can maximize the learning experience relates to the "how" of learning (strategic network), and means differentiating the ways that students can express what they know (action and expression). For example, instead of requiring that all students write an essay to indicate what they have learned about the Canadian constitution, students may choose different forms of representing their "knowing," such as an oral presentation, visual art, or musical rendition.

A third way that educators can reduce barriers to the curriculum is by acknowledging the affective part of learning—student interests and background experiences

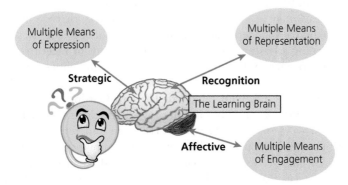

Figure 3.1 Key Components of UDL

Source: Kim Calder Stegemann, Angela AuCoin, *Inclusive Education: Stories of Success and Hope in a Canadian Context,* 1Ce., © 2018, Pearson Education, Inc., New York, NY.

(affective network). This relates to the "why" of learning and means that students need to be stimulated and motivated to learn in ways that are authentic and meaningful, given their unique background experiences (<u>engagement</u>). Note that this particular aspect of UDL/UDI is compatible with the tenants of 21st century learning (Boudreault, Haga, Paylor, Sabourin, Thomas, & van der Linden, 2012/2013; C21 Canada, 2012), which aims for learners to experience deep and authentic learning.

The term **differentiation**, while used by Rose and Meyer, is best associated with the work of Carol Ann Tomlinson (1999). She recommends that teachers consider adjusting three aspects of their instruction to better meet the needs of students with varying abilities and interests—process, product, content. In many ways, these aspects are mirrored in the pillars of UDL. For example, a change in process might mean that the teacher allows students to learn about Egypt by watching YouTube video clips, rather than just reading a textbook (similar to representation in the UDL framework). An example of differentiation of product would be when student understanding of plot in a novel study is presented via a skit, instead of just in writing (similar to the UDL action and expression). Other ways that Tomlinson differentiates instruction is by moving from simple to complex, concrete to abstract, structured to open-ended, or single faceted to multi-faceted.

You may have heard the terms **accommodations** and **modifications.** These were commonly used in Canadian Ministry of Education documents throughout the latter 20th century. Essentially, they refer to making changes to process, product, content, or ways of engaging, responding, and representing. For some provinces or territories, *accommodations* or *adaptations* refer to making changes to the materials, instruction, or activities, so that the learner can achieve the prescribed learning outcomes; while *modifications* refer to substantive changes in the content or curriculum. For example, allowing a student to dictate a detailed three-part story, instead of writing it out by hand, would be a form of adaptation or accommodation because the student is still meeting the prescribed learning outcome. If the student was required to draw a picture of a character in the story, and not create the detailed plot line, that could be considered a modification because the learning outcome has changed substantially from a focus on plot to representing a character in the story. Not all jurisdictions use the terms *accommodation* and *modification* in the same way that we have above. For example, the Yukon uses the term *adaptation* instead of *accommodation* to refer to any teaching and learning adjustments that enable the student to meet the required curriculum. It is best to refer to the Ministry of Education guidelines for your province or territory.

Another aspect of UDL/UDI relates to Howard Gardner's theory of multiple intelligences (MI) (1983). Essentially, Gardner's work has demonstrated that individuals have preferred ways of engaging with curriculum and representing their learning. He identifies eight common intelligences: verbal–linguistic, bodily–kinesthetic, visual–spatial, naturalistic, intrapersonal, interpersonal, logical–mathematical, and musical–rhythmic (see Figure 3.2). Recent work by Gardner and colleagues (Gardner, 2005) has pointed to a ninth intelligence—existentialism—but this has been less widely accepted than the other intelligences. Most people have one or two preferred

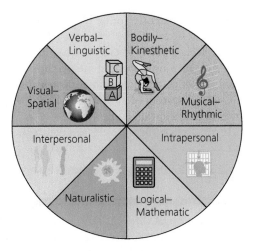

Figure 3.2 Eight of Gardner's Multiple Intelligences

Source: Based on Multiple Intelligences, http://www.educationalvoyage.com/multiintell.html

ways of learning new information, but the preferences depend highly on the context for the learning, the content, and the individual's emotional state. Therefore, when planning lessons, the teacher should aim to match at least one of the preferred intelligences for each learner in the class. It is important to remember, however, that the goal of education is also to expand and challenge learners. Therefore, it is recommended that learners be aware of the need to develop other intelligences.

There are many other theories of intelligence. While these theories are beyond the scope of this text, the reader should be aware of Robert Sternberg and Joseph Renzulli, both of whom have added to our understanding of the complexity and breadth of intelligence. Sternberg (1988) proposed the Triarchic Theory of Intelligence and he suggests that intelligent behaviour is based on an individual's ability to balance analytical, creative, and practical thinking abilities to one's socio-cultural context. Renzulli (1977) is associated with literature on giftedness and he suggested the Three-Ring Conception of intelligence, which consists of cognitive ability, task commitment, and creativity. Personalized learning (choice in representation of learning) and attention to learner interests (task commitment) align with components of UDL.

Response to Intervention (RTI)

Ideally, the vast majority of students should have success in a well-designed UDL/UDI classroom. RTI was designed as a general problem-solving framework to address the needs of those students who continue to experience barriers to the curriculum despite UDL applications. More recently, in the United States, RTI has been incorporated into educational policy at a national level through the *Individuals with Disabilities Education Improvement Act* (IDEA 2004). It is a systematic approach for "establishing and redesigning teaching and learning environments so they are effective, efficient, relevant, and durable for all students, families, and educators" (Sugai, 2007, n.d.).* You may see the terms **multi-tiered system of supports (MTSS)** or **pyramid of intervention**, which are similar to the concept of RTI.

The RTI framework consists of three levels (see Figure 3.3).

1. PRIMARY TIER

At this level all students are exposed to the core curriculum and those who experience academic or social/behavioural difficulties are identified. Key features of this level are a) clear goals and expected outcomes, b) appropriate instruction, c) monitoring, d) feedback and encouragement, and e) error correction (Goodman, McIntosh, & Bohanon, n.d.). Examples of universal, class-wide supports include: audiobooks, alternatives to written assignments to demonstrate knowledge and understanding, advance organizers/graphic organizers to assist with following classroom presentations, and extended time to complete assignments or tests. If the universal supports are not sufficient to meet student needs, a more intensified approach is employed at the next level.

2. SECONDARY TIER

This level provides supplemental academic and social/behavioural support. Typically, a team of educators oversees instruction and intervention at this level. Key features of this level include a) a focus on additional instruction and practice, b) increased structure or explicitness, and c) validated approaches (Fuchs, Fuchs, & Vaughn, 2014).

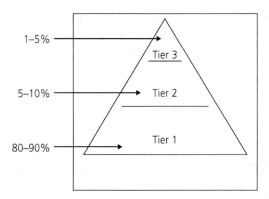

Figure 3.3 RTI Tiers of Prevention

*From School-Wide Positive Behavior Support and Response to Intervention by George Sugai, Published by National Center for Learning Disabilities, © 2015.

Prevention at this level focuses on changes to curriculum, instruction, or the physical environment, so that students are placed in situations that increase the likelihood of increased learning and/or appropriate behaviour. An example of a Tier 2 intervention is the use of an evidence-based program, such as Reciprocal Teaching (for reading comprehension) or Building Blocks for Math with a small group of students. A good source of data about evidence-based practices can be found at the What Works Clearinghouse website (http://ies.ed.gov/ncee/wwc) and the IRIS Center (http://iris. peabody.vanderbilt.edu/ebp_summaries).

3. TERTIARY TIER

The third level of support is individualized and intensive, incorporating specialized methods, strategies, technologies, and materials. Family involvement at this level is essential. An example of this level of intervention is having the learning assistance teacher do short-term pullout with an individual child to work on phonemic awareness using the LiPS Program (Lindamood Phoneme Sequencing).

SUMMARY

At all levels in the RTI framework, assessment and monitoring is central to the instructional process. Decisions about content, processes, products—all aspects of instruction—are based on collected data and problem solving. Student progress is continually monitored to ensure the appropriateness of instruction. Evidence-based interventions are critical at all levels, as is fidelity of implementation. It is estimated that 90 to 95 percent of students can achieve academic and social success at either Tier 1 or Tier 2 (Fuchs & Fuchs, 2006). Therefore, only a very small percentage of the student body should require the intensity of intervention of Tier 3.

In addition to meeting the needs of almost all students at the first two levels, there are other benefits to the RTI framework. It has ecological validity for diagnosis and program planning because assessment and intervention are steeped in the context of the classroom and curriculum. As well, with constant monitoring, it is not necessary for students to "fail" in order to qualify for extra support (Vaughn & Fuchs, 2003). Further, the RTI framework affirms that there is a natural variability among students and that, for the most part, their learning needs can be addressed within the general education classroom. The RTI Action Network provides multiple resources to assist educators in effectively applying a RTI approach.

As you read the case studies in the next chapters, you will see how teachers, support staff, administration, families, and even students reflect principles of UDL/UDI and RTI within their schools. It is fundamental to the success of inclusive education that a solid foundation of social justice and respect for diversity exist within the school climate. You will see that, regardless of how or which aspects of UDL and RTI are employed, the social–emotional aspect is present in all of the cases. As Jennifer Katz (2012) points out in her Three Block Model for inclusion and UDL, the groundwork (Block One) must first be laid to align beliefs and attitudes about diversity and exceptionality.

Key Terms

accommodations The term *accommodations* refers to the adjustments to instruction, assessment, materials, or activities that allow students to have success and achieve the required curriculum outcomes.

differentiation Differentiation is making changes in process, products, or content of learning to match student learning preferences.

modifications Modifications are changes made to learning outcomes in order to address student learning needs.

multi-tiered system of supports (MTSS) MTSS is a comprehensive approach to providing assessment, intervention, and monitoring to effectively provide different types of supports with varying degrees of intensity. (Also known as **pyramid of intervention**.)

Questions to Consider

1. Reflect on your own school experiences. Identify instances where instruction or assessment was adjusted to better match your interests or preferred modes of representation. How did that affect your learning and self-esteem?

   _____

   _____

   _____

   _____

   _____

   _____

2. As we know, intelligence can be viewed in many different ways. Describe your learning strengths (what are you good at?). How do you use these strengths when learning new concepts?

   _____

   _____

   _____

   _____

   _____

   _____

3. Now consider areas where you lack certain skills or knowledge. Imagine that every day of your school life you were required to focus on these areas. What might be the impact on your level of motivation and self-efficacy?

_____

_____

_____

_____

_____

_____

4. How would you design a program of study, using the RTI model, to address your learning needs? Think about increasing levels of intensity and individualization.

_____

_____

_____

_____

_____

_____

5. Imagine that it is your first week teaching in a new classroom of students. What types of activities would you plan to begin to establish a safe and caring classroom climate? How might you increase student self-awareness of the strengths and challenges that each faces?

_____

_____

_____

_____

_____

_____

Useful Websites

CAST
www.cast.org/our-work/about-udl.html#.VnXZ-BLrv4g

Center for Universal Design in Education
www.washington.edu/doit/programs/center-universal-design-education/overview

Center on Response to Intervention
www.rti4success.org

IRIS Center
http://iris.peabody.vanderbilt.edu/ebp_summaries

National Center on Universal Design for Learning
www.udlcenter.org

RTI Action Network
www.rtinetwork.org/learn/what/whatisrti

What Works Clearinghouse
http://ies.ed.gov/ncee/wwc/default.aspx

References

Boudreault, F-A., Haga, J., Paylor, P., Sabourin, A., Thomas, S., & van der Linden, C. (2012/2013). *Future tense: Adapting Canadian education systems for the 21st century.* Retrieved from http://www.actioncanada.ca/wp-content/uploads/2014/04/TF2-Report_Future-Tense_EN.pdf

C21 Canada. (2012). *Shifting minds: A 21st century vision of public education for Canada.* Canadians for 21st Century Learning and Innovation. Retrieved from http://www.c21canada.org/wp-contenet/uploads/2012/02/C21-Canada-Shifting_Minds.pdf

CAST. (2015). *About universal design for learning.* Retrieved from http://www.cast.org/our-work/about-udl.html#.VWcd_ayD5uA

Fuchs, D., & Fuchs, L. S. (2006). Introduction to response to intervention: What, why, and how valid is it? *Reading Research Quarterly, 1,* 93–99.

Fuchs, D., Fuchs, L. S., & Vaughn, S. (2014). What is intensive instruction and why is it important? *Teaching Exceptional Children, 46,* 13–18.

Gardner, H. (1983). *Frames of mind: The theory of multiple intelligences.* New York, NY: Basic Books.

Gardner, H. (2005). Multiple lenses on the mind. In C. M. Huat & T. Kerry (Eds.), *International perspectives on education* (pp. 7–27). New York, NY: Continuum International Publishing.

Goodman, S., McIntosh, K., & Bohanon, H. (n.d.). *Integrating academic and behavior supports within and RtI framework, Part 2: Universal supports.* Retrieved from http://www.rtinetwork.org/learn/behavior-supports/integrating-academic-and-behavior-supports-universal-supports

Katz, J. (2012). *Teaching to diversity: The three-block model of universal design for learning.* Winnipeg, MB: Portage & Main Press.

Renzulli, J. S. (1977). The enrichment triad model: A guide for developing defensible programs for the gifted and talented. *Gifted Child Quarterly, 21*(2), 227–233.

Rose, D. H., & Meyer, A. (2002). *Teaching every student in the digital age: Universal design for learning.* Alexandria, VA: ASCD.

Rose, D. H., & Meyer, A. (2005). The future is in the margins: The role of technology and disability in educational reform. In D. H. Rose, A. Meyer, & C. Hitchcock (Eds.), *A practical reader in universal design for learning* (pp. 13–35). Cambridge, MA: Harvard Education Press.

Sternberg, R. J. (1988). *The triarchic mind: A new theory of human intelligence.* New York, NY: Viking Press.

Sugai, G. (2007, December). *Responsiveness-to-intervention: Lessons learned and to be learned.* Keynote presentation at and paper for the RTI Summit, U.S. Department of Education, Washington, D.C.

Sugai, G. (n.d.). *School-wide positive behavior support and response to intervention.* Retrieved from http://www.rtinetwork.org/learn/behavior-supports/schoolwidebehavior

Tomlinson, C. A. (1999). *The differentiated classroom: Responding to the needs of all learners.* Alexandria, VA: ASCD.

Vaughn, S., & Fuchs, L. S. (2003). Redefining learning disabilities as inadequate response to instruction: The promise and potential problems. *Learning Disabilities Research & Practice, 18,* 137–146.

Chapter 4
Wilson Case Study

Nan Stevens

Wilson has many interests and talents.
Source: Domenicop20/Fotolia

TOPIC COVERAGE:

Autism Spectrum Disorder (ASD)

Individual Educational Plan (IEP)

Modified Program Plan

Psycho-Educational Assessment

The student will:

- State how this case study reflects the philosophical underpinnings of the inclusive educational movement

- Provide examples of barriers to full participation in the general education classroom

- Provide examples of adjustments to the educational, social, and recreational environments in order to reduce barriers to participation

Preamble

Wilson is Nancy and Wes's oldest son. There were complications with his birth and he was delivered four weeks premature via Caesarean section after Nancy suffered from placenta previa during her entire pregnancy. Like all parents, Nancy and Wes had many hopes and dreams for the life they would share with Wilson. From birth Wilson (Wil) exhibited spastic movements and low muscle tone. Nancy became more concerned about Wil's development when he didn't seem to do parallel play with other children and was not acquiring typical early language skills (around age 2). Because Nancy is a teacher and university educator, she was aware of the "typical" developmental milestones for infants and toddlers. The course of Wil's life has taken many twists and turns over the past 11 years, and he now is quite settled in a resource room during school time and in multiple extracurricular activities.

Wilson is 11 years old. He is now toilet-trained, after over nine years of persistence and repetition by his parents, support workers, and care givers. He is unable to wipe himself, and requires assistance to get dressed or put on outside clothes such as boots and coat. He was diagnosed with Pervasive Developmental Disorder-Not Otherwise Specified (PDD-NOS) nine years ago using the fourth edition of the **Diagnostic and Statistical Manual of Mental Disorders (DSM)**. Initially, in the DSM–III and DSM–IV, both PDD-NOS and Asperger's syndrome were included in the autism spectrum disorder. In the latest edition, DSM-5 (American Psychiatric Association, 2015), PDD-NOS and Asperger's syndrome are no longer separate disorders under the autism spectrum disorder classification. Therefore, today, Wilson's diagnosis is autism spectrum disorder (ASD). From the beginning, a clear diagnosis for Wilson was very difficult to ascertain, because his strengths are varied and his needs are very complex. The family sought consultations from numerous medical and community experts.

As you read the case study, pay particular attention to issues related to assessment, funding, and appropriate program planning. Also be sure to notice Wil's strengths. Create an image for yourself of a young lad who has a dynamite smile and a love of biking, horseback riding, and skiing.

Autism spectrum disorder (ASD) and autism are disorders of brain development.

Characteristics

- difficulties with social interactions
- difficulties with verbal and non-verbal communication

- repetitive behaviours
- mild, moderate, severe, or profound cognitive delay
- sensory integration problems or sensory processing disorder

For more information see: Autism Speaks: www. autismspeaks.org/what-autism

Parent Voice

"Wilson is the apple of my eye and has taught me so much about parenting, and life in general. The last 11 years have been very trying, however. Some of the most challenging aspects of having a child with special needs are assessment, diagnosis, and program planning. For example, Wilson scores below 35 on standardized intelligence tests (which are one type of **psycho-educational assessment**). *Although these tests ensure that he receives a variety of educational services, they do not reveal anything about his gifts and strengths. Standardized intelligence tests are deficit-driven and do not consider the whole child. They serve the purpose in terms of screening for services and obtaining an official diagnosis, but cannot possibly assess emotional intelligence, sensory regulation needs, or social skills. Rather, we have relied heavily on assessments which attempt to measure abilities and adaptive functioning.*

Programming has also been a huge challenge for our family. Early on, just after Wilson was diagnosed with autism, we focused on a well-known therapy— **Applied Behaviour Analysis (ABA)**. *This approach is evidence-based and has been proven highly successful for children with autism (especially as an early intervention). My husband and I hired a behaviour consultant from Vancouver at $1000/day, and a team of local university students who the behaviour consultant trained as Behaviour Interventionists (BIs). The BIs conducted discrete trials, recorded ongoing data, and watched videos of each other between sessions to ensure each of them was being consistent—all so that Wilson could learn. However, because of Wilson's level of cognitive functioning, he was unable to retain or generalize any of the skills he learned "at the ABA table." In fact, his behavioural outbursts and overall demeanor drastically declined with this intervention. There is nothing wrong with ABA, per se; it simply was not the right fit for Wilson. Each child is unique, and families need to find the right "fit" for intervention. There were few people to guide us in this process. After an 18 month commitment to a home-based ABA program with minimal results, we were very disheartened given the amount of time, organization, and money required to maintain this kind of program. Other families using this intervention have found success, perhaps because their children are intellectually higher functioning.*

After several years of trying multiple interventions, our focus is on raising a child who is happy, connected to his family and community, who can self-regulate, and who enjoys

learning in natural contexts. Overall health, well-being, and functional life skills are our goal for the foreseeable future."

Sibling Voice

Hank is Wil's younger brother by three years. They are vastly different boys in many ways. Hank is a very bright, precocious, and articulate boy who can't get enough of Star Wars and Transformers. It has been a huge challenge for him to learn how to play and engage with Wil. He is a loving brother and intensely protective of Wil. What sends Hank into a tailspin is when Wil becomes violent and bites him. These unpredictable behaviour outbursts can leave Hank feeling very vulnerable and unwilling to persist and engage with Wil. There have been times over the past several years when Hank has clearly articulated that he feels less important and less loved than Wil.

"Sometimes it can be good, sometimes it can be bad. When it is good, we run around the house and chase each other, sometimes I hide and he says "Where are you?" And sometimes we get to wrestle and spar with each other, which is fun. When it is bad, Wil follows me around everywhere and I cannot get any space. And he grabs or scratches me and it hurts. And sometimes he gets my parents in a bad mood and they take it out on me. Their attention is always on Wil."

Teacher Voice

*"The regular classroom setting is not an easy place for Wilson to be, as it can be completely overwhelming for him. When visiting another class, he may say 'all done' before he has even given it a try. So finding the right fit for **integration** has been very important, and taking time to develop his confidence has also been a key factor. His love for music, and his bond with our music specialist, made it an easy decision to integrate him into music class. Developing his abilities and growing his courage one visit at a time has been a learning experience for Wil and all the other students in the general education class. Not only did Wil need to develop skills in participating with others, the other students needed to learn to accept his differences. We gradually increased his time, and we encourage greater participation as he is increasingly successful. Even when overwhelmed by the busy, noisy music class, Wilson still wants to stay there. He may need a quick walk-a-bout in the hall, or words of encouragement when he is overwhelmed, and we provide that support. He has been successful because he has been allowed to join in the games and songs on 'his own terms', when he is ready. He may dance when others sit, or he may be still as others dance. Wilson may sing along for parts of the song, or just listen to the other kids sing. Wilson regularly demonstrates pride and enjoyment being integrated in music class with the other students, and he truly loves it. It has also been a rewarding learning experience for all students in the general education class. For our staff, integration marks an opportunity to not only teach that being different is okay, but to teach that being different is absolutely and fundamentally what is right with our world.*

*Wilson joins our **Individual Achievement Program (IAP)** two days a week and we all benefit greatly from his presence here. Each of our eight students has special needs, and* everyone is an integral member of our classroom community. Wilson is full of love and curiosity, and he is a keen observer of his environment and the people in it. He needs to move, to be up out of his chair often, to go on walk-a-bouts, or to just stand near his friends. The Individual Achievement Program is a successful placement for him because it allows Wil to be himself, rather than expecting him to fit the mold in a mainstream classroom. Our life skills program works to increase student independence while scaffolding supports to ensure success.

Wilson has a completely modified **Individual Education Plan (IEP)**, which includes goals in the areas of communication, self-care, functional life skills, social/emotional development, and cognitive development. We are able to provide one-on-one support for Wil for parts of the school day, as he works in small groups with his classmates. Small group activities and lessons are designed to promote student participation at their level of ability and access method. Universal design is the norm in our classroom. Our highly skilled support staff is ready to meet his sensory needs on a moment's notice, be it a power walk outside, jumping on the trampoline, or calming words in the quiet room. At times, Wil's need to communicate concern for a classmate or his own discomfort may present as aggression. We are also able to support him through this, providing the space and time he needs to work through his emotions, as well as skilled teaching of replacement behaviours. Unlike a typical classroom, we have a variety of sensory integration materials that he can access at any time, including a ball pit, swing, bean bag chairs, quiet room with low lights, weighted blankets, trampoline, music, and more. Ultimately, the biggest key to his success is that we do not try to change Wil, only to help him uncover his talents and flourish within a supportive and caring environment that fosters true belonging."

Certified Education Assistant Voice

The role of the certified education assistant (CEA) in the resource room is as important as the learning assistance and resource teacher (LART). Although the LART designs and assesses the IEP goals in consultation with the parents/guardians, it is often the CEA who works one-to-one with the student to implement IEP objectives, collect data, and teach routine tasks. Additionally, after-school workers and respite care providers are responsible for similar one-to-one supervision and support. The parents/guardians take on the role of managers for recruitment, orientation, and communication to ensure the school and home support teams are well trained, supported, and coordinated. Thus, outside of a "typical" parenting role, parents of children with complex needs have a greater role to play in the collaboration and management of staff teams and support workers.

"I have had the pleasure to work with Wilson for many years. I am a Certified Educational Assistant in the Individual Achievement Program which he attends two days a week. I have seen this boy grow leaps and bounds into the young man that he is now. This growth is, in part, due to the people that lovingly surround him, but mostly due to the person that Wil is. He is loving, caring, energetic, happy, and empathetic.

In the beginning, Wil found it hard to sit and do both individual and group activities. With time and patience, he is now able to engage in all class activities and seems to be enjoying himself. Although at times he still jumps up, he returns when asked. With Wil, trying something once and giving up is not the way. We will introduce something new and stick with it for a time to see if it will be a successful match for him. We allow him time to adjust in order to meet his sensory needs. Wil is very caring and empathetic towards his classmates and the staff. When a student is upset, he goes to them and tries to show them, in his way, that he cares. We have seen this loving side and are trying to give him a way to appropriately express his feelings to his peers. Wil is allowed to be himself in the classroom. The activities and work are adapted to fit his needs, and not the other way around.

Wilson had the opportunity to join a mainstream class for music. Wil loves music! At first there were some difficulties, but again, we stuck to it. At the beginning we joined for short periods of time and increased the length of stay, when possible. At first, the students in the class showed signs of unease, and maybe fear, as they did not know him. On the first day we explained a bit about Wilson and answered any questions. With time, their feelings turned into curiosity and then to acceptance. Wil is, again, allowed to be himself. He joins the group, sitting amongst the kids, singing and dancing. When outside at recess, or in the hall, these same students will stop to answer Wil's famous question 'how are you?' and talk with him about his love of horses. These children are showing others that, no matter who you are or what differences one has, everyone deserves to be accepted and treated with respect."

Respite Worker Voice

"The best memories that I have of Wilson are from attending camp together. Each summer we go for a week, sometimes two. For the past 5 years the camps that we have attended were for children with exceptionalities—more commonly described as camps for kids with special needs. It was at camp that I watched Wil have the same opportunities as so many other children—camp was an equalizer for all who attended. He ran, explored, swam, sang, and laughed, surrounded by other kids doing the very same. One of the reasons that I believe Wilson enjoyed camp so much was because there was no judgment, no shame in his needs, and no apologies for who he was. It has been my experience that, at times, the social emphasis on inclusion can come at the cost of promoting environments where the sense of true belonging doesn't necessarily occur.

It is in this place of belonging that Wilson did amazing things. During our first year at camp, we tried to participate in the climbing wall, but the requirement of wearing a full harness was too much for Wilson. The tightness of the straps was more than his sensory system could process, and we had to move on to something else. However, the next year we were given free access to use the harness for as long as we needed to, and little by little over a whole hour, Wilson allowed the straps to be tightened enough to safely go on the climbing wall. And climb he did! Wilson's sense of pride was contagious and his fellow campers were ecstatic for him. Our time at camp was filled with countless other 'firsts', and year by year we have built memories that will stay with both of us.

This year, for the first time ever, Wilson has been able to attend a camp which is not exclusively designed for children with special needs. His brother is also attending this camp. I believe that attendance at this camp would not have been possible several years ago. Slowly, we have been able to realize a sense of inclusion into the general stream."

Excerpt from Psycho-Educational Assessment Performed by the Local School Psychologist

RESULTS OF THE BEHAVIOUR RATING INVENTORY OF EXECUTIVE FUNCTION (BRIEF)

The BRIEF is an instrument that helps us to understand an individual's executive functioning. Executive functioning refers to a person's ability to maintain attention and to make decisions. The results in the table below are based on the responses of Wilson's teacher and parent. Both Wilson's parent and teacher showed elevated scores in the negativity index. However, given the nature of Wilson's diagnosis, it is not unusual to see higher than expected scores in these areas. (See Key Terms for definitions of **T-Score** and **Percentile**.)

BRIEF™ Score Summary Table

Index/Scale	Teacher		Parent	
	T-Score	Percentile	T-Score	Percentile
Inhibit	87	> = 99	82	> = 99
Shift	79	98	91	> = 99
Emotional Control	78	98	71	98
Behavioural Regulation Index (BRI)	86	98	85	> = 99
Initiate	84	> = 99	84	> = 99
Working Memory	90	> = 99	80	> = 99
Plan/Organize	74	95	84	> = 99
Organization of Materials	77	96	71	> = 99
Monitor	86	> = 99	79	> = 99
Metacognition Index (MI)	85	> = 99	86	> = 99
Global Executive Composite (GEC)	88	> = 99	88	> = 99
Scale	**Raw Score**	**Cumulative Percentile**	**Protocol Classification**	
Negativity	5	95–98	Elevated	
Inconsistency	2	98	Acceptable	

Note: Male, age-specific norms have been used to generate this profile.

For additional normative information, refer to Appendices A–D in the *BRIEF™ Professional Manual*.

Source: Reproduced by special permission of the Publisher, Psychological Assessment Resources, Inc., 16204 North Florida Avenue, Lutz, Florida 33549, from the Behavior Rating Inventory of Executive Function, by Gerard A. Gioia, Peter K. Isquith, Steven C. Guy, and Lauren Kenworthy, Copyright 1996, 1998, 2000 by PAR, Inc. Further reproduction is prohibited without permission of PAR, Inc.

The scores in the table above indicate that both the teacher and parent see Wilson as having significant executive functioning issues that impact his ability to be independent and self-directed. Given his ASD diagnosis, this is not unexpected and supports the need to be diligent in our efforts to help guide him through his day.

ADAPTIVE BEHAVIOUR ASSESSMENT SYSTEM: SECOND EDITION (ABAS-II)

The ABAS-II provides a comprehensive and diagnostic assessment of individuals with different disabilities that can be compared to cognitive abilities to determine whether they are working within acceptable limits.

The results in the table below indicate that both Wilson's teacher and parent see him as having very limited adaptive behaviour skills. Skills at this level are reflective of individuals with significant disabilities and often reflect cognitive disabilities. Given that Wilson already has a diagnosis of a severe intellectual disability, these results support that diagnosis and indicate the need for long-term support and care for Wilson.

Adaptive Skill Areas	Parent Score	Teacher Score
Communication	1	1
Community Use	1	1
Functional Academics	1	1
School/Home Living	1	1
Health and Safety	1	1
Leisure	1	1
Self Care	1	1
Self Direction	1	1
Social	1	1
General Adaptive Composite	40 ± 4	40 ± 4
Percentile	<0.1	<0.1

Note: Scores that fall in the range of 10 ± 3 are considered to be in the average range. General Adaptive Composites of 100 ± 15 are also in the average range.

Source: Used by permission of Nan Stevens

SUMMARY

The purpose of this assessment was to provide updated information for Wilson's school planning and for future referral to Community Living BC (CLBC). He was previously diagnosed as having a severe intellectual disability and this assessment confirms that he has an intellectual disability in combination with his ASD diagnosis. However, Wilson is not testable in the traditional sense and therefore, we need to rely on the use of other assessment information from observation and from those working with Wilson. Based on the information from the BRIEF and the ABAS, we can state that he continues to present with a significant intellectual disability that continues to affect his ability to learn and progress. As CLBC requires the use of certain language in order to provide support for individuals, we will be referring to the *Diagnostic Statistical Manual for Mental Disorders* terminology to provide a diagnosis for Wilson. Given that Wilson is not testable, it would be more appropriate to diagnose him as having Developmental Delay, Severity Unspecified.[1] This diagnosis will allow him access to community services from Child and Youth with Special Needs as a child, and from Community Living BC once he reaches the age of 19.

Page from a Recent Individual Educational Plan (IEP)

This IEP was prepared conjointly with the Individual Achievement Program (IAP) teacher, CEA, and parents.

Third Long-Term Goal: Wilson will improve his ability to express himself.

Current Level of Performance:

Wilson is not consistent in using his verbal skills. He can use single words and word combinations but needs further support to expand his skills and improve expressive vocabulary.

---

[1] This classification is from the DSM-IV. The DSM-5 classification of "Unspecified Intellectual Disability" would likely be used for these purposes, as stated in his full psycho-educational assessment report.

Action Plan (Objective)	Adaptations/ Strategies/Materials	Personnel	Evaluation
1. 8 weeks from the date of this signed document, Wilson will verbally label nouns for everyday objects or pictures of objects to a level of 80% correct during trials. Objects are: hat, scissors, chair, toothbrush, apple, banana, bowl, plate, cup, fork, and spoon.	■ Use planned activities and the natural environment to present opportunities for understanding these labels. ■ Keep a record of his progress.	Speech/ Language Pathologist Classroom staff IAP teacher CEA	■ Assess progress daily ■ Review objective monthly ■ Assess knowledge in individual session and in daily routines
2. 8 weeks from the date of this signed document, Wilson will verbally label actions that are shown in pictures or demonstrated to a level of 80% correct during trials. Actions are: swim, eat, drink, ride, run, walk, sit, throw.		Speech/ Language Pathologist Classroom staff IAP teacher CEA	■ Documentation sheet
3. 8 weeks from the date of this signed document, Wilson will use an audible volume of voice when naming objects he knows to a level of 50% of the time in trials. Words targeted are: car, bed, pizza, bike, cup.	■ Praise normal volume when used (e.g., used in greetings). ■ Praise an increase in volume even if not fully a normal voice.	Speech/ Language Pathologist Classroom staff IAP teacher CEA	■ Documentation sheet

Source: Kim Calder Stegemann, Angela AuCoin, *Inclusive Education: Stories of Success and Hope in a Canadian Context,* 1Ce., © 2018, Pearson Education, Inc., New York, NY.

General Comments

This case study is a lovely depiction of a young lad who has many gifts and talents to offer his family, school community, and social relationships. It is also a perfect example of our journey, as educators and educational institutions, towards more inclusive practices. One of the overarching goals of inclusive education is for "every individual to feel accepted, valued, and safe . . . [to provide] meaningful involvement and equal access to the benefits of citizenship" (Manitoba Education, 2011, p. 1). It is clear from this case study that Wilson's parents, educators, and caregivers continue to work at creating accepting and safe environments, whether that is in a general or special education classroom. It is also evident that both special needs and non-special needs students have benefited from Wil's inclusion in educational and recreational activities.

As the UNESCO description of inclusive education states, inclusion is a "process of addressing and responding to the diversity of needs of all learners . . . [and] involves changes and modifications in content, approaches, structures and strategies" (United Nations Educational, Scientific and Cultural Organization, 2005, p. 13).[*] Wil's parents have experienced this process firsthand, as they have explored several different educational options. Even though ABA is a research-based intervention, it clearly was not a good match for Wil, who has many complex needs and does not fit the cognitive profile of individuals who have had success with this approach. Similarly, the classroom teacher, certified educational assistant (CEA), and respite worker all provide examples of the slow but steady progress towards more inclusive educational and recreational experiences. Therefore, even though the process of reducing barriers and optimizing opportunities for

participation may seem protracted, it is important to continually take those steps, however small.

It is also important to note that the focus has been on making adjustments to the environment, approaches, structures, and strategies, so that Wilson can develop socially, emotionally, cognitively, and physically to the greatest extent possible. This has required persistence, commitment, and an optimistic attitude that demonstrates the genuine value these individuals have for all children, disabled or non-disabled. Repeatedly, you hear a desire to uncover Wilson's interests and talents, while respecting his unique sensory needs. In the words of the CEA, *"[t]he activities and work are adapted to fit his needs, and not the other way around."*

I also find it interesting that various "voices" use the word *integration* versus *inclusion*. This signals to me that the educational community has not, yet, reconciled its philosophy and practices. As introduced in Chapter 2 of this text, *mainstreaming* and *integration* were the terms used in the 1970s to the 1990s to describe the process of intertwining the special and general education streams. The underlying philosophy was to offer students the "least restrictive" learning environment.

Recently, our profession has grappled with eliminating "special" education (Cochran-Smith & Dudley-Marling, 2012; Fuchs, Fuchs, & Stecker, 2010; Gliona, Gonzales, & Jacobson, 2005; Kauffman, McGee, & Brigham, 2004; Porter, 2010; Zigmond, Kloo, & Volonino, 2009), in favour of a comprehensive public school system where every child belongs (and begins) in the general education classroom. Services and levels of support are then added later, as required. As Ferguson and Ferguson (2012) suggest, the "continuum of less or more restrictive placement should be replaced by a logic of redistributed support and expertise that allows all types of students to learn together in all sorts of arrangements"

---

[*] From Guidelines for Inclusion: Ensuring Access to Education for All. Published by UNESCO, © 2005.

(p. 303).[†] In this particular case study, it may be possible to provide aids such as trampolines, quiet spaces, and weighted blankets in the general education classroom, as well, which could benefit all children in the school. This would require, however, all staff to be trained in the effective use of such aids.

Connections to Theoretical Frameworks

Using a social justice framework, such as Waitoller & Artiles's (2013) three-dimensional conceptualization of justice, which will be discussed further in Chapter 13, one can see that Wilson's educational journey has been one of increased a) access and participation, b) recognition and valuing, and c) opportunities for advancement of the non-dominant group.

Beginning with "Access and Participation," we can see that over time, Wilson has increased participation within the wider school community, and recreationally, progressed into a "regular" summer camp. There are elements of both universal design for learning (UDL) and response to intervention (RTI) in this process. For example, RTI is about establishing and redesigning environments. There is no question that a great deal of progress monitoring has occurred, which has informed changes to Wilson's educational and social environments. Continual problem solving (e.g., moving away from ABA or allowing a slow transition into the climbing harness) has helped to achieve both optimal learning environments for Wilson and increased opportunities in the general education stream. UDL focuses on reducing the barriers to participation and growth, and Wilson's educational team has demonstrated different ways of adjusting the educational or social environment. Participation in a general education music class is a perfect example of this. As the special education teacher notes, *"[d]eveloping his abilities and growing his courage one visit at a time has been a learning experience for Wilson and all the other students in the general education class. Not only did Wilson need to develop skills in participating with others, the other students needed to learn to accept his differences. We gradually increased his time, and we encourage greater participation as he is increasingly successful."*

There are several examples of "Recognition and Valuing," which are consistent with principles of UDL. Both of these approaches are rooted in social justice and the inherent worth of all individuals, valuing of the contributions that diversity can make to the group as a whole. Recall Wilson's parent's comment that the standardized tests, while necessary for funding purposes, *"do not reveal anything about his gifts and strengths."* Wilson's love of music, social and outgoing nature, and kind heart are all acknowledged and valued. The school staff recognizes that Wil has much to teach both staff and students within this caring learning community.

The last part of the Waitoller and Artiles framework is "Opportunities for Advancement of the Non-dominant Group," which could be viewed as personal empowerment. Certainly, Wilson is encouraged to "be himself" and to become the person that HE was meant to become. For example, his parents and teachers encourage him to develop close friendships with other high-needs children within his classroom. The school staff is developing a heightened sense of awareness and understanding about "difference," as noted by the CEA: *"These children are showing others that, no matter who you are or what differences one has, everyone deserves to be accepted and treated with respect."* Although there is not an administrator voice in this case study, one must assume that there is strong leadership both within the school and the school district, with a commitment to excellence and achievement for all staff and students, which supports the notion of empowerment and opportunities for advancement of children and youth with exceptional learning needs.

[†] From The Future of Inclusive Educational Practice: Constructive Tension and the Potential for Reflective Reform. Published by FreePatentsOnline, © 1998.

Summary of Wilson's Case Study

Wilson is, indeed, an interesting young fellow with many strengths and challenges. His family and education team have continually made adjustments to his environment to allow for progressive development and to move towards more inclusive experiences. The addition of sensory regulation breaks throughout the day has been crucial for Wil. He has not been expected to "fit the system," but rather his family and educational team have honoured Wil's personal strengths and current needs. As Wil's mother noted, *"...our focus is on raising a child who is happy, connected to his family and community, who can self-regulate, and who enjoys learning in natural contexts. Overall health, well-being, and functional life skills are our goal for the foreseeable future."*

Key Terms

Applied Behaviour Analysis (ABA) ABA is a systematic approach to instruction that breaks tasks or skills into small, achievable steps. With frequent repetition and corrective feedback, the learner slowly acquires the target skill.

autism spectrum disorder (ASD) ASD describes a range of conditions with varying degrees of delay, typically associated with communication, social cues, intellect, and sensory processing. At one end of the spectrum is Asperger's syndrome, which is a relatively mild degree of impairment, up to conditions such as Rett syndrome, fragile X syndrome, to PDD-NOS (Pervasive Developmental Disorder-Not Otherwise Specified).

***Diagnostic and Statistical Manual of Mental Disorders* (DSM)** This manual provides a standard classification system of mental disorders and is used by mental health professionals in Canada and the United States. The most recent version is the DSM-5.

individual achievement program (IAP) In this educational jurisdiction, IAP refers to a segregated classroom within a school setting for children with multiple complex learning and health needs. The student to certified education assistant ratio is no more than 2:1.

individual educational plan (IEP) Also referred to as an individual program plan (IPP), the IEP notes the student's strengths and needs, and identifies specific goals and objectives, as well as strategies and the personnel who will be responsible for assisting with the goals within a given timeframe.

integration Integration is a term that was commonly used in the 1970s to the 1990s to mean the participation in the general educational environment of individuals with unique learning needs.

percentile rank This is a statistical measure, typically used to report scores on norm-referenced tests, which indicates the percentage of cases that fall below the given score. A percentile rank of 80 means that 80 percent of individuals scored lower.

psycho-educational assessment These types of assessments are typically performed by school psychologists or registered community psychologists to determine current overall level of cognitive ability and adaptive functioning.

T-score A T-score is one of several different standard scores that are used to represent normally distributed data. The mean or average is 50, with intervals of 10 above and below the mean.

Questions to Consider

1. In what ways might Wilson become involved in more activities and events offered within the wider school population? What must the educational team consider before embarking on any new initiatives that foster inclusion?

   _____

   _____

   _____

   _____

   _____

   _____

   _____

2. What administrative support do you assume has occurred and is in place within the school and school district to promote successful inclusive education?

   _____

   _____

   _____

   _____

   _____

   _____

   _____

3. Explain why educators must be cognizant of parental and family stressors when working with children with exceptional learning needs?

   _____

   _____

   _____

   _____

   _____

   _____

   _____

4. How might the special education teacher initiate and develop a co-teaching relationship with general education teachers within the school? Should general education teachers be the ones to seek out co-teaching relationships with special education teachers? If so, what would help to initiate this working relationship? What role can the CEA play in this co-teaching?

_____

_____

_____

_____

_____

_____

_____

5. What is the importance of psycho-educational assessment in program planning? How might this information be valuable in the context of planning for Wilson at home and in the community? How can these assessments act as barriers to social, emotional, cognitive, and physical growth for children with and without disabilities?

_____

_____

_____

_____

_____

_____

_____

Useful Websites

Autism Speaks
www.autismspeaks.org

Community Living British Columbia
www.communitylivingbc.ca

American Psychiatric Association for the DSM
www.psychiatry.org/psychiatrists/practice/dsm

References

American Psychiatric Association. (2015). *DSM*. Retrieved from http://www.psychiatry.org/psychiatrists/practice/dsm

Cochran-Smith, M., & Dudley-Marling, C. (2012). Diversity in teacher education and special education: The issues that divide. *Journal of Teacher Education, 63*(4), 237–244.

Ferguson, P. M., & Ferguson, D. L. (2012). The future of inclusive educational practice: Constructive tension and the potential for reflective reform. *Childhood Education, 74*(5), 302–308.

Fuchs, D., Fuchs, L. S., & Stecker, P. M. (2010). The "blurring" of special education in a new continuum of general education placements and services. *Exceptional Children, 76*(3), 301–323.

Gliona, M. F., Gonzales, A. K., & Jacobson, E. S. (2005). Dedicated, not segregated: Suggested changes in thinking about instructional environments and in the language of special education. In J. M. Kauffman & D. P. Hallahan (Eds.), *The illusion of full inclusion: A comprehensive critique of the current special education bandwagon* (2nd ed.) (pp. 135–148.) Austin, TX: ED-Pro, Inc.

Kauffman, J. M., McGee, K., & Brigham, M. (2004). Enabling or disabling? Observations on change in the purpose and outcomes of special education. *Phi Delta Kappa, 85*, 613–620.

Manitoba Education. (2011). *Towards inclusion: Supporting positive behaviour in Manitoba classrooms.* Winnipeg, MN: Government of Manitoba.

Porter, G. L. (2010). Making Canadian schools inclusive: A call to action. *Education Canada, 48*(2), 62–66.

United Nations Educational, Scientific and Cultural Organization (UNESCO). (2005). *Guidelines for inclusion: Ensuring access to education for all.* France: UNESCO. Retrieved from http://unesdoc.unesco.org/ima

Waitoller, F. R., & Artiles, A. J. (2013). A decade of professional development research for inclusive education: A critical review and notes for a research program. *Review of Educational Research, 83*(3), 319–356.

Zigmond, N., Kloo, A., & Volonino, V. (2009). What, where, and how? Special education in the climate of full inclusion. *Exceptionality, 17*(4), 189–204.

Chapter 5
Gabrielle Case Study

Kathy Howery

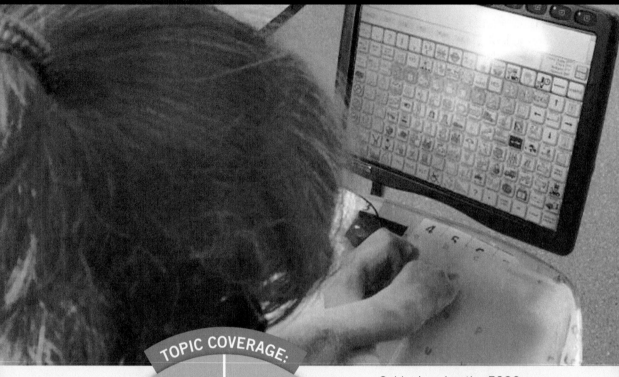

TOPIC COVERAGE:

Assistive Technology

Athetoid Cerebral Palsy

Augmentative and Alternative Communication

Psycho-Educational Assessment

Specialized Supports and Services

Transition Planning

Gabby is using the ECO2 (an augmentative and alternative communication device).
Source: Debra & David Hagen

The student will:

- Describe various assistive technologies and explain their importance for reducing barriers to accessing the general education system and wider society

- Explain how, or if, modified programs fit into the inclusive education perspective

- Provide examples of adjustments to the educational, social, and recreational environments in order to reduce barriers to participation

Preamble

Gabrielle, or Gabby as she likes to be known, is an 18-year-old young lady who jokingly refers to herself as a "cyborg." Gabby uses technology in every aspect of her life. She has been connected to devices and screens since she was born. Her mother Donna tells of spending the first weekend of her daughter's young life glued to the neonatal monitor which read Gabby's oxygen saturation levels as the newborn struggled to learn how to breathe on her own. To this day, Donna still twitches when she hears the ding of an elevator; it takes her back to the neonatal hospital unit and the monitor alerting the nurses to see if Gabby was alright. At the end of that first stressful weekend of watching and listening to the machine, Gabby defied the odds and, you might say, established a lifelong relationship with machines.

Gabby has a diagnosis of spastic **athetoid** quadriparetic **cerebral palsy**, Level IV on the Gross Motor Functioning Scale. She uses a powered wheelchair for mobility; an augmentative and alternative communication device to speak with and text her teachers, educational assistants (EAs), and friends; a computer to write; and an iPad to read! Gabby literally uses her head to control these various devices. She has a switch on either side of her head that she uses to access her communication device and her computer. A device on her wheelchair tray switches her controls of everything from driving her chair, to accessing her **augmentative and alternative communication (AAC)** device, to scanning through apps on her iPad. No wonder she laughing refers to herself as a cyborg! (Some provinces have funding for supports and services for assistive technologies and in particular ACC devices like those used by Gabby. See Useful Websites later in this chapter.)

Gabby lives in a very small town about an hour from the city. There is one elementary and one high school in the town and Gabby has attended both. This year will be her final year in the K–12 education system. In June, she will be awarded a Certificate of High School Achievement, after completing the required **Knowledge and Employability (K & E) courses**, and graduate with the students with whom she began kindergarten so many years ago. In this small town there is no special school or special classes for students with disabilities; inclusion happens because there is no other way.

FAST FACTS ABOUT... CEREBRAL PALSY

Cerebral Palsy (CP) is a neurological disorder caused by non-progressive brain injury or malformation while the child's brain is developing.

Characteristics

- impaired movement of one or more limbs
- may affect one or both sides of the body
- may have hypertonic (stiff limbs) or hypotonic (loose, floppy limbs) muscle tone
- may include involuntary muscle movement

For more information see: Cerebral Palsy at www.cerebralpalsy.org/about-cerebral-palsy/definition

Although Gabby has not attended specialized schools, she has, in large part due to her mother's amazing commitment, been actively monitored and supported by a specialized outreach service provided by the rehabilitation hospital some 150 km away. In her elementary school years, the school team would often accompany Gabby and her mother to the city for appointments and to attend various professional learning opportunities. In recent years, Gabby's EA (educational assistant) has attended most of the visits to the hospital to learn how Gabby's technology works and how to best support its functional use.

As you will read in the case study, Gabby wants to be a writer. She wrote a poem that will be read as part of the graduation ceremonies. It may take Gabby several minutes to write a couple of sentences. She moves her head back and forth to select words and letters from her device, and it is not uncommon to see sweat running down her back from the physical effort. Being a cyborg is hard work! As she explains it, "first I think what to say then I input those words into my device. Once I have what I want to say I push speak to say those words out loud." The cognitive and physical demands of speaking and writing with a speech generating device are tremendous, but as one can see from the sample of her work below, she had tackled those demands with gusto and is harnessing the power of today's technologies to speak with her own voice.

Gabby's Essay

My Beautiful Life in Canada

My name Gabby. I am 18 years old. I was born in a small hospital in the beautiful, wild rose prairie Province of Alberta. You can see golden fields, with bobbing pump-jacks everywhere you look.

I was born in Canada on a warm sunny summer's day. This happy time for my parents could have been darkened by a gloomy and dismal cloud. I came in this world not breathing and I had to be taken by an air ambulance to Edmonton hospital. I stayed at the hospital for many weeks and the great doctors and nurses helped me to live. When my parents brought me home they got lots of support from our family, community, and government programs.

When I was six months old I was diagnosed with Cerebral Palsy. I was immediately put in programs to help me. I tried my hardest and after awhile I didn't walk or talk but the doctors, therapists, teachers and my parent's never gave up on me. Everybody tried to look for different ways to help me. With all the technology Canada has, the great funding programs to help pay for my equipment, and supporting my parents with home care. I soon had an electric wheelchair and was using picture symbols to help me communicate. I was able to attend a regular school and make new friends.

When I was in early elementary school I was the first child in my province to receive a government funded communication device. This opened up the world for me. I finally had a voice. Free to say anything. I could talk to my friends and family. I could do what I love to do, writing, all this made me feel like a proud Canadian.

As technology changes, I've had a few devices. I now can use a computer, Internet and text people.

Being born with Cerebral Palsy has not been easy. I have had to work hard to prove to some people that I'm smart. I've had people who are visiting or moved here from other countries come up to my mom and ask "how is she talking on that machine?" As my mom explains that I use two head switches to scan with, I am quick to reply "My name is Gabrielle. I use a communication device to help me speak." They're always amazed and start talking to me. They tell me how lucky I am to have a talker. Where they're from they have nothing like that to help their disabled people. They always ask how much did it cost and I am proud to say that the government funded my device.

I will always be thankful that I was born in Canada. Canada has strongly supported me my whole life. This year I will be graduating with my classmates and continue my journey to be a writer. This is why I am proud to be a Canadian because Canada has helped me to be proud of myself.

Parent Voice

"Gabby has always been a bit of a mystery. When we first got her definite diagnosis of athetoid cerebral palsy (CP) when she was one, the doctor said it was mild. I asked what that meant and he said 'she'll never be a ballerina'. Then when she was older and saw another doctor he said 'just take her home and love her' which I interpreted to mean that he didn't think she would be able to do much. The kind of CP that she has is not usually caused by oxygen deprivation which is what happened when she was born. She has surprised us.

I have been going back and forth to the rehab hospital since she was two years old. I wanted to make sure she had every opportunity to learn to communicate and learn, and that meant that I would take every opportunity that was offered to her even if I had to drive to the city every day.

I am lucky that I have a job with flexibility, to be able to take her into the appointments and clinics and special classroom happenings at the hospital. And she is our only child. I know that it would be really hard if I didn't have that kind of job or if I had other kids that needed me to be there for them, too.

Elementary school was great. She had good friends and a great principal. They included her in everything. All through grade 1 to 6 she attended every class; she had regular homework just like the other kids. If she started to fall behind, they still kept her in class and accommodated in the class. I remember she was even in the school play. She used her talker to speak her lines.

I worked hard to make sure she had friends. When she was in the preschool program at the rehab hospital they told us not to be surprised if our kids didn't get invited to parties etc. So I made sure we always had parties at our place: birthday parties, Hallowe'en parties, Christmas parties, Easter parties; you name it we had parties, and all the kids were invited.

Grade 7 was not bad. The biggest challenge was her language. In junior high she was pulled out to a different room to do language. The language teacher said she didn't know how to teach her. So this is when she started to get pulled out and I think the EA did a lot of her language programming with her.

She had a tough time in grade 9 because the kids seemed to pull away from her. She was sad and she hated school. They kept making her redo her spelling words and other things. (It seemed like they got hung up on things like spelling. If she didn't get 100 percent on her spelling they would keep her behind.) She told me one day that she hated words. She doesn't hate words any more thankfully. She is learning to use her own words, her own way.

The other day when I picked her up I asked her to tell me about her day. She said, 'I had the most divine day mother'. I loved that! I knew those were her words because no one would have put the word 'divine' into her device. She was saying it in her own voice! That is a day I will always remember.

Two things really made a difference for Gabby in the past couple of years. One is that our town and area got real internet (not just dial-up). I started doing a lot of things with her myself, and she really has made leaps and bounds. The other thing is that she has joined a writing group in a town not too far from here. A group of women get together to write and share their writing

Social media post by Gabby.
Source: Debra & David Hagen

once a week. They have let Gabby join their group and have taught her and me so much. It has just been wonderful! They are going to publish a book and she will have a story in it."

Education Assistant Voices

This year for the first time Gabby has had two educational assistants (EAs) working with her. One of them, Mrs. Beach, has been with her since preschool. The second EA, Miss March, is new to Gabby and was put in place by the school so that Gabby would have experiences working with other people, as she leaves the K–12 system and moves into her next life experiences.

MISS MARCH

"I have loved working with Gabby so much this semester! She has taught me so much! We mostly worked together in cosmetology class. I was so amazed by how she worked with her classmates and how they supported her. It has shown me how caring and thoughtful kids can be. Last week, for example, we were in cosmo class and Gabby was trying to tell me something about grad. I was having trouble understanding; then her friend Jane stepped in and said 'just wait, give her some time, she can tell you'. And Jane was right, I just had to wait for Gabby to construct her message! It is so cool to see how these kids know her so well, how she communicates and how to help her say what she wants. The kids are always coming into her room [Gabby has a room where she comes to do school work, eat, and stretch] and writing notes to her on the white board.

The only thing that I worry about working with Gabby is feeding her. I still feel that is kind of scary. But I am getting better at it, and she is teaching me how to do that, too. Gabby is also bringing me into the technological age. She texts all the time through her communication device. She texts her friends in class, and she texts me. One day I was in the other room and she texted me, 'Miss M I need you now'. Wow, I was so impressed.

The most inspiring thing is reading all of her stories! For her to put down all the amazing things that are in her mind, even when it is such hard work for her. I am so impressed and inspired by her, every day."

MRS. BEACH

"I started working with Gabby when she was just three years old. It was quite daunting at first. Especially when she started to learn Minspeak™[1]. I had to learn all those symbols and figure out everything that was under the symbols. Basically I guess she and I learned her language together.

In the beginning we used the Etran a lot. She would answer questions and do her work by pointing with her eyes. It seemed quicker since she didn't know Minspeak well enough yet.

We really didn't start using technology, like the computer and stuff, until she was in grade 6. That is when Laura, the teacher from the rehab hospital, came out.

---

[1] Minspeak™ is a means of coding vocabulary to a small set of icons that are rich in meaning. Minspeak's use of icons taps into a person's natural tendency to associate multiple meanings to pictures.

A student using Etran eye pointing system to communicate.
Source: Courtesy of Low Tech Solutions

It was hard when she was really little. Little kids don't wait around for someone to take a long time to answer their questions. It was hard for Gabby to keep up. Her good friends came around grade 4. We used to have races down the hallway, Gabby in her power chair and the kids in chairs with wheels. It was a hoot.

There was one girl, Amanda, who always waited to say hello to Gabby. She is her good friend to this day. She actually just got a date for Gabby to go to the prom. A football player no less! These kids have made memories together. Gabby is not the kid in the wheelchair. She is the funny girl, the girl with the weird sense of humour, and the girl who always came up with great ideas for fundraisers when something bad happened in the world.

Things were really good until issues around liability started coming up, for example, when the kids went swimming. Gabby was too cold in the big pool and wanted to go to the hot tub. There wasn't a life guard for the hot tub so it ended up Gabby didn't go swimming with the class. And on field trips it was hard because of her wheelchair. There isn't a wheelchair accessible van in our school.

In grade 8 the principal had an epiphany. He decided that Gabby had to go to a leadership conference with the other kids who were chosen to go. He drove an hour to the main school district office to get the accessible van and then came back to pick up Gabby and her crew, and drove them to Edmonton for a leaders conference. Gabby told me when she got back 'I smiled the whole way!'"

Student Support Facilitator Voice

"I am new to the school this year so I can't say I know Gabby well, but I consider myself lucky to have had this chance to work with her. There have been quite a few challenges and lots of learning along the way, but it has been a great experience.

The continuing challenge with Gabby is that you have to consider the way she communicates. Without Mrs. B I would be lost. How do you do a valid assessment on a student who communicates in such a different manner than the rest of us? We had help from lots of people though. There was the support of the specialist team from the rehab hospital, and *this year our own Assistive Technology team was involved. That team was really hoping to be able to continue to work with her next year, but as the new Education Act[2] did not pass and she turns 19 this summer, our time with her is now over.*

Gabby has been taking a modified K & E program. She has been included in the K & E classroom and will be receiving a K & E Certificate. We have created some locally designed courses so that she will get the credits she needs to graduate. Mostly these have been in the area of Life Skills Math, such as what is a cheque, those kinds of things. We also have been having her involved in some special projects to help her learn about blogging and give her more opportunity for writing experiences. We also have her back at the Elementary School two days a week this semester for work experience. She helps in the library and reads her stories to the various classes. She loves it and the kids love her. They are so excited when she comes to their classes.

I am so happy for Gabby because of the opportunities that there are now for her to connect with things like Facebook. She will have a great social network! I am very hopeful for her future through the use of technology."

Psycho-Educational Assessment Completed for Move to Adult Services

As for other big changes, a **transition plan** is an important tool when a student is leaving school. In anticipation of Gabby's transition to adult services, a transition planning service case conference was held, attended by her parents, the learning support facilitator, her EA, as well as representatives from various departments within Alberta Health Services—AISH (Assured Income for Severely Disabled), Alberta Works, OPG (Office of Public Guardian), and PDD (Persons with Developmental Disabilities)—to identify service needs, based on Gabby and her family's future goals.

The school reports that much of Gabby's work is adapted, including the use of matching and multiple-choice formats to allow her to more quickly and easily answer questions on assignments and tests. Of particular concern to her educational staff is that Gabby tends to quickly forget the information and skills that she has learned, and requires extensive repetition, practice, and linking of new learning to previous learning before she is able to retain new information. Of particular concern to Gabby's mother is that, as an adult, she be able to access the supports she requires in order to pursue her goals of living in Edmonton and attending college.

RESULTS OF PSYCHO-EDUCATIONAL ASSESSMENT: STANFORD–BINET (SB)-5 AND WECHSLER INDIVIDUAL ACHIEVEMENT TEST (WIAT)-III

Prior to attempting cognitive assessment tasks, a brief "trial" was completed by the author with Gabby on her ECO2 AAC device to ensure she would be able to adequately answer formal assessment questions on the SB-5 and WIAT-III. This method

[2] The new *Education Act* allotted for public K–12 education services to be available up to an individual's 21st birthday, instead of the current age limit of 19 years.

Stanford–Binet Intelligence Scale: Fifth Edition (SB-5)—Selected Subtests

As current physical limitations made it difficult for Gabby to interact with the assessment tool, the following selected subtests were administered:

Fluid Reasoning: Both verbal (scaled score 9) and non-verbal skills (scaled score 10) are fairly equally developed, and indicated Average abilities.

Knowledge: Overall skills fell within the Low Average range.

Quantitative Reasoning: Verbal (scaled score 5) and non-verbal abilities (scaled score 5) are evenly developed in the Borderline Impaired or Delayed Range.

STANFORD–BINET INTELLIGENCE SCALE: FIFTH EDITION		
Area	Ability and Background Factors Measured	Scaled Score (Av = 8 to 12)
NON-VERBAL REASONING SCALE		
Fluid reasoning	Ability to solve novel problems using inductive or deductive reasoning, with reduced influence from previously learned material	9
Knowledge	Solve problems using fund of general information and crystallized ability	5
Quantitative reasoning	Reasoning with numbers, facility in mental arithmetic	5
Visual–spatial processing	Ability to see patterns, relationship, or spatial orientations in both verbal and non-verbal areas	Unable to test
Working memory	Ability to store and retrieve visual and verbal information from short-term memory	Unable to test
VERBAL REASONING SCALE		
Fluid reasoning	Ability to solve novel problems using inductive or deductive reasoning, with reduced influence from previously learned material	10
Knowledge	Solve problems using fund of general information and crystallized ability	9
Quantitative reasoning	Reasoning with numbers, facility in mental arithmetic	5
Visual–spatial processing	Ability to see patterns, relationship, or spatial orientations in both verbal and non-verbal areas	Unable to test
Working memory	Ability to store and retrieve visual and verbal information from short-term memory	Unable to test

It is likely due to Gabby's significant expressive speech and motor challenges, including a relative lack of ability to explore her environment and learn with the same ease and frequency as her peers, that her overall learning and development has been negatively impacted over the years. This has likely lead to developmental gaps and disordered and delayed patterns of learning in some areas.

STANFORD–BINET INTELLIGENCE SCALE: FIFTH EDITION				
I.Q. SCORES				
	Score	**Percentile**	**Age Equivalent (Years-Months)**	**Classification**
NON-VERBAL REASONING SCALE	N/A	N/A	-	N/A
VERBAL REASONING SCALE	N/A	N/A	-	N/A
FULL SCALE:	N/A	N/A	-	N/A
FACTOR SCORES				
	Score	**Percentile***	**Age Equivalent (Years-Months)**	**Classification**
Fluid reasoning	97	34	<15-3	Average
Knowledge	83	13	12-3	Low average
Quantitative reasoning	72	3	8-2	Borderline
Visual-spatial processing	N/A	N/A	N/A	-
Working memory	N/A	N/A	N/A	-

*Percentile ranks indicate the percentage of students in the client's age group that obtained a score at or below his or her score.

N/A – Unable to calculate based on scores achieved.

Source: From Stanford-Binet Intelligence Scales, 5e (SB-5) Examiner's Manual by Gale H. Roid. Copyright © 2003 by PRO-ED. Used by permission of PRO-ED.

of communication was deemed adequate for these purposes, thus the assessment was undertaken. It should be noted, however, that the use of the ECO2 during testing represents a departure from the standardized administration of these tests, which may have impacted the results obtained in an unknown way and to an unknown degree. Although Gabby appeared to put forth her very best effort on all assessments tasks and for the reasons stated above, the results should be interpreted with caution.

Wechsler Individual Achievement Test: 3rd Edition (WIAT-III, Canadian Norms)

Adapted Word Reading and Reading Comprehension Subtests

Due to limited time and student fatigue, only two subtests were attempted: Reading Comprehension and an adapted Etran version of the Word Reading subtest.

The Reading Comprehension subtest was attempted at the grade 4 level, but was discontinued due to time constraints. Only the first of three passages were read, as it took an inordinate amount of time for her to read the passage and answer the corresponding questions. Of the three questions that she had time to answer, she correctly answered two recall questions. Significant alterations in the administration of the Word Reading subtest changed the task from one of sight word reading to one of word identification, which is a much simpler task.

The results of recent achievement testing on the Peabody Individual Achievement Test–Revised (PIAT-R), when compared to her intellectual abilities as identified on the SB-5, indicate that Gabby is performing academically at a level *considerably below* her identified abilities and potential. That being said, it is not uncommon for students with the diagnosis of severe CP to experience learning difficulties. Possible reasons for this discrepancy may include school absences due to medical reasons, lack of motivation and effort on Gabby's part, and/or in the absence of information on Gabby's cognitive abilities, a mismatch between educational programming, expectations, and ability.

Summary

Gabby will need continual support and monitoring, significantly more than others her age, primarily because of her significant motor deficits and extremely low adaptive skills, but also to ensure her continued physical health and safety. At present, Gabby is fully dependent on adult support for all aspects of her daily living in all activities and circumstances, and is completely dependent on her AAC ECO2 communication device to reliably communicate her wants and needs to others. Gabby will require ongoing individual support to facilitate her communication and social interactions with others, as well as to assist her in meeting her own personal goals and to maximize her lifelong learning potential.

PAGE FROM A RECENT INDIVIDUAL PROGRAM PLAN (IPP)

This long-term goal is one of two that were added to Gabby's **individual program plan (IPP)** in her last year of school. Each of her goals were similar, in that they focused on her demonstrating knowledge and understanding of the particular Knowledge and Employability course. The excerpt in the table below shares the two short-term goals for her English Language Arts course.

Third Long-Term Goal: Gabby will demonstrate knowledge and understanding of ELA 20-4. Programs of Study

Short-Term Objective	Learning Strategy	Assessment Procedure	Anecdotal Comments
By then end of January, G will work on: ■ Description from images ■ Stories from images ■ Story structure ■ Reading comprehension (grade 2)	1 on 1 support Positive reinforcement Audio-visual cues as needed Modified assignments as needed Raz-Kids Learning A–Z Don Johnson resources Reading & Writing the 4 Blocks Way (Karen Erickson)	Completed assignments Quizzes Anecdotal records	G has met this goal. G has worked well on interpreting images and has developed the skill of connecting emotionally with them.
By the end of June, G will produce written material using the writing process whereby she will brainstorm, draft, proofread, edit, and publish final pieces of writing	EA support Writing process booklet Graphic organisers Blogging support from AT team	Observation, feedback, publication, responses	Gabby has produced various samples of written material using the process. Some of these samples have been entered in various competitions. G has been working hard on sounding out word families using her inner voice to target gaps in her phonological knowledge. G has also composed not only stories but poems also. G has embraced the concept that writing is a process that requires the various stages of brainstorming, proofreading, editing, and producing a final copy. G has also engaged in Raz-Kids to enhance her reading fluency, vocabulary, and reading comprehension and has enjoyed this program immensely.

Source: Used by permission of Debbie Hagen

General Comments

What is inclusion? Definitions abound, revealing two conceptualizations: those based upon key features of inclusion and those based on the removal of barriers to inclusion (Loreman, Forlin, Chambers, Sharma, & Deppeler, 2014). Ultimately, though, schools that exemplify effective inclusion exhibit various features of inclusion, all the while guarding for and addressing barriers that lead to exclusion (Forlin, 2013).

The preceding account of one girl's, Gabby's, experiences, as well as those of her team, illustrates key elements inherent in both conceptualizations and the successful inclusion of Gabby. Context in this case, as in all cases, plays a role. In contrast to lacking resources, this remote and small community and school afforded Gabby and her team opportunities and experiences that were fundamental to her early inclusion and her ultimate achievements. From the outset, Gabby was not excluded or marginalized (Loreman et al., 2014) and there was no segregation or streaming (Nes, 2009). Rather, Gabby experienced school immersed with her same-aged peers—her neighbourhood friends—in a positive and welcoming school and community culture of shared values. Further, she benefited from a consistent, caring, multi-disciplinary, cross-ministry team dedicated to Gabby and working collaboratively to understand and support her needs, while at the same time learning and improving their practice. In Gabby's words, *"The doctors, therapists, teachers and my parents never gave up on me."* Moreover, the broader context of providing resources (i.e., funding, training) for assistive technology was central to Gabby's communication, literacy development, and social interactions, ultimately exposing *her* voice, and enabling independence.

We focus our lens on how the roles of collaborative team approaches and assistive technology, both integral components of the universal design for learning (UDL; Rose & Meyer, 2005) and response to intervention (RTI; Fuchs & Fuchs, 2006) frameworks, defined inclusion for Gabby, allowing her access to education "through the front door."

Connections to Theoretical Frameworks

Collaborative Team Fundamental to Gabby's growth from the very beginning of her schooling was her school–home team. Through the voices of key members who supported Gabby we understand the collaborative way of working that is necessary if students like Gabby are to achieve. Creative and collaborative team partnerships with the common goal of focusing on what is best for Gabby, the *whole* of Gabby (i.e., social, physical, intellectual, creative, emotional), were central to her development; a team working in concert to seek resources and provide opportunities and experiences that develop, indeed uncover, possibilities in Gabby (Mortier, Van Hove, & De Schauwer, 2010). Effective team partnerships are united, flexible, creative, and deliberate in examining and adjusting values and goals, and are accountable (Mortier et al., 2010). We witness this in the team's resourcefulness and creativity in acknowledging Gabby's diverse needs and developing authentic and meaningful educational programs for her (e.g., locally designed courses, writing experiences, work experience in elementary school), reflecting the principles underlying a UDL approach. Moreover, commitment, equality, respect, trust, and advocacy are key principles among team members who effectively include and interact with families (Turnbull & Turnbull, 2015). These ways of working as a team are essential to effective RTI processes at each level, wherein team members work together problem solving; making decisions; and implementing, assessing, monitoring, and evaluating instruction and learning (Fuchs & Fuchs, 2006).

We see these essential qualities in the collaboration of Gabby's school–home team, inspired by the advocacy, drive, and tireless energy of Gabby's mother. Gabby's story reveals what can be achieved when drawing on localized knowledge of parents, school personnel, and provincial resources. Her story demonstrates the need for collaboration and group attention to and reflection on not just the educational goals for the child, but also the barriers that emerge naturally through the course of providing rich and varied experiences and opportunities. Instructional decision-making is embedded within the dynamic context of the classroom and the curriculum, based upon a problem-solving approach, reflecting key principles and processes of both the UDL and RTI frameworks. The success of inclusion lies in the everyday actions on the part of the school team to recognize barriers, and develop and implement solutions to overcome them. Indeed, this focus provides the opportunity to predict and, in turn, pre-empt barriers. As the creators of supports, the responsibility, ownership, and accountability is shared (Mortier et al., 2010).

Role of Assistive Technology Assistive technology (AT) is indispensable in Gabby's life—she has a lifelong, embodied relationship with machines. AT allows her to move in her world, to write, to read, and to speak with her own voice. AT provides independence and the opportunity to participate fully in her world. Largely through AT, Gabby expresses her knowledge, views, and beliefs. Through this communication, the uniqueness that

is Gabby unfolds. The multiple means of engagement, expression, and representation inherent in UDL are clearly reflected in the AT that is essential for Gabby.

We wish to highlight two points related to Gabby's speech-generating device (SGD). First, AT was introduced early with low tech, with Etran training, and gradually and systematically progressed into high tech, the SGD. Early interventions were important steps in the development of Gabby's skills and her inclusion (Guralnick, 2000), as well as the timely, gradual introduction and progress in training that occurred for all members of the team (Green, 2014; Zabala, 2010). Indeed, team member training in the functions and use of AT is one of the most influential factors in the effective and sustained use of AT (Chmiliar, 2007; Chung & Carter, 2013; Copley & Ziviani, 2004; Sharpe, 2010). Without early introduction, systematic and ongoing training and support, Gabby's competent use of technology would not be what it is today (Naraian & Surabian, 2014). All members of Gabby's team required training, especially those who work most closely with her (Mortier et al., 2010). In a less rural setting, peer training may be necessary to promote social interaction and support inclusion (Chung & Carter, 2013; Loreman et al., 2014). While not explicit in this account, there may have been focused discussion for Gabby and her peers, very likely modelling, and no doubt ongoing opportunities and support for social interactions. However, growing up and attending her community school alongside her same-aged peers from year to year figured prominently, naturally supporting her social inclusion.

Gabby acknowledges the importance of her early introduction to a communication device, highlighting the UDL principle of engagement. *"This opened up the world for me. I finally had*

(continued)

a voice. Free to say anything. I could talk to my friends and family. I could do what I love to do, writing. . ." The enabling capacity of communication is illustrated poignantly through Gabby's mother's recollection of hearing Gabby say, *"I had the most divine day mother."* As her mother recalls, *"I knew those were her words because no one would have put the word 'divine' into her device. She was saying it in her own voice! That is a day I will always remember."* From the perspective of students who use AT, experiencing early and immediate social benefits of AT within the context of naturally occurring school activities is of critical importance, and for some, more of a priority than being independent (Hemmingsson, Lidstrom, & Nygard, 2009).

Gabby's SGD, gave her *voice*. And that voice is further evidenced in her essay, *My Beautiful Life in Canada*. As readers we bear witness to Gabby's message through *her* words—the words Gabby chose—as well as the way in which she crafted her sentences, revealing tone and the emotion behind her message. Technology empowers Gabby, revealing her unique thoughts and ideas, her personality. Her SGD provides continued access to social opportunities and connections through the Internet and social media.

Gabby's experience and the results of her standardized assessment raise important considerations for formally assessing students who use alternate ways of communicating. The SGD provided Gabby with the means to respond to the assessment, but challenges and dilemmas were also raised. The development and achievements of students like Gabby are revealed through curricular and social opportunities and the tools that are needed to access, engage, and express learning in multiple ways through the course of each day, as evidenced clearly through Gabby's essay.

Concluding Comments

Education involves understanding the barriers to equal opportunity that some learners encounter, and working to overcome those hurdles. Gabby's story illustrates inclusion *done right*. We must actively seek to identify and rectify inequalities that lead to exclusion so that schools are more available to *all* learners (UNESCO, 2012).

While childhood is such a small part of one's entire life, how do we impress the value of quality of life through the school years? We agree with Turnbull and Turnbull (2015) that an *ethic of dignity* is foremost in the child's developing years. Indeed, more than an education, Turnbull and Turnbull coin "getting a life" as critical academic and social values; thus, including the whole child in the learning process. Through Gabby's voice and her team's accounts, we perceive the growth of the whole of Gabby. Essential to this growth were key components of UDL and RTI instructional approaches that we chose to focus on in our commentary: collaborative team processes and assistive technology. It may sound trite to conclude with the Nigerian proverb, "It takes a whole village to raise a child." But it succinctly describes the team of people at every level (i.e., home, school, community, province) working in concert to understand, problem solve, and provide resources and opportunities for Gabby to "get a life."

Summary of Gabby's Case Study

Gabby is indeed a complex and a uniquely challenging student. An educator might experience working with a student like her only once in their career because children with athetoid CP are rare. The incidence of cerebral palsy has been reported to be about 2 to 4 out of every 1000 live births in the United States; of these, more than half are diagnosed with spastic CP. The percentage of children with dyskinetic (athetoid) is reported to be 2.6 percent of all the cases of cerebral palsy. Gabby is, indeed, rare.

She is, however, as some of the school team pointed out, lucky to have been born at a time when there are remarkable technologies that can help her move, communicate, and learn, despite the challenges that an unruly body presents. But these technologies are not easy to use, and in many cases not easy to access and implement. In conjunction with the assistive technologies, Gabby followed a modified academic program, and all members of her team ensured that there were appropriate environmental adjustments to optimize her educational experience.

Gabby was supported by a dedicated family, who made sure she had regular and ongoing access to the specialized technologies and supports provided by the rehabilitation hospital in her province. For her to actively participate and speak with her own voice, the multi-disciplinary cross-ministry teaming and support truly reminds us "that it takes a village," or perhaps even a province.

Key Terms

athetoid cerebral palsy People with athetoid dyskinetic cerebral palsy experience slow, involuntary, writhing movements of the arms, hands, and legs. They may also experience involuntary facial grimaces and drooling. Sitting straight or walking are difficult. Holding on to objects or performing deliberate actions, such as brushing the hair, are difficult. Some people with the disorder have difficulty speaking. Eating and swallowing can be impaired, making it difficult for the patient to get adequate nutrients. The mixed muscle tone caused by the disorder contributes to these problems; muscle tone fluctuates between being too tight and being too loose. Muscle spasms are sometimes caused by the fluctuating muscle tone. Despite these severe disabilities, the mental ability of patients with athetoid dyskenetic cerebral palsy is seldom affected. These patients usually have normal or even above average intelligence.

augmentative and alternative communication (ACC) These include all forms of communication (other than oral speech) that are used to express thoughts, needs, wants, and ideas. People with severe speech or language problems rely on AAC to supplement existing speech or replace speech that is not functional. Special augmentative aids, such as picture and symbol communication boards and electronic devices, are available to help people express themselves.

cerebral palsy (CP) A neurological disorder caused by non-progressive brain injury or malformation while the child's brain is developing.

individual program plan (IPP) Also referred to as an individual education plan (IEP), the IPP notes the student's strengths and needs and identifies specific goals and objectives, as well as strategies and the personnel who will be responsible for assisting with the goals within a given timeframe.

Knowledge and Employability (K & E) courses These courses are designed for students who meet the criteria and learn best through experiences that integrate essential and employability skills in occupational contexts. The courses provide students with opportunities to enter into employment or continue their education. (https://education.alberta.ca/knowledge-and-employability)

psycho-educational assessment Psycho-educational assessments are typically performed by school psychologists or registered community psychologists to determine current level of functioning in academic areas, as well as overall cognitive ability and functioning.

transition plan Transition plans are a required component of individual education plans (IEPs). Students on IEPs who are 14 years of age and older require a transition plan as part of their IEP to plan for post-secondary activities, except for students who are solely identified with giftedness. Students with autism spectrum disorders (ASD), and other students who need support with changes, will also have a transition plan to prepare for daily transitions between activities or locations, as their specific needs indicate. Transition plans can be utilized for students to help them cope with change.

Questions to Consider

1. Some students with complex needs require the support of many different agencies and specialists. What support services (medical, psychological, mobility, technological) exist in your region? How does a classroom teacher access the expertise available from those agencies?

   _____

   _____

   _____

   _____

   _____

   _____

2. Although **psycho-educational assessments** are used to make decisions about funding, programming, and evaluation of progress, they are typically "normed" on a population of

individuals who are not disabled, nor are they designed for those who require different forms of technology in order to respond. Why would the psychologist have chosen the assessment tool(s) that were used to try to assess Gabby's intellectual capability? How valid are they as measurement tools for students like Gabby? What alternative methods of assessing skills, knowledge, and behaviours would you suggest?

_____

_____

_____

_____

_____

_____

3. Gabby clearly has many skills and talents. However, she was placed on a modified academic program and streamed into the Knowledge and Employability route in high school. In your opinion, was this the best choice for Gabby? Why or why not? Do you think that the rural school setting had any impact on this choice of program?

_____

_____

_____

_____

_____

_____

4. Looking ahead to adult life, what supports will Gabby require in order to live an independent life and attend college? Should the family be responsible for paying for these supports? Defend your opinion.

_____

_____

_____

_____

_____

_____

5.   It can be frightening to work with individuals with multiple physical needs (as expressed by the EA). What experience do you have with people with physical challenges? How would these experiences make you a better educator?

_____

_____

_____

_____

_____

_____

_____

Useful Websites

Alberta Aids to Daily Living Speech Generating Device Benefit:
www.health.alberta.ca/services/AADL-benefits.html

Ontario Assistive Device Program:
www.health.gov.on.ca/en/public/programs/adp

Ontario Teachers' Federation on Transition Planning:
www.teachspeced.ca/transition-plans

Regional Collaborative Service Delivery:
https://archive.education.alberta.ca/admin/supportingstudent/collaboration/rcsd

Special Education Technology British Columbia:
www.setbc.org

References

Chmiliar, L. (2007). Perspectives on assistive technology: What teachers, health professionals, and speech and language pathologists have to say. *Developmental Disabilities Bulletin, 35*(1 & 2), 1–17.

Chung, Y-C., & Carter, E. W. (2013). Promoting peer interactions in inclusive classrooms for students who use speech-generating devices. *Research & Practice for Persons with Severe Disabilities, 38*(2), 94–109.

Copley, J., & Ziviani, J. (2004). Barriers to the use of assistive technology for children with multiple disabilities. *Occupational Therapy International, 11*(4), 229–243.

Forlin, C. (2013). Issues of inclusive education in the 21st century. *Journal of Learning Science, 6*, 67–81.

Fuchs, D., & Fuchs, L. S. (2006). Introduction to response to intervention: What, why, and how valid is it? *Reading Research Quarterly, 1*, 93–99.

Green, J. (2014). *Assistive technology in special education: Resources for education, intervention, and rehabilitation.* Waco, TX: Prufrock Free Press Inc.

Guralnick, M. J. (2000). Early childhood intervention: Evolution of a system. *Focus on Autism and Other Developmental Disabilities, 15*, 68–79.

Hemmingsson, H., Lidstrom, H., & Nygard, L. (2009). Use of assistive technology devices in mainstream schools: Students' perspective. *American Journal of Occupational Therapy, 63*, 463–472.

Loreman, T., Forlin, C., Chambers, D., Sharma, U., & Deppeler, J. (2014). Conceptualising and measuring inclusive education. In C. Forlin & T. Loreman (Eds.), *International perspectives on inclusive education (Vol. 3): Measuring Inclusive Education* (pp. 3–17). Bingley, UK: Emerald Group Publishing Ltd.

Mortier, K., Van Hove, G., & De Schauwer, E. (2010). Supports for children with disabilities in regular education classrooms: An account of different perspectives in Flanders. *International Journal of Inclusive Education, 14*(6), 543–561.

Naraian, S., & Surabian, M. (2014). New literacy studies: An alternative frame for preparing teachers to use assistive technology. *Teacher Education and Special Education, 37*(4), 330–346.

Nes, K. (2009). The role of the Index for inclusion in supporting school development in Norway: A comparative perspective. *Research in Comparative & International Education, 4*(3), 305–320.

Rose, D. H., & Meyer, A. (2005). The future is in the margins: The role of technology and disability in educational reform. In D. H. Rose, A. Meyer, & C. Hitchcock (Eds.), *A practical reader in universal design for learning* (pp. 13–35). Cambridge, MA: Harvard Education Press.

Sharpe, M. E. (2010). *Assistive technology attrition: Identifying why teachers abandon assistive technologies.* (Unpublished doctoral dissertation). Nova Southeastern University, Ann Arbor, MI.

Turnbull, R., & Turnbull, A. (2015). Looking backward and framing the future for parents' aspirations for their children with disabilities. *Remedial and Special Education, 36*(1), 52–57.

United Nations Educational, Scientific and Cultural Organization (UNESCO). (2012). *Addressing exclusion.* Retrieved from http://www.unesco.org/new/en/education/themes/strengthening-education-systems/inclusive-education/browse/1/

Zabala, J. (2010). *The SETT Framework: Straight from the horse's mouth.* Retrieved from http://www.joyzabala.com/uploads/CA_Kananaskis__SETT_Horses_Mouth.pdf

Chapter 6
William Case Study

Dr. Kimberly Maich & Sheri Mallabar

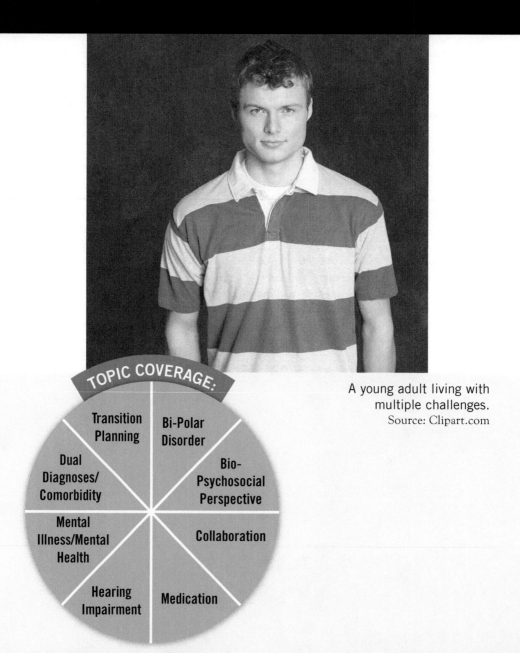

A young adult living with multiple challenges.
Source: Clipart.com

TOPIC COVERAGE:

- Transition Planning
- Bi-Polar Disorder
- Dual Diagnoses/Comorbidity
- Bio-Psychosocial Perspective
- Mental Illness/Mental Health
- Collaboration
- Hearing Impairment
- Medication

The student will:

- Articulate an appreciation of the challenges for students with multiple exceptionalities and their families

- Describe possible approaches to supporting independent living for an adolescent transitioning to adulthood

- Explain crisis planning for extreme emotional and behavioural dysregulation

Preamble

William's is an unusual story, rife with complexities that changed and grew over his tranquil, undemanding preschool and primary school years to his complicated, intense, and incredibly challenging elementary and high school years. His story is also filled with hope and progress as he transitioned to post-secondary life and semi-independent living. His early school experiences were extremely positive to the point where strangers used to ponder, out loud, if William was gifted. During grade four, however, as mental health concerns emerged, this positive experience deteriorated at school, at home, and in the community, where William and his family were pushed to the edges of life in a small community because of his wildly out-of-place behaviour.

FAST FACTS ABOUT... MENTAL ILLNESS AND BI-POLAR DISORDER

Mental illness is a broad term used to include emotional and behavioural disorders which adversely affect thoughts, feelings, and behaviours.

Bi-polar disorder is one form of mental illness where the individual experiences frequent shifts between depression and mania.

Characteristics

- mania may include rapid and/or racing thoughts, feelings of grandeur, impulsivity, hyperactivity, unrealistic ideas, decreased sleep

- depression may include extreme sadness, hopelessness, lack of interest, low energy, difficulty concentrating, significant weight loss/gain

For more information see: Canadian Mental Health Association at www.cmha.ca/mental_health/mental-illness

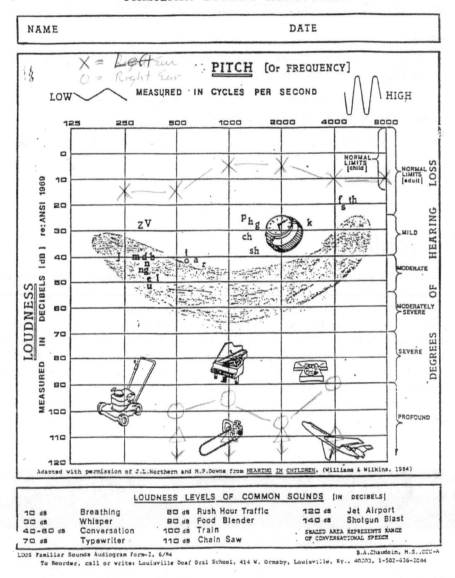

Figure 6.1 William's Familiar Sounds Audiogram

Source: Used by permission of John Maich

This case provides a long-term view of approximately 15 years of William's life. Readers should pay careful attention to the complexities of **dual diagnoses** (hearing impairment, autism spectrum disorder, and mental illness), and the necessity of inter-agency collaboration for multiple exceptionalities. Also note the changes and challenges for William as he navigates life experiences with greater and lesser degrees of inclusion.

Primary School Teachers Voices

- *"Willie is a happy and sociable four year old who is an active participant in all aspects of the preschool program. In conflict situations, Willie is learning to compromise and solve problems through reasoning skills. His creative and unique imagination brings a new dimension to our classroom."*

- *"Willie has had a wonderful year in Kindergarten. He has a very imaginative approach to the solution of all tasks. Willie has demonstrated both affection and kindness with his peers. Well done Willie."*

- *"William is very knowledgeable about the world around him. [He] is an eloquent speaker."*

- *"Overall, an excellent student!"*

The only "hitch" during preschool was the discovery that William was profoundly deaf in his right ear. Preschool educators noticed that he only responded part of the time when he was called. An audiologist completed a Familiar Sounds Audiogram (see Figure 6.1). Later in elementary school, William used a personal headset "FM System," but refused the use of a hearing aid.

Resource Room Teacher Voice

The first two weeks of grade four were different for William. Instead of positive comments, by September 12th, one of the school staff members had recorded a comprehensive log of all of his *"impulsive and unpredictable behaviours,"* clearly indicating the emotional and behavioural **dysregulation** observed in the classroom setting (see Table 6.1).

Table 6.1 Resource Room Teacher's Behaviour Log for William

Verbal Aggression	*—refuses to work by shouting "NO!" at the teacher—fabricates the truth—argues easily—calling others "Idiot!" and shouting at them— asks others if they are as strong as he is—goes to a corner, stands, and cries loudly—yells—is verbally aggressive when told "No"*
Physical Aggression	*—tears up work—locks himself in a private room and becomes very aggressive when he's told that we have to enter—turns out the lights when physically aggressive, so that others can't see where he is—grabs the thermostat and hangs off it—bangs his seat on the floor—uses the shelf in the quiet room to secure the door so that nobody can get in—tries to bite—runs impulsively, inside and outside the school—kicking—hitting with fists—grabs hair and pulls—grabbing at others—stomps feet—threatening peers, like "I will punch you in the face!"—follows peers around, making karate moves and putting his hands in their faces—follows peers around and stares directly in their faces—hits erasers together to get chalk dust on others—locks himself in a bathroom cubicle, cries, and yells while kicking the walls and toilet—pulled the hot air register off the wall—tries to climb shelves—climbs ladder—crawls under book stands—pulls off others' glasses—leaps onto the back of an EA and pulls her down*

(continued)

Table 6.1 (*continued*)

Other Red Flags	*—moody/uncooperative—doesn't want anyone to look at him/talk to him—puts hands over his ears and fingers in his ears—doesn't want anyone to show him how to do his work—enjoys being in a dark room, sitting in the corner on the floor, or under a desk—peers over the high staircase and seems like he is planning something—shuts self in locker—presses scissors to his chest but then slides them down and hides them—puts the cord from the window blinds around his neck—asks the EA for match while peering through a hole in the wall*

Clinical Voice

Grades 4 to 9 were mostly a blur of brief, segmented memories for William and his parents. Their lives centred on multiple assessments and diagnoses, clinician opinions, medications, and interventions. One of these assessments was completed by the school's guidance counsellor in William's grade 6 year, and included formal testing using the Wechsler Intelligence Scale for Children, Third Edition (2004).

EXCERPT FROM PSYCHO-EDUCATIONAL ASSESSMENT

Table 6.2 Excerpt from Psycho-Educational Assessment

Composite Scale	IQ Score	Percentile Rank	Classification
Verbal	107	68	Average
Performance	98	68	Average
Full Scale	103	68	Average

"William is a 12-year-old child who completed the WISC-III. His general cognitive ability, as estimated by the WISC-III, is average (FSIQ = 103). William's verbal and performance ability cores were also both in the average range (VIQ-107, and PIQ = 98)."

Within this time period, 10 diagnoses were given at varied times by a range of diagnosticians, 11 varied medications were prescribed in differing combinations, and William and his family worked with 16 different professional and para-professional support roles, school personnel, and clinicians.

SUMMARY OF DIAGNOSES, MEDICATIONS, AND PROFESSIONALS

Table 6.3 Summary of Diagnoses, Medications, and Professionals

Diagnoses	Medications	Professionals
Adjustment Disorder, NOS[1]	Carbamazepine	ABA Therapist
Asperger's Syndrome	Chlorpromazine	Audiologist
Bipolar Disorder	Dexedrine	Autism Consultant
Disorder of Written Expression	Lithium	Behavioural Aide
Disruptive Behavioural Disorder, NOS	Lorazepam	Behaviour Consultant
	Olazapine	Behaviour Management Specialist
Intermittent Explosive Disorder	Propranolol	
Oppositional Defiant Disorder	Quetiapine	Child Psychiatrist
Pervasive Developmental Disorder, NOS	Risperidone	Clinical Psychologist
	Seroquel	Educational Assistant
Profound Unilateral Hearing Loss	Valproic Acid	Itinerant Teacher for the Hearing Impaired
Traits of ADHD		
		Occupational Therapist
		Pediatrician
		Psychiatric Nurse
		Social Worker
		Special Education Teacher
		Speech-Language Pathologist

[1]NOS – Not Otherwise Specified

During the high school years, William's behaviour became uncontrollable at times. This required additional support plans to be formulated because William would sometimes escape from the school property unsupervised. The crisis plan included a provision for contacting the police if parents or staff were unavailable or unable to calm William.

Behaviour Counsellor Voice

The following behaviour and crisis plan was developed for William by the behaviour counsellor.

BEHAVIOUR AND CRISIS PLAN

Prevention

- At the beginning of each day, staff should work with William to prepare him for his school day. He should be given a daily schedule which outlines times, subjects, and the staff which he will be working with. Staff should ensure that William has the materials that he needs for that day.
- William works well independently. William should be allowed to work on his own, with minimal interruption. Staff should keep their distance and provide support with school work only when he requests it. Only one staff member should provide assistance to William at one time; however, a back-up staff member should be available on request in case William's behaviour escalates.
- William needs to be given choices within his day regarding the order that he will complete his work. For example, he may choose which period he will complete his math work and which period he will complete his English work. This will help give him a sense of control over his school day.
- When possible, William needs to be prepared in advance for changes in the programming or staff. In situations when changes occur with minimal notice (e.g., staff member goes home sick) William should be informed of the change and given a choice how he will deal with the change. He may need to take a break or change the order that he completes his work.
- William presents with a number of sensory sensitivities which affect his anxiety level. Of particular concern is his sensitivity to loud noises, close physical contact and bright light. Care should be taken to reduce William's exposure to these stimuli.

Potential Triggers to a Crisis Situation

The following may trigger aggressive behaviour in William: loud noises/loud talking, bright lights, physical touch; unexpected change; if William is not given the opportunity to make a choice; other individuals speaking rudely to him or acting aggressively towards him.

Indicators that William's Behaviour is Escalating

- William may show the following warning signs as he becomes anxious and before he becomes aggressive: roaming around the classroom/school; cutting people off when they are speaking to him or being rude to others; growling; yelling.
- William does not always show signs of anxiety. He will often brood about something and not share his frustration with others. It sometimes takes William a long time (more than half a day) to recognize himself that he is upset. It is possible for William's behaviour to escalate quickly without warning.

Intervention when Behaviour Is Escalating

If William is working in his room and becomes agitated:

1. Give William the choice of going to the calming area or staying in his room.
2. Once he has made this decision, give William space. Let him know that, in 15 minutes, you will check in to see if he is ready to discuss the situation (using his problem-solving sheet).
3. During this time do not speak to him unless he speaks first or asks for help.
4. Be prepared to remove other students from the immediate area in the event that William becomes aggressive.

If William is outside his room and becomes agitated:

1. Acknowledge William's anxiety and give him choice of going back to his classroom or going to a quiet spot in the immediate area.
2. Once he has made this decision, give William space. Let him know that, in 15 minutes, you

will check in to see if he is ready to discuss the situation (using his problem-solving sheet).

3. During this time do not speak to him unless he speaks first or asks for help.

4. At any point during this process, be prepared to remove other students from the immediate area in the event that William becomes aggressive.

5. Once William has settled in, give him the opportunity to answer the questions from his problem-solving sheet. He should have the choice whether he wants to write the answers or discuss the answers with the staff. He should also have the opportunity to choose the room where he wants to do this.

Intervention for Aggressive Behaviour

■ If William becomes physically (e.g., hitting, kicking, and throwing objects at others) or verbally (e.g., threatening physical harm) aggressive:

1. Remove all students from the immediate area.

2. Speak to William in a calm voice using minimal words. Direct him to go to his room or calming area. Reduce the noise and light level as much as possible.

3. Call the principal to come to the area.

4. Use techniques taught in Non-violent Crisis Intervention to protect yourself and William.

5. The principal will contact William's parents (the children's centre if his parents are not available) and discuss with them the next steps. If it is determined that William needs to go home, transportation will be called to pick him up.

Intervention for Running Behaviour

■ If William leaves school property:

1. Do not chase him but attempt to determine the direction that he has gone.

2. The principal will contact William's parents (or the children's centre if the parents are

unavailable) to let them know that William has left the school property. William's parents (or the children's centre) will let the school know how they would like to proceed.

3. If William's parents or the children's centre is unavailable, the principal may decide to contact the police.

What Is a Crisis?

■ The following is a guideline to use in order to determine that William is in "crisis." In the event of a crisis, follow the procedures as indicated in the Crisis Protocol: William is in an escalated state displaying physical aggression that is threatening the safety of staff or students. He is not responding to interventions as outlined above. He is showing no signs of calming and the principal determines that William presents a safety risk to students and staff.

Crisis Protocol

■ Call the police. Provide as much information as possible regarding William and his presenting behaviour.

■ Contact William's parents and notify them that the police have been called.

■ Continue to follow safety procedures as outlined in the intervention plan above.

Debriefing/Post-Intervention

After the crisis is over, the following staff should be notified:

■ Teacher Consultant – Special Education
■ Principal leader – Special Education
■ Children's Centre

All staff involved need to have the opportunity to debrief in order to determine:

■ What went well
■ What could have been done differently

Staff will also need to meet with William to discuss the crisis and how he and staff might deal with the situation differently if it occurs again.

The following problem-solving steps accompanied William's "Crisis Protocol," to be used as a reflective tool after the crisis.

PROBLEM-SOLVING STEPS	
Identify the problem.	**Brainstorm:**
Explore the problem.	1.
What were your thoughts and how were you feeling?	2.
How did it affect you?	3.
State your objective (what do you really want and is it realistic).	Evaluate each brainstorming idea and select one (circle the best idea).

High School Years

From grades 9 to 12, William's placement was changed from a self-contained ASD (autism spectrum disorder) class, to a self-contained mixed-exceptionality class, to an inclusive placement in a technical high school. In the last placement, William thrived with an applied-level curriculum and hands-on classes such as baking and cooking. No extra support services were provided, other than those available to all students. In this inclusive setting, William successfully finished two independent cooperative placements in local businesses: first, a bakery, and second, a restaurant. He graduated with a high school certificate, went to work, attended literacy classes, and is currently making plans to complete his full diploma with thoughts of doing a career assessment and attending community college. The most recent understanding of William's mental health issues is a diagnosis of **bi-polar disorder**. A psychiatric assessment through a local research study noted that it is likely that most of William's more extreme behaviours and issues were related to the bi-polar disorder diagnosis, rather than the **comorbid** Pervasive Developmental Delay (PDD)-NOS diagnosis. While the Canadian Mental Health Association (2015) notes that 10 to 20 percent of Canadian youths have mental health diagnoses, only 1 percent of Canadians have a bi-polar diagnosis.

Parents' Voices

"A few years before William turned 18, one of our focus areas became supporting him in being as independent as he could be at this time in life. Although he wasn't ready to attend post-secondary education and all of the experiences and milestones that come along with it—including living independently apart from his parents—we figured there must be a way to provide him with some of that positive transition into more independent living. At that point, however, we were concerned that William—who was then struggling in temporary, clinical, residential care—would not be able to live at home again, much less transition in a healthy way to supported, independent living.

William's transitional housing
Source: Dario Lo Presti/ Fotolia

We also worried about trying to figure out something creative for living arrangements within our city bylaws. By scanning online for housing options, we found a house with kind of an 'empty shell' in an outbuilding that was about 300 square feet, plus a same-size basement. We purchased this home with the plan that this space could somehow be converted from its former use as the boiler room for commercial greenhouses into a transitional living space for William. As soon as our purchase was approved, we looked at options that would align with our municipal regulations, but we struggled to find a good fit. So we talked to our local housing support personnel for our municipality, where we were told more about the Canadian Mortgage and Housing Corporation [CMHC] plan for just this type of situation. It was called the 'Residential Rehabilitation Assistance Program [RRAP]: Secondary/Garden Suite' which 'offer[ed] financial assistance for the creation of a Secondary or Garden Suite for a low-income senior or adult with a disability— making it possible for them to live independently in their community, close to family and friends' (CMHC, 2010, para. 1).* What a great fit for William's needs!"

ABA Therapist Voice

"When a person transitions from high school to adult life, there are many new responsibilities that come with this process. These responsibilities may range from finding a full time job, to keeping up with daily cleaning tasks to ensure a comfortable living environment. When it comes to keeping a one bedroom apartment clean for William, a young adult diagnosed with Autism Spectrum Disorder, these responsibilities do not come natural to him, nor do they make much sense. Although William was comfortable with numerous empty cardboard boxes on the kitchen table, hundreds of empty pop cans lined up near his computer chair, and multiple empty pill bottles lying across his counter, many others may question this environment.

In an effort to teach William the importance of keeping a living space tidy for the purposes of entertaining incoming guests, inspections from landlords, and for general health and cleanliness, an Instructor Therapist began to visit William on a weekly basis. Although there were times

---

* From Residential Rehabilitation Assistance Program (RRAP) — Secondary/Garden Suite. Copyright © 2015. Used by permission of the Canadian Housing Information Centre.

where William did not enjoy the suggestions and comments regarding his living space, he was and continues to be willing to make an effort to learn the basics of household chores. To facilitate this teaching, William was encouraged to brainstorm different cleaning tasks to complete and how often each should take place. In a short time, a cleaning calendar was created (see Table 6.4) and William was taught to complete the given cleaning tasks listed for each day. As the weeks progressed, his apartment was transformed! From a clean floor, to the smell of cleaners as he mopped the floors, William began to learn the importance of maintaining a clean living space.

Although there are still moments where William does not enjoy the responsibilities of cleaning his apartment—as many people experience from time to time—he has recognized that taking ten to fifteen minutes out of his day to complete the cleaning tasks goes a long way. As William continues to encounter new responsibilities associated with transitioning into adult life, he is motivated to embrace his independence and seek new opportunities."

Mother Voice

"'They' always say that at times of crisis, you find out the 'good' in people. Sadly, though, I found that this does not apply to mental health crises—apart from rare situations with wonderfully supportive family and friends. What really astounded me, though, was the gap between medical care and effective medical care that I had come face-to-face with the medical model, with its labels and categories. But this was only one moment of many. I could feel the shaming, blaming judgment in all situations. Through all these moments—adding up to about eight years of consistent trauma—it is a wonder that the rest of us were still standing: especially me, the mother, the celebrated target of blame, the pervasive scapegoat. When the point came, however, where William was on his second suicide attempt and the hospital sent him right back home, he threw a battery at my head, threw rocks at cars from the overpass, plucked out all his arm hairs, choked his sister, thought his mother was an alien, and used a rubber molding from the hospital's quiet room as a weapon, and the best suggestions we received from our behaviour consultant were to 'bounce a ball' or 'flick the lights on and off' (Reactive Strategies which were recommended by the Behaviour Management Specialist) to distract him from his constant, dangerous physical aggression, we were truly wore down and began to despair.

Fast-forwarding to today, William is a fairly healthy and pretty content 23-year-old man. It has been nine years since he was effectively medicated—the 'magic pill' that I was repeatedly, vehemently warned did not exist—and four years since he graduated from his technical high school with his Ontario Secondary School Certificate—with honours. He lives in his own apartment adjoining our house, he has a job, and he pays rent. He is giving, compassionate—but not perfect. He thinks ahead, he plans for the future, and he seems content in the present. He wishes for a friend (even one), a family, and children of his own one day. He would like to live in a small town with a nearby lake. As for me? I can hardly believe it. In the midst of those years, what felt like life already in the pit of hell, I wish I had had more hope, more examples, more models, more compassion: someone to show me the way. But now I can give that hope and help to others, and proudly show my imperfect, wonderful, quiet, unsmiling, tall, all-grown-up son to the world with pride in who he has become, and who he will yet still become one day in the future. Like most life-altering situations, raising William was a far tougher task than I could have ever imagined, but its payoff was likewise far greater than my troubled dreams envisioned."

Table 6.4 William's Cleaning Calendar

Sunday	Monday	Tuesday	Wednesday	Thursday	Friday	Saturday
1. Clean bathroom sink 2. Sweep kitchen	1. Recycle boxes 2. Clean toilet 3. Recycle pop cans	1. Sweep bedroom 2. Sweep bathroom 3. Clean off kitchen table	1. Recycle boxes 2. Recycle pop cans 3. Empty garbages (upstairs and bathroom)	1. Sweep downstairs 2. Clean mirror in bathroom	1. Clean kitchen counters and stove top 2. Sort and put away mail	1. Put away grocery bags and food 2. Clean off kitchen table
1. Mop upstairs and downstairs 2. Clean bathroom sinks	1. Dust upstairs and downstairs using Lysol wipes 2. Recycle boxes 3. Recycle pop cans	1. Sweep bedroom 2. Sweep bathroom 3. Clean off kitchen table 4. Clean toilet	1. Recycle boxes 2. Recycle pop cans 3. Empty garbages (upstairs and bathroom)	1. Sweep downstairs 2. Clean mirror in bathroom	1. Clean kitchen counters and stove top 2. Sort and put away mail	1. Put away grocery bags and food 2. Clean off kitchen table
1. Clean bathroom sink 2. Sweep kitchen	1. Recycle boxes 2. Clean toilet 3. Recycle pop cans	1. Sweep bedroom 2. Sweep bathroom 3. Clean off kitchen table	1. Recycle boxes 2. Recycle pop cans 3. Empty garbage cans (upstairs and bathroom)	1. Sweep downstairs 2. Clean mirror in bathroom	1. Clean kitchen counters and stove top 2. Sort and put away mail	1. Put away grocery bags and food 2. Clean off kitchen table
1. Mop upstairs and downstairs 2. Clean bathroom sinks	1. Dust upstairs and downstairs using Lysol wipes 2. Recycle boxes 3. Recycle pop cans	1. Sweep bedroom 2. Sweep bathroom 3. Clean toilet 4. Clean off kitchen table	1. Recycle boxes 2. Recycle pop cans 3. Empty garbage cans (upstairs and bathroom)	1. Sweep downstairs 2. Clean mirror in bathroom	1. Clean kitchen counters and stove top 2. Sort and put away mail	1. Put away grocery bags and food 2. Clean off kitchen table
1. Clean bathroom sink 2. Sweep kitchen	1. Recycle boxes 2. Clean toilet 3. Recycle pop cans	1. Sweep bedroom 2. Sweep bathroom 3. Clean off kitchen table	1. Recycle boxes 2. Recycle pop cans 3. Empty garbage cans (upstairs and bathroom)	1. Sweep downstairs 2. Clean mirror in bathroom	1. Clean kitchen counters and stove top 2. Sort and put away mail	1. Put away grocery bags and food 2. Clean off kitchen table

Source: Used by permission of Rebecca Molly

Summary of William's Case Study

William and his family had a tumultuous school experience as they struggled to understand his biological, psychological, and social needs (**bio-psychosocial perspective**). You will have noticed that the crisis planning protocol that was generated by the behaviour consultant was extremely comprehensive. These types of protocols are useful when faced with very stressful situations. Individuals with multiple exceptionalities present with numerous strengths and challenges that can be difficult to address. Throughout these difficult experiences, William's parents persisted, despite the huge emotional costs. The perseverance paid off, as you can see with William's transition into adulthood and semi-independent living. His goals for the future are similar to most young adults—to have some independence from his parents, earn money, and have some friends. This is a good reminder that all individuals, those with special needs and those without special needs, have far more similarities than differences.

>>> COMMENTARY   By Dr. Jacqueline Specht

General Comments

This case study is all too familiar with the exception that a positive outcome has emerged. William began school with a lot of hope and potential. Comments were positive and he seemed to fit right in. The discovery of a profound hearing loss in his right ear seemed not to interfere with his learning as nothing negative is reported until he reaches grade 4. Many mental health issues arise in childhood. Recent statistics indicate that 23 percent of children between 9 and 19 are reported to be living with mental illness (Smetanin, Stiff, Briante, Adair, Ahmad, & Khan, 2011). Within the school system, we need to be aware of how to create environments where all students feel safe, welcomed, and valued. It appears that from grade 4 onward, the school was far more concerned with creating a safe environment for everyone except William. The case study reports that two weeks into grade 4 all that was being recorded about him were negative instances. I wonder what happened to cause such a negative beginning to the year. It could be that this was the onset of his mental illness or it could be that the environment was not conducive to his learning needs. Regardless, his behaviours

escalated. Unfortunately, as soon as a student is labelled as having externalizing behavioural issues, people begin to see only those behavioural issues and not anything positive that the child brings. It poisons the environment for him and all of the other students and teachers.

Roger Slee (2011) discusses the issues of inclusion in his recent book *The Irregular School*. His view is that "schools have become fertile fields for the discovery of abnormalities" (Slee, 2011, p. 128). At the end of his book, he presents the idea that schools are communities that continue to promote a culture of indifference. We perpetuate the ideas that people are labelled and categorized for their own benefit, instead of truly celebrating diversity and personal characteristics on a continuum rather than as categorically good or bad. We see these issues in the many labels that William has been assigned. There appears to be an inherent need to discover what is "wrong" with William rather than discovering what he needs to thrive. Interestingly, when he is placed in an inclusive technical high school, he is successful. Was he "cured" or did they just stop looking for abnormality and create a welcoming environment?

Connections to Theoretical Frameworks

Attention to social and emotional issues has become a necessity for teachers and schools in meeting the challenge of teaching students in a changing and complex world (Hymel, Schonert-Reichl, & Miller, 2006). Creating a classroom environment where students feel safe, secure, and have a sense of belonging helps reduce alienation, stigma, fear, and anxiety (Curran, 2003; Dwyer, 2002).

One of the key challenges for teachers is to address all of the needs of their students. CAST's model of UDL is most useful for instructional design, but it does not focus on the social and emotional needs of students. The Three Block Model of UDL (Katz, 2012) addresses this critique by synthesizing decades of research on inclusive educational practice into a framework for UDL that builds upon the CAST model and highlights important elements of inclusion. This model explores the learning environment in holistic ways—seeking to build a truly inclusive learning community in which ALL students feel a sense of belonging and competence, and are challenged to learn and grow. In other words, this model brings together theory and research to create a school system that is both socially and academically inclusive.

Valuing diversity underpins the model in Block One by developing community/social and emotional well-being. Block Two, which closely resembles CAST's model, ensures that instructional and assessment practices are effective for all students. Systemic structures and strategies for supporting inclusion are inherent in Block Three. The three blocks are interrelated and together are necessary for effective inclusion (Katz, 2012). In order for William to feel valued, his mental health issues should have been addressed from a perspective of diversity rather than viewed as abnormal and bad. A focus on Block One was needed in his classes and at his school in order to reduce the barriers to his learning. The segregated classes and the constant focus on what was wrong with William would do little to help him feel that he could be successful. Of course, the correct medication seems to coincide with the movement to less and less segregated environments so it is difficult to know for certain why he became successful. Nonetheless, it all relates to getting what you need. William found his niche at the technical high school.

Prior to his success in the technical high school, he was clearly at Tier 3 in the RTI model with respect to his behaviour. He needed intensive support (in the form of medication and behavioural therapy). As his mood changed, so too did his ability to engage in school. He appeared to move from requiring Tier 3 supports to Tier 1 supports. That is, he could be successful with general classroom instruction. This change illustrates that students can move in and out of the tiers, depending on their needs. We should not assume that all students will remain where they started. It is up to the adults working with the students to determine their needs and act accordingly.

In special education, we tend to focus on asking what is wrong with the child. We focus on deficits. We diagnose diversity and we tolerate the differences. The call in inclusive education is to ask what is wrong with the environment, focus on strategies to help the student learn, value diversity, and embrace difference (Philpott, 2007). When William's environment met his needs, he thrived. His outcome is what we want for all of our students. We need to work using the theoretical models of UDL and RTI to get us there.

Key Terms

bi-polar disorder A type of mental illness where the individual experiences extreme fluctuations between mania and depression.

bio-psychosocial perspective The bio-psychosocial framework or perspective considers all aspects of biological development and functioning, psychological well-being, and social context when attempting to assess, evaluate, diagnose, and program plan.

dual diagnoses This term is used when an individual has two diagnosed exceptionalities (typically, medical and psychological) which impact his/her day-to-day functioning. The term comorbidity is sometimes also used to indicate that two or more diagnoses are co-existing.

dysregulation This term refers to an inability to self-regulate, such as emotional dysregulation (e.g., negative affect) and behavioural dysregulation (e.g., externalizing behaviours). Self-regulation is foundational for both mental and physical health, whereas such dysregulation tends to be related to psychopathology (Macklem, 2008).

mental illness A broad term used to include emotional and behavioural disorders which adversely affect thoughts, feelings, and behaviours.

psychotropic medications These medications are used to treat mental disorders such as depression, ADHD, schizophrenia, and bi-polar disorder.

Questions to Consider

1. Children and youth with multiple exceptionalities or dual diagnoses pose great challenges to all educators. What role should educators play in the development and delivery of effective programming? Are there roles that educators should avoid? Explain your answer.

   _____

   _____

   _____

   _____

   _____

   _____

2. The use of **psychotropic medications** for children and youth is often contested by parents and educators. What are your beliefs about the use of medication to manage behaviour and emotions?

   _____

   _____

   _____

_____

_____

_____

_____

3. Physical aggression by students can be alarming for peers, parents, and teachers. How well prepared are you to handle a crisis? What actions can you take to ensure that you develop the necessary skills?

_____

_____

_____

_____

_____

_____

4. Transitioning from high school can be stressful for all students, whether or not they have exceptional learning needs. What must be considered before creating a transition plan for the student?

_____

_____

_____

_____

_____

5. One of William's goals as an adult is simply to have a friend. As a teacher, how can you support the development of social networks for students with exceptional social, emotional, and academic needs?

_____

_____

_____

_____

_____

Useful Websites

Canadian Mental Health Association:
www.cmha.ca

Help Guide:
www.helpguide.org

References

Canadian Mental Health Association. (2015). *Fast facts about mental illness.* Retrieved from http://www.cmha.ca/media/fast-facts-about-mental-illness/#.VnYL2cArI1I

Canadian Mortgage and Housing Corporation (CMHC). (2010). *Residential Rehabilitation Assistance Program (RRAP)—Secondary/Garden Suite (On-Reserve).* Retrieved from http://www.cmhc-schl.gc.ca/en/ab/hoprfias/hoprfias_010.cfm

Curran, M. E. (2003). Linguistic diversity and classroom management. *Theory Into Practice, 42,* 334–341.

Dwyer, B. M. (2002). Teaching strategies for the twenty-first century: Using recent research on learning to enhance training. *Innovations in Education and Teaching International, 39,* 265–270.

Hymel, S., Schonert-Reichl, K. A., & Miller, L. D. (2006). Reading, 'riting, and relationships: Considering the social side of education. *Exceptionality Education Canada, 16*(3), 149–192.

Katz, J. (2012). *Teaching to diversity: The three-block model of universal design for learning.* Winnipeg, MB: Portage & Main Press.

Macklem, G. L. (2008). *Practitioner's guide to emotional regulation in school-aged children.* Manchester, MA: Springer.

Philpott, D. F. (2007). Assessing without labels: Inclusive education in the Canadian context. *Exceptionality Education Canada. 17*(3), 3–34.

Slee, R. (2011). *The Irregular School: Exclusion, schooling, and inclusive education.* London, UK: Routledge.

Smetanin, P., Stiff, D., Briante, C., Adair, C. E., Ahmad, S., & Khan, M. (2011). *The life and economic impact of major mental illnesses in Canada: 2011 to 2041.* Prepared by RiskAnalytica on behalf of the Mental Health Commission of Canada. Retrieved from http://www.mentalhealthcommission.ca/English/system/files/private/document/MHCC_Report_Base_Case_FINAL_ENG_0.pdf

Chapter 7
Jake Case Study

Dr. Sheila Bennett, Maureen Sabin & Charmaine Chadwick

TOPIC COVERAGE:

- Social Inclusion
- Applied Behaviour Analysis (ABA)
- Modified Program Plan
- Autism Spectrum Disorder (ASD)
- Gradual Entry

Jake is ready for school.
Source: Bruce Shippee/Fotolia

The student will:

- Identify ways to educate students and staff about the realities of living with an exceptionality

- List potential adjustments to classroom instruction that support the success of students with exceptionalities in the general education classroom

- State the importance of inclusive educational practices for students with and without exceptionalities

Preamble

Jake is currently a high school student in an inclusive school board earning credits towards graduation. Jake is a young man with **autism spectrum disorder (ASD)** and like many students, he demonstrates strengths in some areas and challenges in others. It took many years to recognize these features because Jake's entry to elementary school was tumultuous.

A slightly built boy with brown hair and bright smile, Jake made an impression that was swift and definitive. Entering into a kindergarten classroom with 20 classmates of varying backgrounds and skill sets, Jake quickly set himself apart as a student. It was clear Jake would need a great deal of support and this would challenge all of the educators who were to work with him. Fortunately for Jake, he entered a school setting and a classroom where the question of whether he fit into the existing structure was not asked. Within the policy framework of this particular

FAST FACTS ABOUT. . . AUTISM SPECTRUM DISORDER (ASD) AND AUTISM

Autism spectrum disorder (ASD) and autism are disorders of brain development.

Characteristics

- difficulties with social interactions
- difficulties with verbal and non-verbal communication
- repetitive behaviours

- mild, moderate, severe, or profound cognitive delay
- sensory integration problems or sensory processing disorder

For more information see: Autism Speaks at www.autismspeaks.org/what-autism

educational setting was a fundamental adherence to inclusive practice. Foundational support for such an orientation is clearly delineated in the *Canadian Charter of Rights and Freedoms* (Government of Canada, 1982), which provides direction to all Canadians in relation to discrimination. Protection from discrimination is supported in the "duty to accommodate" outlined in the *Canadian Human Rights Act* (CHRA) (Barnett, Nicol, & Walker, 2012). The CHRA focuses on equality for all individuals and the provision of equal opportunities for each person to access a life of their choosing without discriminatory interference. In this inclusive school system every child fits; the structure might need tweaking, but the notion that Jake "belonged" elsewhere was not entertained.

Jake presented with persistent deficits in social communication and social interactions across multiple contexts. He exhibited challenges with both verbal and non-verbal communication, and had difficulties understanding peers and/or social situations. He had an extreme inability to cope with change, was rigid, and had restricted patterns of behaviours that interfered with all areas of functioning; these challenges match the characteristics of ASD, as outlined in the current *Diagnostic and Statistical Manual of Mental Disorders* (DSM-5) (American Psychiatric Association, 2013). This case study presents the voices of various educators, peers, and the parent at key transition points in Jake's education—from intensive one-to-one therapy before starting school, to inclusion with a modified program, and after the first few years of high school. Note the specific emphasis on developing peer relationships, as well as the way that general education teachers made simple adjustments to ensure Jake's success.

Applied Behaviour Analysis Lead and Teacher Voices—The Primary Years

*"The first few years of school Jake was basically non-verbal and he communicated via tantrums, aggression, and destructive behaviours. For every demand, transition, environmental noise, or for reasons that were unclear at the time, Jake would either scream, drop to the floor, run out of the classroom or a combination of any one of these. The in-school team, with the support of the Applied Behaviour Analysis (ABA) Lead, set to work on putting in place strategies and resources to address the situation. As mandated by Ontario Ministry of Education's Policy/Program Memorandum No. 140 (PPM 140) sound evidence-based behavioural interventions (**Applied Behaviour Analysis, ABA**) were used to identify reasons for the outbursts and teach appropriate replacement behaviours. The first few years of ABA programming were crucial in setting clear behavioural expectations that ensured that Jake develop skills to communicate his wants and needs in a socially acceptable way. These were the prerequisite skills that Jake needed in order to access and engage in the academic learning environment.*

Even in the primary years, a great deal of attention was paid to long term planning. The goal of Jake not being on a special bus, being shadowed by an adult or being separated from the class in any way, was clearly articulated by team members. The ultimate goal for Jake was full and meaningful inclusion. Concerned that he was not socializing and that his behaviour was creating a barrier between himself and his peers, the team consolidated their efforts to find solutions. Jake's classroom experiences were set up carefully to encourage independence and peer interactions. **Differentiation** of instructional and social engagement opportunities widened the learning experiences, not only for Jake but for his classmates as well. ABA strategies such as reinforcement, use of visuals, prompting, modelling, shaping, task analysis and data collection were incorporated into and guided the regular academic programming. This meant that Jake could actively participate and achieve curriculum learning expectations (**academic inclusion**). Social rules and expectations were explicit and presented in multiple ways and always clearly posted for all students. The culture created was one that highlighted Jake's strengths and talents, as well as those of his peers, which levelled the playing field and allowed all participants an opportunity for success (**social inclusion**)."

When Jake entered the late primary years, enough progress had been made so that academics could finally become a major focus of intervention. Jake's environment had been adjusted to allow him to function more fully in a school setting without behavioural outbursts disrupting his ability to learn. Jake began to demonstrate that he was, indeed, very bright and astonishingly accomplished, especially in the area of mathematics and technology.

"Having been provided the behavioural support he needed, Jake began an upward trajectory that would intimately involve his peers in strategic and meaningful ways, taking all those involved to unexpected heights and truly exploring what can be accomplished in an inclusive setting. His academic skills were no longer masked by socially inappropriate behaviours. To address Jake's academic needs, whole class tasks, assignments and tests, were very open ended. All students were given the chance to tailor work to their specific interests and levels of ability. Jake was now involved in the same academic activities and had similar expectations as his peers; therefore he had context and a reason to communicate with them. Jake had now learned to verbally answer questions and socially talk to his peers. Jake submitted quite a few assignments in all subject matters, several which showcased his in-depth interest and knowledge of video games!

As his school years continued, so did his progress. In grades K to 2 Jake's program was essentially alternative, which meant that he was not working to achieve curriculum expectations, but behavioural goals. In grades 3 to 6 there were clear academic goals set out for him, however these expectations were modified, in that they were not at grade level. By grade 7 and 8 Jake was meeting grade level curriculum expectations with instructional, assessment and learning resource accommodations (see Excerpts from Jake's IEP). The diversity training that Jake and his peers participated in to understand the challenges associated with ASD offered them all an opportunity to build positive social relationships. This consistent messaging and training for students, teachers, and community members allowed everyone to share essential understanding and knowledge. Previously Jake had had a full time Educational Assistant (EA) who sat beside him. By the end of grade 8 Jake did not have an EA—there was one assigned to the classroom, but Jake was just one of many students who the EA assisted. At the beginning of grade 7, Jake's mom would often attend school trips with him; if not, an EA would attend. By the end of grade 8 Jake attended the school's year-end four-day trip independently with his peers and had a fantastic time. At the end of grade 8 Jake received his diploma, along with his peers, for completing the grade 8 curriculum."

EXCERPTS FROM JAKE'S INDIVIDUAL EDUCATIONAL PLAN

Grade	Subject Area	Performance Task
8	Language (Modified)	Reading: Jake will read a variety of texts using his iPad and/or laptop. He will share his thoughts about what he reads in the form of a reading response. *(Grade 4—OE: 1/SE: 1.1, 1.3, 1.4, 1.5, 1.6, 1.8)* Media Literacy: Jake will create a simple advertisement using his laptop to include in his magazine. *(Grade 8—OE: 3/SE: 3.4)*
8	Math	Data Management: Jake will collect data (survey, experiment, etc.), organize it in an appropriate way (graph, chart, table, etc.), and communicate about it, providing at least three pieces of information. *(Grade 8—OE: 1, 2/SE:1, 3, 4, 6)* Patterning and Algebra: Jake will create, solve, and represent/model linear sequences/patterns using scatter plots, tables of values, and algebraic expressions and equations. *(Grade 8—OE: 1/SE: 2, 3)*
8	Alternative—Behaviour	Jake will respond verbally to peers and adults when asked a question or engaged in a conversation. Jake will independently type homework and reminders in his email at the end of each day using his iPad and independently check and follow through with homework and reminders at home. Jake will independently copy down classroom notes in all subject areas using his iPad.
5	Alternative—Behaviour	Jake will respond to peers individually and in a small group when prompted. Jake will participate in whole group activities with visual prompts. Jake will take appropriate texts and/or work out of his desk with visual prompts. When encountering a group of adults or peers, Jake will walk around the group and use "excuse me" when he needs to move through the group with verbal prompts. Jake will hold the door for others when he is first in line.

Mother Voice

"When Jake entered school I was aware that there would be challenges. Those early years were isolating for Jake. He often kept to himself, and he displayed his frustration through tantrums. The school children did not understand this kind of behaviour and shied away from him."
  Despite these challenges, Jake's mother, even from early on, expressed appreciation for the opportunity Jake had to be in an inclusive school system. The introduction of the P.E.E.R. Pals Program (Peers Establishing Effective Relationships) at the beginning of grade 3 was a turning point for Jake and herself. While Jake had received support throughout those early years, this circle of support was now being systematically widened to engage his entire class and school community. Inclusion stopped being just about Jake fitting in and began to be about everyone fitting together.

PEERS ESTABLISHING EFFECTIVE RELATIONSHIPS (P.E.E.R.) PALS PROGRAM

The P.E.E.R. Pals Program is a peer-mediated social skills program intended to:

- Enhance social communication skills for all students
- Educate peers on how to successfully interact with students with Autism Spectrum Disorder (ASD)
- Increase school-wide disability awareness
- Promote a strengths-based perspective in both attitudes and behaviours

In the P.E.E.R. Pals Program, social communication skills are taught in the classroom, trained student leaders run structured games at recess for all to participate in, and skills practice and diversity training are provided for the entire school. This diversity training focuses on disability awareness, overcoming challenges, and building on strengths. The P.E.E.R. Pals Program provides educators with guidance in teaching social skills and how to create opportunities for all students to practice these skills in the classroom, and other environments, throughout the day. It is not an add-on program, but is embedded into the curriculum. Schools adapt the program to best suit their particular needs and school cultures.

(Thames Valley Children's Centre, 2008, p. 2)

Source: From The P.E.E.R. Pals Program Manual, 2008, pg. 2. Copyright by Thames Valley Children's Centre. Used by permission of Thames Valley Children's Centre.

"Jake's classmates learned about autism and participated in many sensitivity activities; such as wearing scratched glasses, and wearing gloves to try and screw in nuts and bolts. They began to understand a little of what it was like for Jake to engage in tasks that were challenging for him. A reward system was developed for Jake and used to motivate him to complete difficult tasks. He was then able to choose a reward, which often was time on the computer or iPad." This was an activity he absolutely enjoyed. As his engagement with the class grew, so did the opportunities for Jake to model and participate in positive social interactions. From his mom's perspective, *"the truly important part was that Jake's peers demonstrated in a clear way that they accepted him*

for who he was as a person. The children really like him and always look out for him. Their total acceptance allowed Jake to not be ashamed of whom he was and to be the happy kid that I knew he was all along."

As he began to accomplish more academically, his classmates discovered that Jake was not only able to participate academically, but could also display a clever and appropriate sense of humour and interact in meaningful ways. His peers also discovered Jake's other skills and talents.

"Jake was a whiz on the computer and in mathematics, and willingly helped his fellow students when he noticed they were having problems. This inclusive teaching process has been the best thing that had happened to Jake. He has grown into a fine young man who positively enriched many people's lives along the way. I have difficulty understanding why other parents have to struggle to have inclusive classrooms for their children. I sympathize with other parents who struggle to get what Jake has naturally been given and indeed what every child deserves from being a member of a school community. All children with special needs should have the right to be included."

At Jake's grade 8 graduation celebration, his mom was proud of her son and his accomplishments. *"Jake was included in a way that made him totally comfortable to be at the event. Jake's love of Mario (the video game) was incorporated by the parents and the students when the event was planned. The evening focused on a Mario theme for decorations in the hall. The whole hall was decorated with Mario materials; students each wore a Mario hat and a moustache. Jake and his friends enjoyed every minute of this special graduation designed specifically to include everyone in the class."*

Observations of Peers

In grade 8, Jake and his peers created presentations and a video about successful inclusion and peer supports and went on to present at their school board and high school, and at various gatherings such as the Geneva Summer Institute, Community Alliance for Developmental Disabilities and Autism (CADDA), and other special education related events. Most of the following observations from Jake and his peers are taken from those presentations: these are their words, lightly edited and profoundly meaningful.

Student Voices

- *"In JK, K, grade 1 and grade 2, Jake did not always do the things that other kids in our class did. He sometimes made loud noises, got angry and threw tantrums. He didn't speak very much or do much school work—really he didn't communicate with us at all. Now, Jake is totally a part of our class. He is our friend and we are his friends. We play together, talk to each other, and share LOTS of laughs! He doesn't react to things the way he used to, and he even follows all of the classroom rules, most of the time ... but hey, I don't follow all of the rules all of the time either!"*

- *"We basically started working on our relationship with Jake in grade 3. The first thing that we needed to do was to learn more about disabilities. This way we could understand how we could help. We got to experience different challenges by doing some activities like trying to write a test with lots of background noises, screwing nuts and bolts together while wearing big gloves and even writing some words with glasses that were all scratched up. I think this was called diversity training, because it showed all of us the diverse needs that exist in our world and allowed us to put ourselves in other people's shoes. From this experience we learned that many people have challenges and by understanding this we were able to help each other to do the best we could. We learned to support each other as a class. We learned about autism. In grade 3 and 4 we did not get too many details ... like what we know now, but we definitely got enough to better understand why Jake did some of the things he did."*

- *"He does the same schoolwork as we all do. He goes on trips with us, rides the regular school bus with us, and plays with us at recess. He has a great sense of humour and likes to play tricks on us..."*

- *"We definitely know a lot more now but back then what we learned was that students with autism needed help socially, had trouble communicating both with words and with understanding others. It just meant that some students had routines or movements that they did and had some real intense interests in things."*

- *"In elementary, on the schoolyard Jake usually walked around by himself.... Sometimes he would even spend his recesses just holding hands with the yard duty supervisor. He had to wear an orange vest so that the supervisors would know where he was. Once he became our friend, he didn't need the vest anymore. We looked after each other."*

- *"By grade 5 and 6 we didn't need our teachers to cue us to talk with Jake as much as we did in the past, although it was still nice that they noticed and told us we were doing the right thing."*

- *"He started to do a lot more schoolwork and didn't need his EA to help him as much ... mostly because we all helped each other!"*

- *"This was also the year that Jake started riding the regular school bus instead of a special bus. There were some students in our class, including me, that are on the same bus as Jake. I can speak for all of them when I say that having Jake on the same bus as us was a very important part of building our friendship with him. We laugh and joke and talk all the way to and from school! Right now Jake is even beginning to have back and forth conversations with us on the bus—he says good morning and goodbye to our bus driver and calls her by her name. Back in grade 5 when Jake first started on our bus, and today, Jake knows that if he is confused, upset, or simply having a bad day ... we are there if he needs us."*

General Education Teacher Voice

"Jake finds transitions difficult. When we do not prepare him, his day does not go as smooth as usual. We provide a predictable daily routine. This might simply be an agenda for the day on the blackboard or a specific one for Jake. We schedule a time for talking or playing with things that interest Jake. Jake likes to use his iPad to check his schedule. This allows him to transition without as much stress. We provide lots of positive reinforcement for the good things! Jake participates in school dances, parties, extracurricular activities, field trips, band,

and everyday schoolwork, where he excels in math. He initiates conversation all the time and is always teaching us new imaginative and creative games to play. In the beginning it seemed that there was a great deal that we had to teach him. Now we know that there is so much more that he has taught us."

Applied Behaviour Analysis Lead and Teacher Voices - The High School Years

"Even in an inclusive high school that is accustomed to dealing with diverse populations successfully, challenging behaviours such as aggression, screaming and flailing of a student in the hall way can be jarring. Jake's first few weeks of transition into this new setting were marked by such incidences. Once again it was essential that educators, family, and peers worked together to develop appropriate strategies and accommodations that welcomed Jake into this inclusive environment and allowed him to excel, just as they would for all students."

"Despite somewhat of a bumpy start, when Jake began high school, he responded well to structure. Many of the relationships that had been strong in elementary school remained so. The close circle of support that had worked so well in elementary school needed to be re-examined however, incorporating Jake's wishes, and considering the more independent culture of a high school setting. Teamwork was an essential component to maintain inclusion. Important information and strategies were shared, and while the first few weeks were an adjustment for everyone, having that information, and a team approach, proved essential.

With the support of the special education teaching staff and educational assistants, as Jake's high school teacher, I soon learned what things worked for Jake and what didn't. As for his peers, we all talked to the students about autism so they could understand Jake. His peers came to learn that it was just a normal thing for Jake to act and react like he did,

Jake during computer time.
Source: Haz/Fotolia

and how to interact with him. The students became very comfortable with Jake. They always greeted him and worked with him.

Behaviourally the use of visual cues helped in assisting Jake to learn appropriate behaviour in the high school setting. An example of this is when Jake first began grade 9 he attempted to touch a teacher's computer, and he was stopped. He presented with challenging behaviours and it appeared as though he was not following the teacher's direction. Jake actually possessed such a passion for technology, and one of his ritual behaviours was that he wanted the computer screen to be displayed in a precise manner. Jake did not have the functional communication skills to explain it that way to the teacher. However his peers did. They explained the situation to the staff, on Jake's behalf, and came up with a viable solution by suggesting that the teacher place the universal sign for 'not available' on the computer and this would stop him from trying to access things that he should not touch. This signage allowed Jake to visually remember the rules and made for a quieter classroom.

Using the same strategies as in elementary school really helped Jake focus on what he had to do. The only change was that the materials were altered to suit this age group. For example, a checklist was made up and as Jake worked away he would get check marks rather than stickers or tokens. When he reached the agreed upon number, he would get the reward that he chose (he was given 3 choices). The students in the class also got used to his routine and accepted and supported it. With proper accommodations, Jake was able to acquire regular high school credits in many subjects."

Along with these more standard types of accommodations, Jake also required some finessing in his school environment. One teacher related that, "when I was taking roll call I would ask an attendance question of the day. During this routine activity, Jake's classmates and I had to try to avoid several buzzwords that would trigger Jake into a mini episode. One trigger word was 'deal'. Every time he heard this word he would shake the hand of the person who said it. The first student of the class was named Neil and I would always start out the roll call by saying Mr. Campbell (his last name) as Jake would hear _deal_ instead of _Neil_. Jake also did not like the word 'watch' or 'listen', and I would often have to express myself differently when getting the attention of the class by blowing a whistle or getting everyone's attention in a different manner than usual. However, once these procedures were established, they became the new normal and there was virtually no difference for the regular classroom setting.

Once when an **occasional teacher** was teaching a physical education class warm-up session the occasional teacher said something to the effect of 'if this is a race, you don't want to be the last one to finish'. Jake interpreted this statement to mean that he could not participate in the rest of the class if he was last in the warm-up jog. On several occasions following that day, I would have to clearly say 'It is not a race' and that eliminated the outbursts of Jake laying down and saying he could not 'do gym because he lost the race'. After this incident Jake continued, despite reassurances, to try very hard to not finish last and I smiled when occasionally he cut a corner short in a small jog to ensure he would stay ahead of other class members.

Jake did not enjoy physical education but he did love technology. To encourage him to participate in class, the educational assistant filmed me demonstrating the correct procedure and technique in a particular sport. Jake could then watch that short video several times and emulate the action. The class educational assistant also filmed Jake, so he could see himself in action. This proved to be a valuable tool, as Jake noticed mistakes in his technique and would improve his next attempt.

Music was a safe place for Jake who had a love of music coming into high school. It was not a tough job convincing Jake that music was awesome. He loved the structure and routine in the grade nine class and the frequent space to explore while taking brief breaks. In Jake's grade nine year there was a good number of his elementary school peers in the instrumental music class with him. I would frequently ask them 'what would his grade 8 teacher do?', 'what would you guys do in class last year?' etc.... It was a great help and the use of familiar routines made Jake feel comfortable. I would also ask Jake's former classmates to be exemplars to the class in terms of how to actually be inclusive (for instance verbal cuing). Occasionally, I would also talk to students individually and ask them to 'step up' or 'step in' when necessary and get a little more involved."

"It was important to show Jake's classmates that I saw the ability within Jake. I worked hard to drive home the positives on a daily basis, stopping the class to celebrate Jake's achievements and explain to the class why what Jake said or did was an example of learning that was often above where the class was at. One day in class Jake did not like the melody that lead up to the end of a song. After the class played through it quite a few times the melody line was driving Jake nuts. Finally in a burst of frustration he ran up to the front of the room and grabbed a pencil and composed an alternate ending. He went to the second-last bar of the piece and arranged the last two bars to form a more melodic resolution. The classmates loved seeing what Jake had come up with and they tried out his adaptations. It provided the class with a way to allow Jake to demonstrate his learning and was just one example of how effective creative practices can be for all involved."

JAKE'S ONTARIO SECONDARY SCHOOL DIPLOMA STATUS – GRADE 11

	Eng	Fre	Math	Sci	Art	Phys Ed	Civics	Careers	Hist	Geog	Grp 1	Grp 2	Grp 3	Comp	Elect	
Required	4	1	3	2	1	1	0.5	0.5	1	1	1	1	1	18	12	30
Earned	3	0	2	2	1	1	0.5	0.5	1	0	0	1	1	13	3	16
On Track*	4	0	3	2	1	1	0.5	0.5	1	0	0	1	1	15	12	27

*Includes earned, current, and next year courses.

Summary of Jake's Case Study

Each year of a student's life is a journey that needs to be re-examined and new goals set. As the students move into the grade 10 year, some become more socially conscious and seem more reluctant to interact in the familiar patterns of elementary school (not a situation specific to Jake, certainly). As Jake moved into grade 10 (the point in which this case study finds him), social issues once again come to the forefront.

"As students move in different circles and have different interests and their worlds broaden, new strategies and relationships need to be nurtured. There also needs to be a recognition that Jake may, at times, just want to be alone as many teenagers do."

Finding the line between connection and respect for autonomy is a challenge for any adolescent. This requires discussion and collaborative efforts, as Jake continues to move towards adulthood. All members of the educational team needed to be 'on-board' and informed about Jake's social, emotional, and academic needs. Recall the various classroom adjustments that teachers made in order to ensure Jake's success in the general education classroom. Ultimately, all members of the school community benefit from the inclusive educational experience.

COMMENTARY   By Monique Somma

General Comments

This case is a beautiful illustration of a community that came together in order to provide a child with a successful school experience. Not without its challenges, the growth and successes described provide the reader with a tried and true example of what inclusion can look like for a student with needs across various domains. This case is also a representation of the growth that occurred not only for Jake, but also for all members involved including Jake's mother, various teachers, and his peers. This growth is articulated eloquently by one of his teachers saying, *"In the beginning it seemed that there was a great deal that we had to teach him. Now we know that there is so much more that he has taught us."*

In reading Jake's story, three factors stand out as being the keys to the success of this example of inclusion. These factors include the use of RTI initially, followed by UDL, teamwork, and the power of peers. I will speak to each of these factors in greater detail.

Connections to Theoretical Frameworks

RTI and UDL Jake was part of an inclusive setting right from the beginning, and components of UDL are clearly embedded in the pedagogy of this school. When Jake entered school there was an early focus on specific areas of his adaptive functioning; his social interactions and the importance of peers in his education are foundational in inclusive school environments (Wolfberg, DeWitt, Young, & Nguyen, 2015). In following the first level of the RTI framework, as mentioned in Chapter 3, Jake was included in his early primary classes where he was exposed to the same curriculum as the other students in order to establish his specific learning needs. It was also identified that ABA was implemented and accessed in Jake's early years as a form of early intervention that follows the third level of RTI, where Jake was receiving one-on-one support for a period of his school day.

The level of commitment to successful inclusion is evident in comments made throughout the case study, such as that of a teacher: *"All students were given the chance to tailor work to their specific interests and levels of ability."* This statement exemplifies the teacher's investment in UDL, where she was changing the program and the structure of the lessons and expectations in order to meet Jake's needs and, at the same time, was meeting the learning needs of all the students in the class. Whole class tasks and open-ended assignments and tests were key strategies used on a regular basis in order to meet Jake's specific learning needs, but also the learning needs of the rest of his classmates. By implementing strategies of UDL, *"Jake was now involved in the same academic activities and had similar expectations as his peers; therefore he had context and a reason to communicate with them."* Jake's teachers differentiated by using a personal schedule and tailoring activities to align with Jake's interests, such as the Mario graduation party which encouraged Jake's full participation. By imbedding opportunities for Jake to teach the class games and share his interests

with his classmates, his teachers encouraged his socialization and helped to facilitate his autonomy and broaden his scope within the classroom.

Teamwork As in most cases, students with exceptionalities will have teams of people working with them in various capacities as they move into and throughout their education. Porter (2010) discussed the importance of teams of support for schools and teachers working towards fully inclusive classrooms. In Jake's case, teamwork was identified as *"an essential component to maintain inclusion."* Teams composed of classroom teachers, resource teachers, parents, administrators, community organizations, and often students are crucial in the successful inclusion of students with exceptionalities. By sharing important information and strategies, transitions are often smoother and more successful. The support of a team was invaluable when planning and programming for Jake.

The Power of Peers The belief system embedded within this case is that of a rights-based inclusive framework, which was clearly articulated by Jake's mother: *"All children with special needs should have the right to be included."* This belief system, founded on each child's right to attend his/her neighbourhood school with same age peers, set the precedence of Jake's inclusive school experience (UNESCO, 1994). In combination with positive teacher attitude and the implementation of the P.E.E.R. Pals Program, Jake's classmates were given the tools they needed in order to build positive relationships with Jake and with each other.

An example of the power of peers is described in this case where Jake's peers were actually able to advocate on his behalf when a new teacher was trying to establish expectations about not touching the computer. Because of their experience and time spent with Jake in their classroom, the students had a better understanding of Jake's needs and were able to come up with successful

strategies that were valued by teachers. This will prove to be an important component to Jake's success in secondary school when his peers can advocate for him and for each other in suggesting modifications or accommodations to teachers who only see their students for one period a day.

When reading this case, I really appreciated the clips from Jake's classmates and how simple and obvious their relationship with Jake was. When Jake's peers identify that an important component to their friendship with Jake was when he started to ride the same bus and that once they were friends, Jake didn't need to use the vest at recess anymore, the benefits of inclusion become so obvious. Jake's parents and teachers could spend countless hours teaching him how to have a rehearsed conversation with someone but within a few years of riding the bus with his classmates, he is having conversations spontaneously. These examples depict how powerful peers can be in inclusive settings.

This case identifies a crucial factor involved in any example of successful inclusion: belonging. Jake's mother noted that, *"the truly important part was that Jake's peers demonstrated in a clear way that they accepted him for who he was as a person. The children really like him and always look out for him. Their total acceptance allowed Jake to not be ashamed of who he was and to be the happy kid that I knew he was all along."* In reading this story, we are reminded, as educators, of the great opportunity we have to facilitate a world where young people look at each other on the basis of what they can do rather than on the basis of what they cannot do. Where they accept unique qualities rather than differences in each other and take what we teach them about caring, compassion, and humility and carry it with them as they move out of the education system. As described in this chapter, the opportunity to create classrooms where all students feel this sense of belonging is truly invaluable to all involved.

Source: Used by permission of Monique Somma

Key Terms

academic inclusion The purpose of including students with disabilities in the general education classroom is to increase academic achievement of all students.

applied behaviour analysis (ABA) ABA is a systematic approach to instruction which breaks tasks or skills into small, achievable steps. With frequent repetitions and corrective feedback, the learner slowly acquires the target skill.

autism spectrum disorder (ASD) ASD is a term used to describe a range of conditions with varying degrees of delay, typically associated with communication, intellect, and sensory processing. At one end of the spectrum is Asperger's syndrome, which is a relatively mild degree of impairment, up to conditions such as Rett syndrome, fragile X syndrome, to PDD-NOS (Pervasive Developmental Disorder-Not Otherwise Specified).

differentiation Differentiation means to make changes in process, products, or content of learning to match student learning preferences.

occasional teacher This term is used to refer to teachers who temporarily teach a class, in place of the full-time teacher. Some jurisdictions use terms such as substitute teacher and teacher-on-call.

social inclusion The purpose of including students with disabilities in the general education classroom is to enhance the social-emotional intelligence of all students and encourage the development of social networks between those with and without disabilities.

Questions to Consider

1. Inclusive education teaches all students and staff about social justice, compassion, respect for diversity, and valuing the contributions of all group members. How did the educators and parents in this case ensure that that Jake's classmates developed these skills and attitudes?

    _____

    _____

    _____

    _____

    _____

    _____

2. What experiences have you had with someone (or a group) who is very different from you (language, culture, race, academic skills, socio-economic status)? Were you instantly comfortable with this person? How did you overcome any stereotypes or pre-conceived

attitudes/beliefs that you held about this individual? What may have helped to bridge the gap?

_____

_____

_____

_____

_____

_____

3. Using the RTI framework, how would you classify the intense type of intervention that Jake received in primary school? Where would you place the type of adjustments that the high school teachers describe in the last section of the case study?

_____

_____

_____

_____

_____

4. Some authors have distinguished between social inclusion and academic inclusion. Why would some educators prefer to make this distinction? In Jake's case, which type of inclusion was the focus?

_____

_____

_____

_____

_____

5. What dispositions are critically important for inclusive educators? If you were to write an advertisement for a teaching position in an inclusive high school, which qualities would you deem essential?

_____

_____

_____

_____

_____

_____

_____

Useful Websites

Autism Speaks
www.autismspeaks.org/what-autism

Ontario Ministry of Education resource guide: *Effective Educational Practices for Students with Autism Spectrum Disorders*
www.edu.gov.on.ca/eng/general/elemsec/speced/autismSpecDis.html

References

American Psychiatric Association. (2013). *Diagnostic and statistical manual of mental disorders* (5th ed.) Arlington, VA: American Psychiatric Publishing.

Barnett, L., Nicol, J., & Walker, J. (2012). *An examination of the duty to accommodate in the Canadian human rights context*. (No. 2012-12-E). Ottawa, ON: Canada Library of Parliament. Retrieved from http://www.parl.gc.ca/Content/LOP/ResearchPublications/2012-01-e.pdf

Government of Canada. (1982). *The Charter of Rights and Freedoms. A guide for Canadians*. Ottawa, ON: Minister of Supply and Services Canada.

Porter, G. L. (2010). Making Canadian schools inclusive: A call to action. *Education Canada*, 44(1), 62–66.

Thames Valley Children's Centre. (2008). *P.E.E.R. Pals*. London, ON: Author.

United Nations Educational, Scientific and Cultural Organization (UNESCO). (1994). *World conference on special needs education: Access and quality. Final Report*. Paris, France. Retrieved from http://files.eric.ed.gov/fulltext/ED384189.pdf

Wolfberg, P., DeWitt, M., Young, G., & Nguyen, T. (2015). Integrated play groups: Promoting symbolic play and social engagement with typical peers in children with ASD across settings. *Journal of Autism and Developmental Disorders*, 45(3), 830–845.

Chapter 8
Margaret and Vance Case Study

Sophie Pitre-Boudreau

As siblings, Margaret and Vance support one another.
Source: Dmitry Naumov/Fotolia

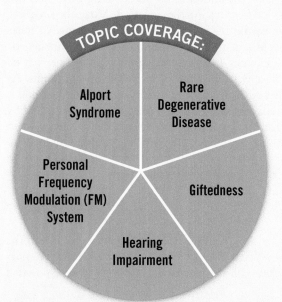

TOPIC COVERAGE:

Alport Syndrome

Rare Degenerative Disease

Personal Frequency Modulation (FM) System

Giftedness

Hearing Impairment

The student will:

- State the symptoms and characteristics of Alport syndrome

- Explain the implications of assisting students who have "hidden" disabilities

- Describe the benefits that a personal frequency modulation (FM) system can have in the classroom

- Explain the benefits and the complexities of having multiple children with disabilities in the same family

Preamble

Vance is 11 years old and Margaret is 10 years old; two easy pregnancies and deliveries that happened without a glitch. Growing up, Margaret always wanted to be exactly like her brother: they learned to read and write at about the same age, they were both passionate about winter sports, and Margaret always tried to get Vance to admit that she is as good as he is in everything they do. With Margaret being **gifted** in mathematics, she can now rightfully boast of her academic abilities. Their parents are very proud of their personal connection and rivalry that seem to bring them closer.

From a very young age, traces of blood could be found in the children's urine, and this worried the medical team. A follow-up appointment revealed an abnormality in Vance's hearing, and soon after, the same was found in his sister. Additional checkups quickly confirmed a progressive loss of hearing. At the age of 8, Vance began using hearing aids and, a few months later, so did his sister. Meanwhile, other medical tests diagnosed the cause for the children's loss of hearing, **Alport syndrome**, a rare genetic **degenerative disease** that affects the kidneys, hearing, and sight. Ninty-five percent of those with this disease are boys, while only five percent of girls develop symptoms. As a teacher, their mother thought of the consequences this could have for their learning.

Margaret and Vance's story is a success story, but it was a difficult journey led by the big brother, who eased the way for his sister, two school years behind him. When Vance was in grade 3 and Margaret was in grade 1, they made a multimedia presentation for their respective classes about their condition and what it meant. Each, in their own way, responded to their friends' and teachers' questions.

Parents' Voices

"We are very proud of Vance and Margaret, to the point that we often forget their differences. The feeling of powerlessness, however, is very difficult. They don't look sick at first sight, and anyway they're still typical pre-teenagers. Nevertheless, their numerous appointments with the pediatric

FAST FACTS ABOUT... ALPORT SYNDROME AND HEARING IMPAIRMENT

Alport syndrome

Characteristics

- rare degenerative genetic disease
- end-stage kidney disease and hearing loss
- in some cases can also affect the eyes
- visibly bloody urine and protein in the urine are common features
- occurs in approximately 1 in 50 000 newborns
- significant hearing loss, eye abnormalities, and progressive kidney disease are more common in males than in affected females

For more information see: www.alportsyndrome.ca

Hearing impairment

Characteristics

- partial or total inability to hear
- may occur in one or both ears
- can affect ability to learn language
- can be temporary or permanent

For more information see: Canadian Hearing Society at www.chs.ca

---

nephrologist outside of the province, with the audiologist in a neighbouring town, with three ENTs [ear/nose/throat specialists] located in different places across two provinces, and with the ophthalmologist in yet another town have been overwhelming. Despite this, they still want to keep up their sport activities. For now, their sight doesn't seem overly affected. Both children have the beginning of cataracts in their right eyes. When they don't feel well, we always have this heaviness in the pit of our stomach and we wonder: Is this when we'll have to tell them that they'll have to quit their activities? Will they really be 12 years old when they start dialysis? What kind of teenage life will they have nailed to a hospital chair four hours a day, every second day? Despite the severity of the degradation of their kidneys, as parents, it's the loss of sight and hearing that are the most heart breaking. How do you comfort an 8 year old whose friends no longer want to play with her because they are tired of repeating the same instructions? How do you comfort them when they are told that they are 'not listening' in class?

As parents, we have had to sit down with teachers to make a clear distinction between 'hearing' and 'understanding' when it comes to loss of hearing. Most of the time, the teachers grasped the concept, but only after the fact, that is, after denying the children their recess, giving them extra homework, or taking away that special activity. How many tears did we have to wipe away? We felt so helpless! Like other parents, we want our children to grow up healthy, but we mainly want them to be happy with their peers, at school, and in life.

There is no cure for this disease; a good diet, exercise, and experimental drugs only seem to slow its progression. And of course, we feel guilty—how could we not know that we had this gene and that we would transmit it to our children? Let alone to both children!

To fight against this feeling of helplessness, we started to look at what we could have an influence on. As a teacher, I took advantage of how they enjoyed reading. By the age of 8, they were already excellent readers, reading material 2–5 years beyond their grade level, and maintaining good academic performances despite their frequent absences. Also, noticing the

Accommodations to Consider to Address the Access and Learning Needs of Students with Hearing Loss

Amplification Options:

- Personal hearing device (hearing aid, cochlear implant, tactile device)
- Personal FM system (hearing aid + FM)
- FM system/auditory trainer (without personal hearing aid)
- Walkman-style FM system
- Sound-field FM system

Assistive Devices:

- Telecommunications device for the deaf (TDD)
- TV captioned

Communication Accommodations:

- Specialized seating arrangements
- Obtain student's attention prior to speaking
- Reduce auditory distractions (background noise)
- Reduce visual distractions
- Enhance speech reading conditions (avoid hands in front of face, moustaches well-trimmed, no gum chewing)
- Present information in simple, structured, sequential manner
- Clearly enunciate speech
- Allow extra time for processing information
- Repeat or rephrase information when necessary
- Frequently check for understanding

Physical Environment Accommodations:

- Noise reduction (carpet, other sound absorption materials)
- Specialized lighting
- Room design modifications
- Flashing fire alarm

Instructional Accommodations:

- Noise reduction (carpet, other sound absorption materials)

Use of visual supplements (projected materials, whiteboard, charts, vocabulary lists, lecture outlines)

- Captioning or scripts for announcements, television, videos, or movies
- Speech-to-text translation captioning (e.g., computer on desk)
- Educational interpreter (ASL, signed English, cued speech, oral)
- Buddy system for notes, extra explanations/directions
- Check for understanding of information
- Down time/break from listening
- Extra time to complete assignments
- Step-by-step directions
- Note-taker

Curricular Modifications:

- Modify reading assignments (shorten length, adapt or eliminate phonics assignments)
- Modify written assignments (shorten length, adjust evaluation criteria)
- Pre-tutor vocabulary
- Provide supplemental materials to reinforce concepts
- Provide extra practice
- Alternative curriculum

Evaluation Modifications:

- Reduce quantity of tests or test items
- Use alternative tests
- Provide reading assistance with tests
- Allow extra time

Other Considerations:

- Supplemental instruction (speech, language, pragmatic skills, auditory, speech reading skills)
- Counselling

- Sign language instruction
- Transition/vocational services
- Family support
- Deaf/hard of hearing role models
- Recreational/social opportunities

- Financial assistance
- Monitor progress periodically by a specialist

(DeConde Johnson, Benson, & Seaton, 1997, p. 448)

Source: Individualized Education Program/504 Plan Checklist: "Accommodations and Modifications for Students who are Deaf and Hard of Hearing". In Cheryl DeConde Johnson & Jane B. Seaton (2012), *Educational Audiology Handbook,* 2e., 528-529. Revised CD Johnson, 2014.

progression of the illness at each appointment with the pediatric nephrologist, we tried to take everything into consideration, to take advantage of life as much as possible, never letting opportunities for trips or activities slip by, so that they didn't feel like they lost part of their adolescence. But most of the time, we live in a state of denial, imagining them in postsecondary studies like any other young person, aging with children of their own, worrying what the coming years have in store for them."

The first years when we [Margaret and Vance's parents] discovered the situation, Vance always made sure that his little sister wore her hearing aids and adapted well. Vance was always a very reasonable and protective older brother, despite his comical and teasing personality. He was very aware of her feelings, the progression of her illness, and her well-being. He would be the one to ask his sister if she felt better after hard episodes, and he would be the one to caress her back or forehead to soothe her or bring her a glass of water. The 15 months that separated them no longer existed when one or the other felt bad. As the older brother, he asked doctors many questions and sometimes did some online research regarding the symptoms, treatment, and quality of life of people with this condition, which increased his anxiety.

Brother and Sister Voices

Vance's experience at school was more difficult, despite excellent academic results in the regular program. *"I would like school if I didn't have to write. I hate writing!"* But his difficulties were mainly due to his heightened sensitivity and anxiety. *"I don't understand, and I know they [adults and pupils] are tired of always repeating."*

Thus, his lack of understanding led to consequences for unfinished tasks or tasks incorrectly completed. Another difficulty Vance had in the classroom was managing his tone of voice. *"We had a fight because I was yelling. Well, there was already so much noise in the classroom that I didn't know what to do to be heard. Then if I speak softer, they say that I'm whispering."* In addition, because he was in a combined class with 54 other pupils, he often had headaches and difficulty staying focused. Rather than remain in a permanent auditory cacophony, *"I remove my hearing aids and I read, hiding my book under by desk. It relaxes me, and my head hurts less."* Because of this, he became late doing his homework and started avoiding the task entirely, which earned him other rebukes. In spite of this, he was able to stay in the upper average range of his class.

In some ways, his sister has a very different academic profile. Margaret loves to read, writes easily, and shows special aptitudes for languages. However, since

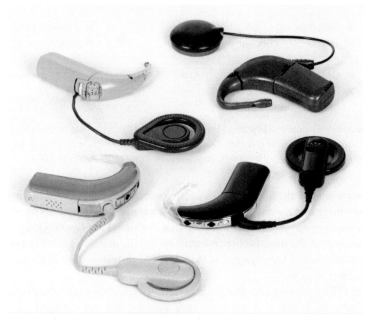

Hearing aids
Source: Elsahoffmann/
Fotolia

she would also hesitate to ask people to repeat instructions, she would imitate her teacher or her peers to make sure she complied with the instructions. *"I look at what my friends are doing and I imitate them. If I don't understand, I ask my friend sitting beside me, but usually when the teacher speaks in the microphone, I understand what I need to do."* A bit more charming, her main concern is that her friends should not know how different she is. She is very shy when people point out her illness and prefers to speak little of it in front of others. *"I don't like to speak about kidneys: that's where your pee comes from! I prefer to say that I need to go to the washroom rather than to say that I don't feel well, because the students know that my kidneys aren't working well… The other day, we were speaking about kidneys during Sciences class: all of them looked at me! I turned beet red."* Despite this, with the burden of anxiety (like her brother), she follows her heart, performing well in sports and at school with energy and a contagious smile, without mentioning or worrying about her illness.

Teachers Voices

TEACHER VOICE: VANCE AND MARGARET

"First of all, I have to tell you that my situation is a bit particular. I had the opportunity to be Vance's teacher twice. I was his teacher in kindergarten and in 3rd grade. I still remember the first time we met. Vance had a large smile and seemed very happy to start school. He was a very motivated pupil and he enjoyed learning. From the first day, I noticed it was easy for Vance to establish friendships. After a few weeks, he also demonstrated a good understanding of everything that has to do with literacy. By the end of the year, his achievements were

Wireless microphone system
Source: Photopixel/Shutterstock

remarkable. He could read little books without any difficulty. If I remember correctly, he was one of the pupils who wanted to be challenged in order to learn more about reading.

Vance was in second grade the first time that I was informed about the challenges he was facing; they installed an **FM system** *in the classroom. This was to help him hear better and thus improve his understanding of what was said.*

The next year, at the end of August, I got the list of names for my new grade 3 class. I noticed Vance's name. I met with school management to see what would be done with the FM system; the room transfer request had been made. Vance started the year by making a presentation to his classmates to help them grasp his situation. He was a pupil filled with curiosity and potential who found it easy to express himself. He gave the same presentation during a staff meeting. It was important that all personnel be aware of Vance's situation since he would be in contact with all of them. It was also to clarify that he sometimes had difficulties hearing us and wasn't trying to ignore us. Imagine the problems if we weren't aware of his situation!

I knew that this [FM] system was very important for Vance's well-being. Unfortunately, despite the transfer request, many weeks passed before the system was installed. We were lucky that Vance was still a motivated pupil because hearing and understanding instructions correctly without a system was a big challenge. After a few weeks, Vance's parents came to see me and to explain their worries. They knew that this was a crucial resource for Vance. I can sincerely tell you that I shared their frustrations. Vance's mother came to see me to give me all of the information that she had on Vance's condition. Not all parents have the skills required to learn as much to help their child and the teacher to better understand the situation. Even with the best intentions, some things can go unnoticed.

The equipment in the rooms other than the classroom was also quite a challenge; it was only after several discussions among teachers, parents, management, the district specialist for the hearing-impaired, and the pupil that we finally understood that a system should be installed in the gymnasium. It took a long time before it was installed, but it was very useful.

I have to say that Vance was very patient with us and ready to do whatever he could do to help himself and us. Everybody involved in Vance's school life learned something. I met a few times with the teacher specialized in hearing impairment. It was useful, but we always wish for more resources, to help us but mainly help our pupils. It was the first time that I worked with this type of system. I can tell you that this system was a tool that could help all of the pupils to understand better. After a few days, I realized that it wasn't just the teachers who could use the system, but also the pupils. The pupils started to use it for verbal communications, presentations, etc.

This system has become an indispensable tool in the classroom, despite a few stumbling blocks: the first time that I was absent, I hadn't explained the importance of using the system to the substitute teacher. I admit that it may have seemed a bit strange for someone who has never had the opportunity to see this type of system. There is also the time Vance took off his hearing aid to go to the washroom and we thought that he had lost it. We had the chance to see how Vance was appreciated by his classmates; all of the pupils from both grade three classes looked for his device. I should also add that the microphone had to be connected at the end of each school day. This could become a problem if the user forgot to connect it. Of course, Vance's situation was not always ideal, but he was and still is a boy capable of overcoming challenges.

Two years later, it was Margaret's turn to be in third grade, and I had the pleasure of having her in my class. Margaret's situation was similar to Vance's, but there were fewer problems regarding the tools needed. The FM system was already installed in my classroom, and her brother was there to help his little sister. I was a bit more used to it because I had had the opportunity to work with Vance, his parents, and the specialized teacher. After a few weeks, they even added something to the system. We got a microphone. The pupils could use it for several of their oral activities. It was very interesting, and the pupils really liked using it. Even though the system was already there, it doesn't mean that we didn't have a few problems: the FM system did not meet all of Margaret's needs, so she was given a personal system that we had to connect to the bigger system. At some point, she could hear the teacher in another class because she was on the same frequency. Her personal system also had to be connected at the end of each day, and sometimes we forgot.

I have to add that this tool helped other pupils enormously. Here are some of the positive points that I noticed: the sound of voices is much clearer, most pupils are more attentive, shy pupils didn't have to speak louder as much with the microphone, the personal system allows the child to hear only the person who is speaking, better understanding of instructions, and the person speaking doesn't have to strain his or her voice.

Information and support is primordial for these children to succeed. It's important to understand that each child is different, and that we have to find the tools and the means to meet their needs. In my opinion, this system is a tool that has positive effects in the classroom. I believe that every classroom should have this type of system. This way all pupils could benefit from it, and we would know more about how to use it."

TEACHER VOICE: MARGARET

"Margaret began her 4th year in September 2014. From the start, I noticed that she was organized, helpful, and took her role as a pupil seriously. She was very self-confident and was comfortable explaining to me how the hearing system worked. Margaret has two regular teachers. I teach her mathematics and English as a second language as well as sciences and technology. Mrs. Leblanc teaches her French, humanities, and art. Her group goes to Mrs. Leblanc's classroom and comes back to mine every day. Every room is equipped with an audio system.

Margaret's academic performance is average to superior. She has a number of academic strong points, particularly in mathematics, where she was chosen a few times to be the teacher's assistant. During March, she participated in making educational video clips in mathematics that were posted online on the school's blog.

My pupils change places every two months. Margaret is not an exception to the rule; however, she is always given a place from where she can hear well. Most of the time when I teach, pupils sit on the floor at the gathering place. Having a place to gather and sit on the floor enables every pupil to be close to me. I have been using this strategy for two years, and I believe that pupils understand me better. The better they understand, the more meaningful the learning becomes.

The two teaching strategies that are mainly used in class are explicit and **reciprocal teaching**. These two strategies promote fundamental learning (reading, writing, and counting) among pupils with learning difficulties and those at risk of failing. When using **explicit teaching**, I model a concept by writing it step by step on the board. Writing the steps enables all pupils in the classroom, but most particularly Margaret, to visualize the parts that might have been less well understood if said out loud. Reciprocal teaching makes it possible for pupils with difficulties to get help from their peers. For those like Margaret who are gifted, it allows them to further consolidate their knowledge."

Resource Teacher Voice

"I had the pleasure to meet Vance two years ago when he started his 4th year at our school. At that time, I had a 7th grade homeroom, but I had the opportunity to meet him during recess and during the tutoring sessions in mathematics that I gave in my class. Although I have a hard time remembering names, I learned his pretty quickly: Vance, come down from the hill! Vance, don't play there! He was a 'real' little boy full of energy who wanted to discover everything in his new environment. I quickly got to know him better, and I realized that the sweet little Vance that I saw in the schoolyard was also a little man filled with nice qualities and knowledge.

I started working as the new resource teacher in my school at the beginning of this school year. So it is as a resource teacher that I greeted Margaret when she started school with us this year. I was a bit worried about how this little blond girl who seemed so shy at first sight would adapt to her new school with new teachers and new challenges. However, my worries soon dissipated when I began to get to know sweet Margaret. This little go-getter never hesitates to come to ask me to replace the batteries in her hearing aids or to check if her transmitter isn't working. We had to remind her a few times at the beginning of the year to tell her teachers the moment something doesn't work well, and she expresses herself better now. Then there is Vance who doesn't want to bother me with his daily setbacks. A preadolescent boy is not necessarily happy at the idea of telling his teachers that he can't hear well, or to leave the classroom to come tell me that he is having problems with his hearing aids. So, I make sure to visit Vance in his classroom more often to check the equipment.

Regarding how they work in the classroom and at school, these two children follow the same routine as all the others. They participate in all classes, including physical education, they play like any other child during recess, and they progress well academically. They are two typical children who are curious, mature, and perseverant. We are lucky to see them on a daily basis because, although we don't realize it, they teach us more than we can ever teach them."

Psychologist Voice

Vance's mother made a request for a private individual psychological follow-up for Vance when he was in grade 5.

"Vance seemed to have difficulties adapting to his split class containing 54 pupils, and sometimes got warnings for his behaviour. He experienced stress regarding everything that had to do with his hearing problems. He said there was a lot of noise in the class, and a lot of echo because of the size of the room. He often complained about headaches, and would consequently turn off or remove his hearing aids in the classroom, which meant that he sometimes wouldn't get to work or would try to guess the instructions.

In short, Vance is an extremely endearing boy with great sensitivity. He always showed up with a large smile and positive and optimistic attitude. It was easy to establish rapport with him, and he had a good energy about him. He made excellent visual contact, and his eyes were full of wonder for even little simple experiences. He expressed himself easily, and never took on the role of a victim. He was open to expressing his feelings, and he found solutions. When I talked with him about thoughts that influence feelings, Vance quickly realized that he had some control over the way he perceived life and challenges. He also understood that he had power over how he felt. He always showed great motivation and maturity to work on himself. It was a privilege for me to accompany Vance through the hardships he had to face."

Audiologists Voices

Two audiologists have been treating Vance and Margaret since they were very young.

"Vance was the first to be diagnosed in July, five years ago. The referral came from the mother. She had already noticed that her son often asked her to repeat. According to her, he was healthy and attending school. The mother's relevant observations quickly enabled us to give the diagnosis of a moderate unilateral hearing loss on the left side. Indeed, it was known that Vance was less attentive when the teacher was on his left side. Then, his hearing degenerated gradually on both sides. At every appointment, changes were noted until the decision was made three years ago that he would use a hearing aid on the left side. Binaural fitting was added in fall of that year. Vance was about nine years old at the time. Margaret was also diagnosed with a moderate unilateral hearing loss on the left side four years ago. The source of the hearing loss was conductive (blockage) at first and then became sensorineural (permanent).

Margaret received the initial device in May, and in December of the same year she received a binaural fitting. She was almost eight years old. At each appointment, it was very difficult to tell the family the changes that we noted. The otological [hearing test] investigation with respect to the etiology of the hearing loss was long and difficult. The family had to overcome many disappointments in a very short time. The fact that the hearing loss table did not fit with the difficulties normally encountered by most hearing impaired persons complicated the parents' expectations and provoked many questions from us. Several difficulties—related to school and adaptation to the hearing loss—could not be explained by the degree of loss suffered by Margaret and Vance.

The journey was difficult. In hindsight, it is possible to say that the rapid changes in hearing observed could, in part, explain the difficulties noted at the time. Given their hearing loss, Margaret and Vance used both hearing aids and a frequency modulation system in the classroom. The use of such a system makes it possible to counteract the effects of distance, reverberation, and noise in the classroom. There have been many technical problems with this type of equipment: from intermittent audio signals, distortion, and equipment breakage, to teachers simply refusing to use the system. All of this has caused much frustration from everyone, many delays, and many appointments in audiology. This additional challenge could have had more adverse effects if Margaret and Vance had not been such academically gifted pupils to start with. Now their hearing loss profile seems more stable. Because of their diagnosis of Alport syndrome, Margaret and Vance still go for regular checkups at the Health Centre in Halifax.

It's always a pleasure to work with them; with their multiple participation in various activities [Vance plays hockey and Margaret figure skates], in addition to family trips, we hear many stories. The real value of our job becomes clearer when working with this kind of family. We are lucky to have the opportunity to see and participate in these children's development."

Summary of Margaret and Vance's Case Study

Much can be learned from Margaret and Vance's story. First of all, we understand that gifted students can also be faced with important challenges at school. In Margaret's case, even though she was in the top percentile of her math class, she did not always understand what was being taught because she could not always hear what was being said. As with most diseases, Alport syndrome produces no distinctive feature that can easily be spotted. Prior to being diagnosed, common behaviours associated to the symptoms of visual and hearing loss, and of kidney failure, could have been misunderstood for misconduct on the part of the student. Vance and Margaret are fortunate to have been followed since an early age by doctors who collaborated closely with their parents to keep them informed. In turn, this enabled the parents to collaborate with teachers and school personnel to make sure that the needs of both of their children were met as soon as they entered school.

As we have seen in this story, devices can sometimes help students overcome certain obstacles. In Margaret and Vance's case, an FM system was installed in each of their classes; one was even installed in the gymnasium. After a while, not only were the teachers using the system, but students were also comfortable using it when doing presentations in front of the class. Since the FM system permits the user to speak more softly and the listener to hear only the person who is speaking, it becomes an indispensable tool for everyone in the classroom.

This story is different from the others that you will find in this book because it deals with two siblings. While it might be helpful in some ways for parents and teachers to have an older brother pave the way for his younger sister, it must be very difficult for parents to accept the consequences associated with a disease, such as Alport syndrome, for both of their children. Teachers need to keep this in mind and be very thoughtful when dealing with the parents. Special care should be taken when the family returns from their doctor appointments, as they will have received results not only for one of their children, but for both. Margaret and Vance's mother shares that they often forget their differences. With the help of their teachers and devices that can be used in the classroom, their "differences" will hopefully become part of the norm!

General Comments

This case study is truly refreshing as well as a good reflective tool. It is refreshing because it clearly illustrates that having special needs doesn't mean that the child has no strengths or a worthy personality. In this case, Margaret and Vance are well liked for their characters (Margaret: helpful, sweet, organized, self-confident, go-getter, contagious smile; Vance: large smile, comical, easy friendships, curious, full of energy, capable of overcoming challenges), as well as for their academic potential (Margaret: reading, writing, languages, mathematics; Vance: reading, knowledge, and curiosity). That in itself is crucial in inclusive education—the capacity of the school community to recognize and appreciate every part of the individual instead of focusing only on their differences (Combs, Elliott, & Whipple, 2010; Paterson, 2007).

This case study is also a good reflective tool as it addresses collaboration, organizational issues, self-knowledge, learning aids, and teaching strategies, all of which are central components to inclusive education. This collaboration is threefold: home–school collaboration, home–medical specialists, teacher–learning specialist. Collaboration is a key condition to effective inclusion as is self-knowledge and the capacity to express oneself (Logan, 2006; Sokal, 2012; Wehmeyer, 2003). In this case, we are witness to Vance and Margaret's ability to express themselves on their medical condition and what it means for them—we are also witness to Vance and Margaret's parents' ability to collaborate with the school and other specialists to better support their children both in school and in their day-to-day lives.

That being said, let's address the two theoretical frameworks presented in Chapter 3 of this book as they relate to this case study.

Connections to Theoretical Frameworks

Universal Design for Learning (UDL) Two ideas come to mind when analyzing Margaret and Vance's case study in light of the UDL theoretical framework. First, based on the basic premise of UDL—that is to reduce barriers to learning that occur when students interact with the curriculum (Rose & Meyer, 2002)—it could be argued that the use of a FM system plays an important role in Margaret and Vance's learning experiences. Foremost, it emphasises the distinction between listening and understanding, an important point made by the parents at the onset of the case study. Therefore, it is a tool reducing at least one barrier to learning. Furthermore, the use of the system seems to be associated with benefits for the whole class, the pupils being more attentive to what is happening in class. Second, the use of explicit teaching *and* reciprocal teaching are good examples of two different modes of teaching *and* learning. This being said, the case study doesn't allow for a more in depth analysis of means of representation, action and expression, and engagement in the classroom. However, accordingly with UDL principles, it is nice to acknowledge the important role of the school staff in identifying the learning profile of their students, namely their strengths, weaknesses, and interests (Rose & Mayer, 2002). This case study leads us to believe that the classroom teachers and the resource teacher are fully aware of Vance and Margaret's learning profiles.

Response to Intervention (RTI) Analyzing Margaret and Vance's case study in light of the RTI theoretical framework, it is interesting to pay attention to the Secondary and Tertiary Tiers. As it relates to the Secondary Tier, Vance's resource teacher's support in mathematics is a good example of additional instruction and practice. (That is, if that support occurs in the classroom; otherwise, this additional support would not qualify for the Secondary Tier.) As for the Tertiary Tier, the installation of the FM system in the gymnasium, following *"several discussions among teachers, parents, management, the district specialist for the hearing-impaired and the pupil,"* is a good example. It isn't surprising that it took a long time before this support was implemented. This illustrates the complexity of responding to the child's need in a structure (the school organization) that is not always flexible. Another example of this tier is the personal system given to Margaret in addition to the FM system.

In conclusion, it is essential to address the important role that Margaret and Vance's parents play in this case study. *"Not all parents have the skills required to learn as much to help their child and the teacher to better understand the situation"* report the teachers. As mentioned earlier, inclusive education strongly relies on collaboration. In this case, the parents' voices were strong enough and articulated enough to play a crucial role in both Margaret and Vance's school experiences. In part, they contributed to the coordination of all individuals playing an important role in their children's day-to-day lives. They also contributed to the education of the school staff by explaining their children's

medical condition and its impact in school—a very important contribution as recent research identifies the lack of knowledge of certain conditions (learning, developmental, medical, etc.) as an obstacle to inclusive education (Bhatnagar & Das, 2014; Morrison & Burgman, 2009). They sought help when confronted with their son Vance's anxiety, which was impacting his well-being. Furthermore, without inhibiting their children's qualities, strengths, and self-confidence, they taught them the skills necessary to be able to talk freely about their medical condition and help the school (staff and pupils) better understand their reality, a capacity strongly related to self-determination. The parents' level of commitment and collaboration certainly needs to be acknowledged. This being said, when working with parents, no matter the level of commitment they demonstrate, it is always necessary to uncover the whole profile of every child. Not only is it necessary but it is also a great privilege to be trusted by them!

Key Terms

Alport syndrome Alport syndrome is a genetic condition characterized by kidney disease, hearing loss, and eye abnormalities. These symptoms are more common in males with Alport syndrome than in affected females. It occurs in approximately 1 in 50 000 newborns.

degenerative disease The result of a continuous process based on degenerative cell changes, affecting tissues or organs and that will increasingly deteriorate over time.

explicit teaching Explicit teaching is an instructional strategy used to meet the needs of the students and engage them in unambiguous, clearly articulated teaching. Teachers plan for explicit teaching in order to make clear connections to curriculum content, through a concise focus on the gradual and progressive steps that lead to a student's development and independent application of knowledge, understanding, and skills.

giftedness Giftedness is when a person has a striking talent or an intellectual ability significantly higher than average.

personal frequency modulation (FM) system The personal FM system consists of a transmitter microphone used by the teacher and a receiver used by the student. If the student is wearing a hearing aid, the sound is transmitted directly to the device.

reciprocal teaching Reciprocal teaching refers to an instructional activity in which students become the teacher in small group reading sessions. Teachers model, then help students learn to guide group discussions using four strategies: summarizing, generating questions, clarifying, and predicting.

Questions to Consider

1. How would you describe the relationship that Margaret and Vance's parents have with school personnel? What factors facilitate a good working relationship between parents and teachers?

_____

_____

_____

_____

_____

_____

_____

2. Do you think the FM system could benefit all students in the classroom? Explain your answer by providing examples.

_____

_____

_____

_____

_____

_____

3. How can teachers become more aware of whether students feel accepted in the classroom? Do you know of any method that could measure a student's level of inclusiveness?

_____

_____

_____

_____

_____

_____

4. What lessons can we learn from this case study in terms of "hidden disabilities"? How can it have an impact on the way we should work with all of our students?

_____

_____

_____

_____

_____

_____

_____

Useful Websites

National Kidney Foundation
www.kidney.org/atoz/content/Alport

American Speech-Language-Hearing Association
www.asha.org/public/hearing/Effects-of-Hearing-Loss-on-Development

California Ear Institute
www.californiaearinstitute.com/hearing-device-center-listening-device-classroom-bay-area.php

My Read
www.myread.org/explicit.htm

References

Bhatnagar, N., & Das, A. (2014). Attitudes of secondary school teachers towards inclusive education in New Delhi, India. *Journal of Research in Special Educational Needs, 14*(4), 255–263.

Combs, S., Elliott, S., & Whipple, K. (2010). Elementary physical education teachers' attitudes towards the inclusion of children with special needs: A qualitative investigation. *International Journal of Special Education, 25*(1), 114–125.

DeConde Johnson, C., Benson, P. V., & Seaton, J. B. (1997). *Educational audiology handbook*. San Diego, CA: Singular Publishing Group.

Logan, A. (2006). The role of the special needs assistant supporting pupils with special educational needs in Irish mainstream primary schools. *Support for Learning, 21*(2), 92–99.

Morrison, R., & Burgman, I. (2009). Friendship experiences among children with disabilities who attend mainstream Australian schools. *Canadian Journal of Occupational Therapy, 76*(3), 145–152.

Paterson, D. (2007). Teachers' in-flight thinking in inclusive classrooms. *Journal of Learning Disabilities, 40*(5), 427–435.

Rose, D. H., & Meyer, A. (2002). *Teaching every student in the digital age: Universal design for learning*. Alexandria, VA: ASCD.

Sokal, L. (2012). What are schools looking for in new, inclusive teachers? *McGill Journal of Education, 47*(3), 403–420.

Wehmeyer, M. L. (2003). *Theory in self-determination: Foundations for educational practice*. Springfield, IL: Charles C. Thomas Publishing Company.

Chapter 9
Jennifer Case Study

Dr. Steve Sider

Jennifer has strong self-determination.
Source: Artranq/Fotolia

TOPIC COVERAGE:

- Accommodations
- Assistive Technology
- Visual Impairment
- Individual Education Plan (IEP)
- Transition Planning
- Itinerant Teacher
- Self-Advocacy

The student will:

- State how this case study reflects the philosophical underpinnings of the inclusive educational movement

- Provide examples of barriers to full participation in the general education classroom

- Acknowledge the importance of transition planning during school moves, as well as upon high school graduation

- Illustrate the development of self-advocacy skills as a student transitions through secondary school

Preamble

In this chapter, we consider Jennifer, a student who has partial sight and is nearing graduation from an urban Catholic secondary school. Jennifer has one brother who is two years younger. Her mother is a teacher in the same school system in which she attends. Jennifer is in the process of transitioning into university, possibly to be a teacher. Jennifer was born with cataracts and now experiences blurred and cloudy central and peripheral vision, and visual fatigue.

Jennifer's school trajectory has been similar to her peers: she started school in kindergarten at the age of 5 and progressed through elementary school and secondary school without being retained or accelerated. Her visual impairment was identified before school commenced so an **individual educational plan (IEP)** has been in place since grade 2. The school team decided that an IEP was not necessary in kindergarten and grade 1 since teachers were using books with large-sized font and there was an emphasis on oral language.

FAST FACTS ABOUT... VISUAL IMPAIRMENT

Visual impairment is vision loss ranging from partial sightedness to complete blindness caused by genetics, illness, environmental factors, or injury.

Characteristics

- legal blindness in Canada is defined as worse than or equal to 20/200 with best correction

in the better eye or a visual field of less than 20 degrees in diameter

For more information see: Canadian National Institute for the Blind (CNIB) at www.cnib.ca

In addition to her IEP, starting in grade 2, a special area in Jennifer's classroom was designed with a computer, scanner, and printer for her use. A Special Equipment Amount (SEA) vision claim was approved to support the purchase of these items. She was also provided with **assistive technology (AT)** software, such as **ZoomText** and **Kurzweil 3000**. These kinds of assistive technologies can help students access class materials that they would otherwise struggle with. For example, Jennifer can use Kurzweil 3000 to take written materials (handouts, books, websites) and turn them into auditory form. She can use ZoomText, a screen magnifier, to make the font size on computers and tablets easier to read. Jennifer used the computer daily and spent more time using computers in her elementary schooling years than the other students in her class.

In addition to Jennifer's insights, we also consider the perspectives of her mother and an administrator from her secondary school. The three viewpoints, as well as artefacts such as the individual education plan (IEP), provide rich understandings of the ways in which teachers, staff, and school administrators can support students with visual impairments.

Student Voice

"Some teachers I think just don't really understand that I really can't see if I'm not sitting in the front. I've had teachers reluctant to move me because teachers have their seating plan already and they don't want to mess it up on the first day, but most teachers are generally pretty good about it if I say I need to sit at the front. In grade 9 I had a teacher who didn't want to move me, I'm not sure why exactly but I kind of just stayed where I was. It was Math, so it wasn't a big deal, I could just basically listen and it was a lot of repeating of what we had done the year before so I already knew what was going on. But if it was a different class or now I would definitely push more to make sure I was at the front. I go to all my teachers on the first day of the semester, just to let them know of my needs."

In elementary school, Jennifer had an **itinerant teacher** with a specialization in supporting students who were blind or had low vision, and she came in to Jennifer's class once a week. Jennifer comments that, *"A lot of what she did when I was little was helping me learn how to type really well and learning programs with the computer that could help. As I got older there wasn't as much that we could do and now in secondary school we still meet but just once or twice a year."*

On having an itinerant teacher and using a computer in class, Jennifer comments: *"Everyone wants to fit in. I don't think the stigma is as bad in secondary school, it was probably worse in elementary school. But it was worse in elementary school because I had a whole table with a bunch of equipment. I still use the computer enough, just not in class as much. In elementary school we had a lot more time to do work in class whereas now we do a lot of our work at home so if I'm writing an essay, we don't write it in class, we write it at home. I will type it on the computer still or we have a work period in the lab. Just to take notes I don't find that the laptop is too helpful."*

In her comment, Jennifer speaks to the issue of **social inclusion**. One of the challenges with having specialized support people and resources for a student with vision impairment is his or her sense of not fitting in. It is important for educators to be aware of this challenge and to find ways to best support the student without bringing further stress into the school experience. One of the other challenges Jennifer has experienced in secondary school is a sense of being overwhelmed at times in the year, such as midterm and final exams.

"I always get large print tests now. Some teachers are better than others, some teachers just forget which is understandable, and I also get extra time. I also get printed notes and some exams I've written on the computer, not often but I have done that in the past. Tests with lots of writing, such as the provincial Literacy Test, I have done on the computer. Anything with a lot of writing and reading is not enjoyable. It is too hard to read, like a chore."

Throughout elementary and secondary school, Jennifer participated in all subjects, even those such as physical education that might be a challenge for someone with a visual impairment. Jennifer comments that, *"In elementary school certain things I wouldn't do all the time like if we played baseball I wouldn't play outfield. I would just bat because I don't like getting hit with baseballs."* The school purchased orange balls so that she would have an easier time hitting them.

Instructional, Environmental, and Assessment Accommodations

Other accommodations include a laptop, class notes provided by the teacher, online course notes accessible to all students, and enlarged hard copy pictures.

For Jennifer, part of what helped develop a sense of support in the school was a tour that was provided when she transitioned from grade 8 to 9. The tour was arranged specifically because of her vision impairment in order to help her find her way around the secondary school. The tour included finding classrooms and particular places such as the library and main office. Since the school operates on multiple floors, she also was provided with a tour of the stairwells so she could navigate them once school started. Having a tour was part of Jennifer's **transition plan** (see Figure 9.1), a required part of her IEP. Other aspects of her transition plan included preparing for the standardized literacy test (grade 10) and career preparation such as completing assessments on personal aptitudes, interests, and career options. Each of these aspects speaks to the importance of helping a child with vision impairment develop **self-advocacy** skills (see Table 9.1). Jennifer was encouraged from her early

Table 9.1 Instructional, Environmental, and Assessment Accommodations

Instructional Accommodations	Environmental Accommodations	Assessment Accommodations
■ encourage to self-advocate ■ use bold print ■ provide copies of notes ■ watch for signs of visual fatigue and allow for breaks ■ provide enlarged print	■ use furniture adapted for vision needs ■ arrange classroom to optimize learning ■ reduce glare	■ additional time ■ quiet place to work ■ large print ■ reduce glare

The following have been barriers to success for the student: Check as appropriate.

☐ attendance	☐ social/interpersonal issues
☐ test preparation	☐ homework completion
☐ organization	☐ emotional/personal health
☐ study skills	☐ behaviour
☐ note-taking	☐ attitude
Other: Please list	

The following assist the student to achieve success. Check as appropriate.

☑ attends regularly	☑ excels at hands on activities
☑ able to sustain attention	☑ cooperates with staff
☑ completes tasks	☑ takes part in extra curricular activities
☑ interacts positively with peers	☑ asks question when needs help
☑ participates positively	
Other: Please list	

Figure 9.1 Excerpt from the Transition Plan for the Grade 8 IEP

elementary school years to speak up for those things she needed. However, the transition plan also highlights the specific steps that schools can take to help students be more self-reliant. For example, specific support in completing interest assessments allows Jennifer to have confidence when she requests a resource or accommodation to help her be successful in striving toward those areas of interest and aptitude.

EXCERPT FROM THE TRANSITION PLAN FOR THE GRADE 8 IEP

Academically, Jennifer has done well in school, often receiving A level grades in the various subjects. Although an IEP continues to be developed for Jennifer each semester (Figure 9.2), the only accommodation that she continues to request and receive is extra time to complete assignments and tests. We see here Jennifer's development of self-determination skills as she advocates for her own needs. From time-to-time, Jennifer will request other supports such as printed notes or larger size print and she has generally found that teachers are willing to accommodate her.

The motto of the school board of Jennifer's school is "success for each and a place for all" and this has resonated with Jennifer. She has felt socially included and successful in school life and is looking forward to transitioning from secondary school into university, where she is considering studying education so that she can become a teacher.

Mother Voice

As a teacher, Jennifer's mother Mona has a good understanding of the challenges that teachers experience. This has helped her to support Jennifer through the challenges she has experienced with teachers and course materials. Mona recognizes that teachers have different teaching styles and expectations and has been able communicate some of these aspects to Jennifer. This helps Jennifer have a better understanding of why she may be experiencing certain reactions from teachers.

Individual Education Plan

Student : Jennifer

Assistive Technology (AC1): Assistive Technology: Alternative Curriculum

Note: The following information represents the starting point for the development of this IEP. The information serves as a baseline and will not change for the duration of this IEP.

Baseline Level Of Achievement for Alternative Program:

- is proficient in keyboarding, and creating and editing Word files including tables. She types using correct fingerings with 91% accuracy.

Annual Program Goal: A goal statement describes what a student can reasonably be expected to accomplish by the end of the school year in a modified subject, course or alternative program.

- will be proficient in assistive technology skills that will enable her to access the curriculum in e-Text and KESI formats. She will create MS documents of increasing complexity.

Learning Expectations	Teaching Strategies	Assessment Methods
Term 1		
will create headers and footers.	– Learn by doing – Describe the steps – Review often – Provide functional opportunities to teach the skills	– Demonstration with Rubric/Checklist – Observation with Checklist
will view multiple documents side by side. She will also switch between multiple open documents.	– Learn by doing – Describe the steps – Review often – Provide functional opportunities to teach the skills	– Demonstration with Rubric/Checklist – Interview – Observation with Checklist
will review all tool bars and all previously acquired skills in MS Word.	– Provide functional opportunities to use acquired skills. – Insist on good posture, light touch and correct Fingerings	– Assignment(s) – Checklist
will set page dimensions and margins of MS Word documents.	– Learn by doing – Describe the steps – Review often – Provide functional opportunities to teach the skills	– Demonstration with Rubric/Checklist

Figure 9.2 Excerpt from Grade 8 Individual Educational Plan (IEP)

Source: Used by permission of Lisa Brown

"I remember in grade 4 when her homework really started, and her teacher gave her a lot of homework which probably wouldn't have been a big deal except it was very heavy visually so I remember a few nights of tears until we contacted the teacher and she was mortified that we had gone two nights through that. That's when there was a big push for her to become a self-advocate. They really encouraged her to self-advocate because no one knew what she needed, they could make guesses but if she wouldn't speak out they wouldn't [know] how to best support her." Mona is reluctant to speak to teachers about concerns because she does not want to damage their professional relationship. She has relied on her husband, from time-to-time, to assist with these situations.

"Jennifer has always done well in school, both elementary and secondary. Mathematics is a subject area that Jennifer has done particularly well in, consistently receiving grades in the 80s and 90s. Jennifer has not enjoyed reading, largely because of the size of print. It was only in secondary school that the use of a tablet became an option for Jennifer and then she just took off reading. It was amazing. I just thought she was never going to be a reader. It was the size of the font after all. The rest of us were all readers so I was shocked when she wasn't a reader. It's sad we didn't realize that was the only thing holding her back."

Jennifer's parents have provided input into the IEP at times. Certainly, Mona's knowledge of the IEP process has helped them in identifying what strategies are working and should continue to be a focus and what areas should be changed. The parents have asked for some things to be removed from the IEP, such as access to a computer, and have focused more on ensuring that accommodations such as increased size of print and extra time to complete tasks are included in the IEP (see Figure 9.2).

School Administrator Voice

Kate is one of two vice-principals at Jennifer's secondary school. Kate indicates that teachers review Jennifer's needs each year and also consider the effectiveness of the accommodations that have been put into place. The school team also considers Jennifer's achievement in the classroom and makes adjustments to her academic program as necessary. As part of this process, the **special education resource teacher (SERT)** distributes a one-page feedback form to each teacher who has Jennifer in his or her class. This is done at midterm and end of term and the SERT then considers the input of the teachers when she reviews the IEP and develops a new one. This dynamic process allows the school, as students grow and mature, to alter accommodations on a regular basis in a way that best meets the needs of the student.

Parental input is a key part of this process. After an initial IEP is developed in early September, it is sent to the parents by September 30 and input is solicited. This input is considered and incorporated to the greatest degree possible and a final copy of the IEP is then returned to the parents. After Jennifer's parents have signed off on the IEP, a copy is stored in Jennifer's official file. Each of Jennifer's teachers receives a copy of the IEP within the first week of September, updated in October, and again in semester two.

Kate is clearly interested in the best academic program for Jennifer and wants to ensure that she is successful in school. When she heard about the challenge for Jennifer to use a microscope in Biology class, Kate states:

"This is really good learning for me because one of the pieces of technology that I know exists but I'm not quite sure why it's not hooked up is an eye piece for a TV screen. The eyepiece *hooks directly on the microscope and on to the TV. The TV screens are 64 inches and you can see what's in the microscope: You move the microscope, it moves on the TV. I know that technology exists at one of our sister schools and we need to ensure it is in place here too."*

The school's administrative team has supported Jennifer's progress through secondary school by ensuring that there are regular reviews of Jennifer's IEP. As well, Kate provides support and encouragement to teachers to ensure that the accommodations within the IEP are being acted upon.

Summary of Jennifer's Case Study

Jennifer has received consistent support from classroom teachers, special education resource teachers, and school administrators. This, coupled with the support she has received from her family, has helped with transitions in school and in ensuring that appropriate accommodations were in place. Jennifer indicates that this support has included simple, but high-yield strategies, such as printing off notes or posting class materials online. The on-going communication between family and school has also been an important contributor to Jennifer's success.

In addition to support, Jennifer was encouraged to develop self-advocacy skills starting in grade 4. This support appears to have helped her gain the confidence to ask for certain accommodations. As Jennifer notes, *"When I was in grade 9, or even in elementary school, the Special Education Resource Teacher was more of a voice for me. I would go through them and they would talk to the teachers, whereas now I go to my teachers on my own."* Her self-advocacy skills have also contributed to her sense of confidence in building relationships. As a result, Jennifer has developed a strong sense of social inclusion. She has also become more aware of her own learning preferences, such as preferring listening to writing, and she has been able to advocate for herself in adapting assignments to meet these preferences. In many ways, Jennifer has become a self-determined person who has a strong sense of her future goal direction.

It is critical that teachers understand that a student with a visual exceptionality may not like a subject such as English due to the challenges of reading text and not because of the content area. Jennifer has now developed an enjoyment for reading, but the overload of information when presented in a traditional printed form contributed to her previous dislike for the subject area. As well, life beyond the classroom

Assistive technologies are always changing.
Source: Nsfotogyrl/Fotolia

in secondary schools can be overwhelming. Awareness of a student's needs must go beyond the classroom to include the cafeteria, gymnasium, the outdoor context, and bus transportation. A child with vision impairment is going to be impacted beyond what happens in the class, thus office staff, bus drivers, teachers, and school administrators need to be aware of the student's needs. As Mona stated when asked about her advice to teachers, *"Just remember the whole child and the whole school experience, not just your particular 70-minute period."* Good words of advice for all educators!

⟫⟫ COMMENTARY   By Dr. Sheila Bennett

General Comments

The inclusion of students with diverse learning needs encompasses a large variety of situational and environmental factors. Students with visual impairments represent a small subpopulation of students within the school system but their requirements for differentiation, accommodation, and modification in terms of service delivery are important and should be no less valued than our expectation for all students. In this case we meet Jennifer, a very academically successful student. Her program contains elements of universal design for learning (UDL) that allow her to participate more fully in educational experiences. We also see her being maintained, for the most part at the Primary Tier of response to intervention (RTI), which is characterized by being maintained in core curriculum with monitoring and feedback. Based on what we read about Jennifer, we can clearly see that she has an excellent support system at home and, for the most part, adequate support in the school setting.

Connections to Theoretical Frameworks

According to the American Foundation for the Blind (2015) Josephine L. Taylor Leadership Institute, three factors form the basis for successful service delivery for students with visual impairments. These factors include: a team approach, a range of services that support the development of the IEP, and skills and training of personnel. This framework of successful practice for working with students with visual impairments will form the basis for analysis of Jennifer's case study.

Factor 1: A Team Approach Students with visual impairments are each unique and require a collaborative response to programming (Sharma, Moore, Furlonger, Smith King, Kaye, & Constantinou, 2010). Parents, educators, other professionals, as well as the student themselves are essential components for success. The Primary Tier of RTI has as a central focus a monitoring and feedback loop that allows the students' work to be adjusted and supplemented where necessary. A departure from the regular curriculum is not required but communication is key. Within the case study it is clear that Jennifer's parents were well informed and supportive. It is interesting to note that there was some reluctance on the part of Jennifer's mom, a fellow teacher, to intervene at certain points. This is understandable, indeed, but does speak to the need for communication and collaboration to be constructed in a way that allows for the free flow of information. Early work by Friend and Cook (1992) discussing the characteristics of successful collaboration note that collaborative groups need to have mutual goals, share responsibility for decision making, and share accountability for outcomes. In the case of Jennifer, an open and mutually respected collaborative process would have invited all participants in for a discussion that was represented by equality, absence of judgment, and shared responsibility.

It is encouraging that, in keeping with the intention of RTI, Jennifer's case was reviewed regularly by the in school team. It seems clear that the school had Jennifer's best interest in mind and set it as a priority to keep current. While not mentioned, the reader is compelled to question

whether Jennifer was part of these meetings; this is not common practice, but it is certainly not unprecedented. Given Jennifer's ability and her intimate understanding of her needs, her voice would be a valuable one in these reviews. Her participation in these discussions would promote her self-advocacy skills, an important skill to hone as she moves into post-secondary schooling and adulthood.

Factor 2: A Range of Service Delivery that Support the Development of an IEP Resources, equipment, and program adaptation are only some of the considerations for creating a robust and personalized program for Jennifer. From an inclusive perspective, it seems laudable that for her primary years a decision was made to dispense with an individual education plan (IEP). Certainly, many of the types of learning experiences that take place in those early years can be easily adapted for a variety of students. However, it may be important to take a moment to consider whether this choice, had it been different, may have had positive consequences.

The development of an IEP can be an opportunity to formalize a discussion that allows for the sharing of information. While Jennifer could adapt and fit in for those early years, could more have been done? Jennifer, herself, notes that her elementary years were more awkward for her, as she felt more singled out in terms of equipment use. Would the introduction of this equipment earlier, and integrated into the classroom more unobtrusively, have assisted her adjustment and the adjustment of the other students to see this as a regular part of their day? Would Jennifer have come to love reading at a younger age had she been provided with more diverse ways to interact with print earlier? Would the introduction of a process that formalized the discussion of Jennifer's needs led to an expansion of services such as the provision of tactile and auditory modifications to promote the full range of experiences in those early years that would have assisted Jennifer but also benefited her classmates?

Adopting a framework of RTI, we might be able to look at Jennifer's school experience, as noted earlier, contained primarily within the Primary Tier of RTI. When we examine her needs early in her school experiences, would it have been beneficial to move into more of a Secondary Tier approach to allow for the introduction and assimilation of equipment use within those formative years? The fluidity between tiers in RTI is sometimes difficult to navigate. Perhaps the introduction of technology use could have been done without any disruption to curriculum delivery or perhaps a short, more intensive intervention might have been necessary for long-term results that would have made Jennifer's use of technology more seamless and inclusive. Using a team approach through RTI allows educators to collaboratively make those decisions. As often noted in educational circles when discussing differentiation, practices for students with special needs are almost always "essential for some, good for all." It is interesting to ponder whether a more formalized approach earlier was left undone as an inclusive measure or as one of expediency. Jennifer was able to cope and participate to the extent that was possible for her and while there was much merit in this, was there opportunity lost?

Factor 3: Skills and Training of Staff and Personnel Throughout Jennifer's educational experiences it is clear that many individuals personally and professionally worked to ensure a positive and academically robust program. On a positive note, the IEP was updated frequently and a solid process for review and interaction was established. It is disturbing to note though, that despite these positive mechanisms, Jennifer experienced situations where teachers were reluctant or unwilling to accommodate for her needs and decided to act in a way counter to her preferred learning modality. *"I've had teachers reluctant to move me because teachers have their seating plan already and they don't want to mess it up."* Better understandings of Jennifer's visual impairment would have allowed these educators to

(continued)

make more informed decisions. Earlier planning and wrap-around intervention may have allowed for more training and skill development for school staff. Training also allows for staff and parents to expand experiences and feel more confidence in supporting and providing opportunities, for example in Jennifer's participation in athletics (Herold & Dandolo, 2009).

Having the necessary expertise and confidence in UDL to allow students to participate fully in all aspects of curriculum is an important goal for educators. Using the communication and monitoring of the Primary Tier of RTI would allow participating educators a way of communicating difficulties and collaboratively problem solving. While this did take place, it would seem that in some cases more support, learning, and communication was needed. Success in teaching students with visual impairments has been linked to knowledge and skill, support, and attitude (Sharma et al., 2010). Information, resources, and training are essential components of providing optimum support for students like Jennifer.

Concluding Comments

Universal design for learning is more than an approach that requires educators to think of different options for process, product, and content. At its most basic level, UDL could look like providing large print books. Within a school environment one hopes that UDL encompasses the entire experience of the student. Jennifer's educational experience included being out on the playing field for baseball, sitting in a row of desks, in the incorporating of technology into a classroom community. The story of Jennifer, while filled with positives, is also filled with possibilities. How might the technology have been introduced so that it was not embarrassing and intrusive? Did her need to advocate for herself make her more adept at utilizing advocacy skills or was it an unnecessary inconvenience that at times forced her to settle for less than optimal instruction? Was Jennifer's academic excellence enough and because of it, did we feel as educators that we had done enough? Finally, is "enough" what we need to aim for?

It is clear that we are reading a successful story here and much credit goes to Jennifer, her parents, and her teachers. By examining some of the nuances of the story though, it does allow us to expand our thinking with regard to universal design for learning and response to intervention, and all that it implies for students in our classes.

Source: Used by permission of Sheila Bennett

Key Terms

assistive technology (AT) These specialized devices or software are designed to provide access to materials. Examples include speech-to-text software (e.g., Dragon NaturallySpeaking), text-to-voice software (e.g., Kurzweil 3000), screen magnifiers (e.g., ZoomText), large keyboards, and concept-mapping software.

individual educational plan (IEP) Also referred to as an individual program plan (IPP), the IEP notes the student's strengths and needs, identifies specific goals, objectives, and strategies, and the personnel who will be responsible for assisting with the goals within a given timeframe.

itinerant teacher These educators have specialized training to support students with special educational needs. Typically itinerant teachers might support students with vision, hearing, or behaviour needs on a weekly or monthly basis.

Kurzweil 3000 Kurzweil 3000 is one of many different software programs that enable accessing written language. www.kurzweiledu.com/default.html

self-advocacy Self-advocacy is the ability to speak for one's own views, desires, and interests.

social inclusion The purpose of including students with disabilities in the general education classroom is to enhance the social-emotional intelligence of all students and encourage the development of social networks between those with and without disabilities.

special education resource teacher (SERT) Across Canada, different titles are given to those teachers who have special training to support the needs of students with exceptionalities. Other common titles are learning assistance teacher, resource teacher, and educational assistance teacher.

transition plan A transition plan is a formal or informal process of identifying individual needs and required services to assist transitioning in or out of a school setting. Ideally, this plan/document would become part of the student's file.

visual impairment Vision loss ranging from partial sightedness to complete blindness caused by genetics, illness, environmental factors, or injury.

ZoomText This is a magnification and reading software. www.synapseadaptive.com/aisquared/zoomtext_9/zoomtext_9_home_page.htm

Questions to Consider

1. Jennifer's teachers did not always understand the effort required for her to process written material. How could all school staff and students become more aware of these challenges?

_____

_____

_____

_____

_____

_____

2. Assistive technology (AT) is essential for many students to experience full inclusion in the general education classroom. What types of AT are you familiar with? Which would you like to investigate further?

_____

_____

_____

_____

_____

_____

3. Jennifer developed strong self-advocacy skills at an early age. Can you identify when you developed skills of self-advocacy or an example of when you demonstrated self-determination? How could a general education teacher create a class climate that would promote self-advocacy among all of the students? What specific actions or activities could develop these skills?

_____

_____

_____

_____

_____

_____

4. Jennifer's early dislike of reading had less to do with the subject content and more to do with processing of print material. What ATs or adjustments could a general education teacher make that would reduce the reading and writing barriers for all students? Under what circumstances would you use these accommodations? Are there times when you would not use the accommodations? If so, explain why.

_____

_____

_____

_____

_____

_____

5. Mona was an educator in Jennifer's school board. This proved to be useful. Are there times when having a parent working in the school could be problematic for the student or for the teachers? What type of boundaries would you want to establish if you were Jennifer's classroom teacher?

_____

_____

_____

_____

_____

_____

Useful Websites

Canadian National Institute for the Blind (CNIB)
www.cnib.ca

SNOW – Education, Access, and You!
www.snow.idrc.ocad.ca/content/inclusive-technology

Teaching Students with Visual Impairments
www.teachingvisuallyimpaired.com

References

American Foundation for the Blind. (2015). *Educating students with visual impairments for inclusion in society: A paper on the inclusion of students with visual impairments*. Retrieved from http://www.afb.org/info/programs-and-services/professional-development/teachers/inclusive-education/1235

Friend, M., & Cook, L. (1992). *Interactions: Collaboration skills for school professionals*. Toronto, ON: Copp Clark Pitman.

Herold, F., & Dandolo, J. (2009). Including visually impaired students in physical education lessons: A case study of teacher and pupil experiences. *British Journal of Visual Impairment, 27*(1), 75–84.

Sharma, U., Moore, D., Furlonger, B., Smith King, B., Kaye, L., & Constantinou, O. (2010). Forming effective partnerships to facilitate inclusion of students with vision impairments: Perceptions of a regular classroom teacher and an itinerant teacher. *British Journal of Visual Impairment, 28*(1), 57–67.

Chapter 10
Drake Case Study

Monique Somma

Drake thrives in a school that
understands him.
Source: Lisa F. Young/Fotolia

TOPIC COVERAGE:

- Tourette Syndrome
- Transition Planning
- Teacher–Student Relationship
- Autism Spectrum Disorder (ASD)
- Specific Learning Disorder
- Attention Deficit/Hyperactivity Disorder (ADHD)
- Medication

The student will:

- Explain how multiple diagnostics impact a student's learning

- State how the universal design for learning (UDL) and differentiated instruction (DI) enable the student who might otherwise be struggling to become part of the regular classroom

- Explain how developing a positive teacher–student relationship benefits the teacher as well as the student

- Describe inclusive strategies to use with students who struggle with social/emotional and behavioural abilities

Preamble

Numerous assessment reports indicate that Drake fits the DSM-5 criteria for **attention deficit / hyperactivity disorder (ADHD)** as well as **Tourette syndrome**, which are commonly paired. Here is a child who struggles with following through on instructions and paying attention appropriately to what he needs to attend to; appears not to listen; is disorganized and misses details; has trouble starting tasks or with tasks that require planning or long-term effort; appears to be easily distracted or forgetful. These behaviours are paired with motor tics, such as body jerks and tense muscles, and vocal tics, such as yelling, humming, and echoing, which may be masked by the aforementioned behaviours. A 2011 psychological assessment indicated that Drake's intellectual potential is in the average range but his cognitive profile revealed deficits and his academic performance is below grade level in core subjects including language and math. It was at that time that the diagnosis of was also included on Drake's profile due to his difficulty in socialization with peers and the repetitive and almost ritualistic behaviour that had been noticed since he was a small boy (according to the DSM-5, Asperger's is no longer recognized as a separate category under **autism spectrum disorder (ASD)**). The following case sheds light on the importance of developing trusting relationships with students, as well as the essential implementation of strategies for UDL and differentiated instruction.

Teacher Voice

"One year after teaching Drake in grade 5, I walk into his grade 5/6 split class where he is working at his desk, quietly and quite focused, on a writing assignment. He showed me his work and was very proud to share his piece. I compliment him on his focus and hard work. Having difficulty accepting a compliment for his work, he shrugs his shoulders and

FAST FACTS ABOUT... ATTENTION DEFICIT / HYPERACTIVITY DISORDER (ADHD) AND TOURETTE SYNDROME (TS)

Attention deficit / hyperactivity disorder (ADHD)

Characteristics

- attention deficits, hyperactivity or impulsiveness
- often results in poor school performance
- most commonly studied and diagnosed psychiatric disorder in children and adolescents

For more information, see National Institute on Mental Health at www.nimh.nih.gov/health/topics/attention-deficit-hyperactivity-disorder-adhd/index.shtml

Tourette syndrome (TS)

Characteristics

- a brain-based condition
- causes people to make involuntary sounds and tics
- many who have TS have one or more other conditions as well

For more information, see Tourette Canada at www.tourette.ca/what-is-ts

continues with the illustration he was working on. His report card for term one indicates that he 'needs improvement' in the Learning Skills areas for independent work, organization and self-regulation. 'He is often unable to self-initiate his work and stay on task without frequent prompting and reminders', is a comment that is not new for Drake and will likely be stated in a variety of ways on subsequent report cards for the rest of his formal schooling.

Drake entered my grade 5 class part way through the first term from a French language school. He was 10.9 years old at that time. He had been raised solely by his mother in the same city since he was two years old. In the past few years mom has developed a rare connective tissue disorder that causes her to be in extreme pain most of the time unless she takes medication and has therapy. This allows her to be home and available for Drake but at the same time prevents her from being able to drive him to and from activities. Fortunately, he has been able to participate in some community programs where transportation is included. Mom has also hired a tutor to assist with homework and work on developing skills.

It was indicated by his mother before coming to the new school, that Drake has some issues that have an impact on his learning. Although his Ontario Student Record (OSR) was not available beforehand, not having access to it provided an opportunity to get to know him in an authentic way before reading the formal and informal assessments and other information regarding his academic history and current program. It was interesting to note once the OSR did arrive that it was listed on the Individual Education Plan (IEP) that he was receiving support for at least one period per day. In this class, there was little support available outside of the classroom teacher, the Educational Assistant who is responsible for a high needs student, and limited time with the educational resource teacher.

Beyond the IEP, there was much more information in the OSR that filled in the gaps of Drake's challenges at school. Assessment reports were included indicating a diagnosis first of Attention Deficit/Hyperactivity Disorder, Tourettes Disorder and later Asperger's which I knew to be a form of Autism Spectrum Disorder where the individual struggles mostly in

FIRST PORTION OF DRAKE'S IEP

Assessment Type	Grade	Result
DRA	Grade 4	Scored 63 on a level 40 indicating his comprehension is at a late grade 3 level.
Psychological/Psychiatric Assessment	Grade 3	Assessment results indicate that intellectual potential is situated within the average range. His cognitive profile reveals deficits and his academic performance is below expected levels in all core subjects.
Medical/Health (Hearing, Vision, Physical, Neurological)	Preschool	Was diagnosed with Tourette syndrome.

Strengths & Needs

Areas of Strength	Areas of Need
■ compliant with adult requests ■ gross motor abilities ■ processing speed ■ participation	■ expressive language (speaking) ■ receptive language skills ■ literacy skills ■ organizational skills ■ perseverance ■ attention ■ self-control ■ social interaction

Characteristics Necessitating Special Education Program

Literacy and numeracy skills are below grade level. He also has difficulty with attention and social interaction. Has been diagnosed with Tourette syndrome, ADHD, and Asperger's syndrome.

Personal Characteristics

■ peer helper – enjoys school

the social domain. Since it was evident that Drake was also about one grade level behind in Language and Math, these identifications would help to guide what approaches and strategies would best suit Drake's learning and social development in grade 5."

Mother Voice

"As a toddler Drake was an extremely energetic and talkative child. He never really talked like a baby. He just started talking and had very good speech. I always thought this was the reason why he seemed to relate better to adults and older kids in the neighbourhood. He was running all the time. He had so much energy and often seemed to struggle with what to do with it. For example, from a very early age Drake was aggressive with other children and animals. That is why I had to get rid of our two little dogs. He would kick dogs or cats that crossed his path and when he was three he took a chunk out of another child's back from a bite. I didn't know where this aggression was coming from. Although I recognized that this behaviour was not only due to his high energy, and many friends had tried to convince me to look into it further, I was in denial and afraid of what a doctor would say. It was his preschool teacher who finally convinced me to see a doctor and have him assessed. She talked to me about different characteristics to watch for and as I watched him I did notice what she was talking about. Drake was diagnosed at four years old with ADHD and Tourette's and although they suspected Asperger's at the time this label was not added until he was nine. He was also diagnosed by the school board with a specific learning disorder[1] when he was in grade 3.

Even though I was opposed to using medication, at the age of six I started Drake on stimulant medications. [Central nervous system stimulant medications which affect chemicals in the brain and nerves that contribute to hyperactivity and impulse control, such as Ritalin, Adderall, and Concerta, were prescribed in an attempt to help him control his impulsive and aggressive behaviour.] *Drake took these medications in various doses and combinations for almost four years until I recognized the impact they were having on his health. Drake had become very skinny and was not eating or sleeping regularly, which are common side effects of these medications. And although the school believed that the medication was having some impact on Drake's behaviour, when the medication was finally stopped, the teacher provided contradictory reports on his progress. In fact she indicated she had noticed improvement in Drake's behaviour in class when I had actually stopped the medication. This proved to me that the medication wasn't helping him at all."*

When Drake was four he entered junior kindergarten at the local French language school. *"Since I was from a French background, I valued that Drake also be bilingual. Early on in school, Drake didn't interact with the other children very much and he preferred to play alone. Although he began to interact more with peers as the years went on, Drake struggled with his teachers the most. In the early primary years he became very stressed about going to school. He would come home crying every day that his teacher put him in the corner and yelled at him all the time. The messages communicated to me by the school were always the same; that Drake couldn't sit still, he was always disrupting the class, and he has to learn to stop talking out loud and follow directions. The teachers would get mad at him in front of the class which made him very embarrassed. There was negative stigma attached to Drake by all staff members. This time destroyed his self-esteem, and took away my boy. At one time Drake disclosed to me that he wanted to kill himself. Reflecting back, I realize that I should have moved him sooner when he had asked me several times to change schools.*

---

[1] In the DSM-5, learning disability is now referred to as specific learning disorder.

It was the way Drake came home upset and often crying, the way the school made me feel like they were judging me and that I was a bad parent, and that their solution always came back to pushing the medication. The final straw was in the Identification, Placement and Review Committee in June of his grade 4 year and I remember very clearly that each member in the meeting took their turn trying to convince me about the medication issue. I felt ganged up on and made to feel like an incompetent parent. So after six years of battling with a school system that was not meeting his needs, I finally decided it was time to try something else and give Drake a fresh start. He is a good boy and is smart and he has a heart of gold. I wanted him to be in a place that could see this about him. When I first visited the new school, I knew in my heart that was the right place for Drake. I knew I had made the right decision when Drake came running down the street from the bus after his first day at his new school with a smile I could see from the corner. 'I love my new school mom, my teacher is an angel. Thank you so much mom.' Drake no longer comes home crying. Now I worry about high school and if I will pick the right one; a school that will understand him like the school he is at now.

The strategies that I use with Drake really come from my own personal experience with having ADHD myself. I always make sure that he is looking into my eyes when I am giving him an instruction. When he is looking at me I know he is more likely to remember what I have asked him to do. I have taught him the importance of following the same routine every day to help ensure that he doesn't forget things. He gets frustrated when he forgets to do things, so following the same simple and logical routine every day helps to keep him on task which really helps me as well. He still gets distracted, but since it is the same routine every day, he is able to more easily get back on track. Because the routine stays the same everything is predictable [and] he is less worried about what comes next and better able to focus on the task at hand. I also teach him to breathe. Breathing helps him to calm down when he gets on a roll with this talking. He talks very fast and often about two–three things at the same time. I remind him to breathe so that he can slow down and tell me one story at a time."

Teacher Voice

"The grade 5 class was a dynamic vibrant environment filled with diverse learners. Since my former teaching experience was mostly in self-contained classes, I felt it was particularly important to do whatever I could to ensure that all students had the opportunity to be as successful as they possibly could. Lessons and activities were developed with the learning needs and strengths of all students as the focal point. Students were often given the opportunity to choose the outcome they wanted to produce. They worked collaboratively or on their own to create an end product that demonstrated not only their skill level but also their interests and strengths. Over the course of the year several project based activities allowed for the flexibility that many of the students including Drake needed in order to truly be themselves and to feel successful.

The classroom as a family was established early on in the school year and was visually displayed in the classroom. The fall consisted of in-depth discussion and activities around social justice and human rights for everyone (especially the right to go to school, feel safe and learn with peers) and we had a consensus that it was our responsibility to make sure that all of our classmates' rights were being respected. Within the dynamics of the class, there was a child (Sam) with many physical and learning needs and in order for the other students to get to know him and for him to be included, each student had a chance to learn about his activities, ask questions and then have an opportunity to work with him on his academic tasks. This allowed them to see Sam's abilities, develop patience, compassion and understanding and ultimately change the way they view individuals with learning needs that are different than their own. Although this was a process that spanned the year, the understanding which they developed helped the students to recognize and focus on the strengths of each other. I really tried to instil the value of their responsibility for each other.

The opportunity to work with Sam allowed Drake feel good about doing something good for someone else, but also to recognize that he had skills and talents that he could use to help others. Drake had a natural ability to help. His non-judgemental personality allowed him to model to his peers what it looked like to truly appreciate and understand the strengths and abilities of some individuals that are often overlooked by most. It also allowed him an outlet to simply be himself without having to worry about what others might think.

This learning environment encouraged and challenged Drake and all the students to take risks and explore their interests. Many identified feeling safe and comfortable within the classroom. Drake was no exception. He seemed at ease and was always smiling. Although I recognized his struggles academically and socially, I would not have ever imagined the sad child described by his mother. I now know that the community built from within the classroom allowed all students including Drake to feel important, safe and included."

SOCIAL/EMOTIONAL

"In the grade 5 classroom, Drake enjoyed talking and socializing and was generally liked by his peers. Although he was liked by his peers he strove for their attention and was concerned about and tried to be involved in everything they were doing. At times this became a challenge for his peers, especially when they needed some personal space. On one occasion another student who was not aggressive, shoved Drake in the classroom and shouted for him to 'get out of my face'. It wasn't as though this student disliked him, as up until that point they interacted amicably. He strove for acceptance from his peers and even though they liked him for who he was, he lacked the confidence and self-esteem to see it."

BEHAVIOURAL

"Drake often spoke out of turn, spoke in a louder than indoor voice and engaged those sitting around him in conversations during independent work. He often had a difficult time concentrating on independent work due to most regular classroom distractions. Organization was also a challenge for Drake in the classroom. Work that was completed was unorganized and messy. He had a difficult time keeping track of his belongings and learning materials including books, completed work and work in progress, as well as writing tools and supplies. Materials were often scattered on his desk or on the floor and he often needed help to find what he needed to complete and activity such as the proper notebook and a pencil.

During group work Drake struggled to remain on task and was easily distracted by the other students. His voice level often became quite loud as he competed to be heard and became excited about talking with his classmates. He often engaged in conversations not related to the topic of the group work assignment that many of the students needed in order to truly be and feel successful."

REMAINDER OF DRAKE'S IEP

Behaviour (Alternative) Individual Education Plan for continued teacher: Term 2

Level of Achievement

Requires programming in the area of behaviour due to his extreme difficulty concentrating, staying on task, completing work independently, and lack of age appropriate social interaction skills.

Annual Program Goals

By the end of the school year, will further develop strategies for on task behaviour to complete work, organizational skills for preparedness, and positive interaction with peers during group work.

Term 1

Performance Tasks	Teaching Strategies Where different for this student	Assessment Methods Where different for this student
■ Will demonstrate on-task behaviour four times per day for 10 minutes without requiring a prompt to stay on task.	■ positive reinforcement ■ individual seating when necessary	■ anecdotal notes ■ self-evaluation
■ Will demonstrate self-initiative by being prepared and ready to learn with all his books and materials (pencil, book, etc.) at the beginning of each period 50% of the time without teacher prompting.	■ visual checklist on his desk ■ peer model nearby	■ anecdotal notes ■ reference to checklist
■ Will respond and interact positively when working in a whole class or group situation (he will wait his turn to speak, listen to others who are speaking, and complete his share of the work) 75% of the time.	■ positive reinforcement ■ non-verbal cues ■ reminders of desired behaviour beforehand	■ anecdotal notes ■ self-reflection

(continued)

Term 2

Performance Tasks	Teaching Strategies Where different for this student	Assessment Methods Where different for this student
■ Will respond and interact positively when working in a whole class or group situation (he will wait his turn to speak, listen to others who are speaking, and complete his share of the work) 75% of the time.	■ positive reinforcement ■ non-verbal cues ■ reminders of desired behaviour beforehand	■ anecdotal notes ■ self-evaluation
■ Will demonstrate on-task behaviour three times per day for 10 minutes without requiring a prompt to stay on task.	■ positive reinforcement ■ individual seating when necessary	■ anecdotal notes ■ self-evaluation
■ Will demonstrate self-initiative, organization, and readiness by being prepared and ready to learn with materials (pencil, book, etc.) at the beginning of each period 50% of the time with a single teacher prompt or no prompt.	■ weekly desk organization with a peer ■ peer model in front for him to see ■ visual cues ■ proximity	■ anecdotal notes ■ reference to checklist

ACADEMIC

"According to his previous IEP and other reports, it indicated that Drake was working approximately one grade level below in most curriculum areas. So in combination with the fact that he has just entered full English instruction for the first time and that he is already working below grade level posed learning challenges for Drake. At times I would watch him think and I could see that he was spending a lot of time thinking about how to write what he wanted to write in English. I began to spend time talking with Drake about what he would write down. This strategy supported his learning where he was successfully completing written tasks rather than feeling frustrated and as a result disengaged. I decided to try pairing students up in order to work though their writing process with a peer. This was an effective strategy [and] proved to be beneficial for many students. It was apparent that Drake needed

help with organization as well as strategic placement in the classroom and within groups in order to maximize his success at school."

STRATEGIES

"The seating arrangement changed over the course of the year but Drake was always strategically placed away from other distracted students and in close proximity to the work area of a student who was supported with an Educational Assistant in order to cut down on the number of verbal prompts that I was giving him. He was also always placed beside a reasonably strong student who demonstrated patience and with whom Drake seemed to get along. This student changed throughout the year as he found common interests with others and gained new friendships. An instructional strategy that was used on a regular basis was teacher proximity. I began teaching lessons while standing beside his desk. Just the proximity of my presence helped him to regulate and focus without being verbally prompted to do so. These simple adjustments to the physical environment promoted a more universally designed space for Drake and the other students to learn.

Drake received modified work for Mathematics and Language; although usually with the proper accommodations, he could complete language activities. Accommodations that were most often used for Drake included a scribe for written work. Drake was a very verbal and creative boy and having the opportunity to tell his story verbally was very helpful. Using technology for writing and having alternative methods for output were also strategies that were available to all students. Use of technology wasn't always the best tool as he was still required to self-regulate and maintain focus on his work. At times he would choose to wear headphones, plug them into the computer to look like he was listening to something, in order to help block out the background noise and help him to focus on his task at hand. Even if it was a completely self-selected task that was of high interest to him, he often experienced challenges completing tasks without human support for redirection. Most of the times, if he was provided with support to focus on his tasks, he could complete them. In order to minimize adult supports, Drake, as well as others in the class was paired with a classmate while completing work. In the beginning groupings were teacher selected and students who had greater ability to support by redirecting were paired with students who needed more direction. Through this modelling, as well as contributing factors of what was happening in the classroom with our rights and community work, other students were able to adopt these 'helping' skills. Students including Drake were more willing to accept 'help' from a classmate when they also had the opportunity to 'help' someone else with something which they excelled in.

Using differentiated instruction through project based tasks helped me as an educator to meet the needs of all of the learners in the class. These projects provided the opportunity to meet the students where they were at and build on their learning skills. The students were working on at least one project in various subject areas at a time over the course of the year. The projects were developed sequentially in that based on the results, outcomes and feedback I received from one project, I developed the next project with these in mind. For Drake these differentiated projects had many purposes. I was able to provide him with a format for learning a topic of high interest, various methods of output and various methods of assessment. He was working on the same projects as all of his classmates and although his expectations may have been modified in my assessment of his process and product, he was able to produce work that aligned with what everyone else was doing and have a product he seemed proud to share with his classmates.

Although most of these strategies were very successful in helping Drake to be successful, it is important to recognize the impact of how Drake came to school. Since he was happy to come to school most days, he had an eagerness about him. He was willing to learn and trusted that he would be supported. He learned quickly that I would never try to center him out, yell at him or make him feel inferior. He was respected just as the rest of his classmates were."

Another Teacher Voice

"Drake is a very lively and social person who enjoys socializing with his peers and being a part of the group. I have strategically placed him away from most students but near a peer that does an effective job of keeping Drake's behaviour in check. Drake has a very big heart and likes helping with Noah (a student with a developmental exceptionality) and will often volunteer to help the Educational Assistant when given the opportunity.

It didn't take me long to understand that Drake is a visual and kinaesthetic learner. At times he will exhibit impatience and have a propensity to talk out and he seems to understand things better when he sees them visually or has an opportunity for hands on experiences. A few weeks ago, I was explaining translations of objects, specifically slides on the two-dimentional plane. Using the smart board and a few motioned graphics, he seemed to have a better comprehension of the concept. Drake also had the opportunity to use a 10 strip to move around in various slide rules. He was able to tell that the shape did not change in size or orientation after the slide. These types of kinaesthetic strategies seem to work best for understanding difficult concepts. Cooperative work situations are always his preferred method of task accomplishment, although, he also looks forward to working one on one with Mr. Newman, the resource teacher, since it allows him time to focus and work through more difficult processes.

With regard to programming for Drake in all subject areas, the biggest strategy is the use of concrete examples and guiding questions. In his writer's journal, I give him an example of a paragraph and put emphasis on the conventions, such as capitals and punctuation, by bolding them. The guiding questions include a list of prompts such as, who are you writing about? where does it take place?, and what is the problem?, which all help him to formulate his ideas for the paragraph. At times, I may point out small things to correct in his paragraph such as capitals or a grammar error. I only pick one for him to focus on in the next submission.

In mathematics, I like to give many examples of samples for the work they will be performing. I allow Drake to reference his samples in order to do his work on the page. As much as possible, I use chunking with him to break down [a] larger process. Division is an example of an operation that took Drake weeks to master, but he now has a good understanding. Drake also gets some one-on-one time with the Educational Resource Teacher to focus on Math skills.

Other general strategies that I use on a regular basis include trying to be very supportive of Drake by listening and asking him questions and providing him with opportunities to feel successful and helpful. I also try to help him organize his things in order to get ready at the beginning and end of each day. Since April I have encouraged him take more control of this task and start to develop some independent organization skills. Drake has definitely improved his organization in some areas; yet, some areas still require more attention. Routine is also a key strategy for Drake. This helps him to be more organized if he knows what to expect each day. I also provide Preparatory or Cue commands such as 'in five minutes we are going to be switching to Science' or 'I am going to come to you for this answer'. This provided Drake with time to think about what is coming next and also be more prepared to handle the transition when it happens.

As much as possible, I have it appear that I treat him the same way as I do the rest of the class. It should seem as invisible as possible to his peers that he is receiving anything 'different'. It is important to note that all of the strategies I use in the classroom are based on a Universal Design for Learning model. Drake is one of a small group of students that these strategies are intended for but these strategies are available and benefit the learning of all of the students in the class.

Although Drake still needs to focus for greater periods, initiate tasks in a quicker manner, and independently seek help when he needs further understanding, he has made notable progress over this current school year. In independent work, I have noticed that he is able to stay on task for three 15-minute intervals without cues or reminders. This is up significantly from two 10-minute independent work periods. At the beginning of the year, I was emailing his mom for homework reminders and for other important school related items and since April, I have not sent an email. Homework since the last week of April has been completed and submitted on time. The few minor incidents when homework was not completed were recognized by Drake and he accepted the responsibility of finishing the work on his recess time. He has been taking more responsibility to keep his materials more organized and in the past few months he has made a concerted effort to place his notes in order in their respective duo-tangs.

Drake's greatest strength is his heart. He has certainly touched mine this year. He is about as genuine as they come. He has a personality and smile that seems to draw his peers to him. Even when he has conflicts, he will be the first to apologize or forgive."

Student Voice

Drake uses Bitstrips, an online comic creator program, to design and write his own comics. He selects the background and characters and writes the script. He does this for fun.

Figure 10.1 It's Billy Joe, by Drake

"What I like about school is Math and Science. I get to hang out with my friends and do lots of fun activities and organized sports. I also like Language, like story writing and making comics using Bitstrips on the computer. I like to write stories. I like the imagination part of writing stories. I get lost in the story and when I am writing I am not distracted by other things going on around me.

I especially like using technology for learning things like the SMART board and the laptop for doing my work like writing. I can just go on the laptop and start writing a story or find information for a project. I can also play games that help me get better at Math like division and Reading. I find it easier to focus on my work when I am using the laptop; it keeps me focused. I work better in groups because I can concentrate better and I don't have to do all of the work. I can do most of the work but I don't have to do all of the work. I like that I can work through the problems with other people. It helps me to learn something that I wasn't sure of and find out that I know the right answer before giving it to the teacher.

It helps me the most when teachers just talk to me. Talking to me alone, not centering me out to make me feel embarrassed; because when I feel embarrassed I can't do anything in the classroom, I just want to hide. When the teacher talks to me one-on-one and reminds me of what I need to do—because I need reminders, or explains something to me, I understand it better. Sometimes I need the teacher to explain it to me again or explain it better if they didn't explain it good enough the first time.

The only things that I don't really like about school are Social Studies and memorizing things. When I am not interested in the topic, for example, Social Studies, it makes it harder to learn. Also, there seems to be a lot more memorizing that I need to do for tests and things in Social Studies. When teachers just give us the work without explaining it, it makes it hard. Sometimes they don't explain it well or they go too fast and I don't get it. When it's really noisy in the classroom I can't think. Most of the time it is really noisy and I just can't concentrate on anything no matter how hard I try. Until the teacher notices and makes the noise stop, I just can't think. It's still really hard to be organized. I need the teacher to help me organize my things like cleaning out my desk otherwise I spend a lot of time looking for my stuff and then I eventually find it. If it's something I like, for example, my video games, I will organize it. I don't like organizing at school.

I feel successful when I get a good grade. When teachers are nice to me and I can make friends, I feel good. I like going to school now. The teachers understand me better!"

Summary of Drake's Case Study

Drake's story reminds us as educators that despite all of the strategies we put in place to make our classrooms inclusive, we need to remember that the child with the exceptionality can often tell us what works best for him or her. Teaching all students to be advocates for their learning needs and recognizing what they identify as needing is crucial for students to feel successful and have a sense of belonging at any age. Although students with ADHD can at times be scattered, unorganized, and speak out of turn, it is important to remember that our reactions to this behaviour can impact how other students will view and treat them. When including students with ADHD, it is also important to recognize that their self-esteem may have been negatively impacted by their previous school experiences. This is especially true when the student faces multiple challenges as a result of multiple diagnostics. By focusing on the student's strengths and needs rather than diagnoses, differentiated learning opportunities can be developed in order to maximize student success. By modelling inclusive behaviour and acceptance of students with exceptionalities, teachers create classrooms that are communities of belonging. When a teacher makes use of universal design for learning (UDL) and focuses on differentiating instruction (DI), all students in the class can be fully included in the curriculum. Since UDL is based on the assumption that difficulties in learning are due to problems with delivery of curriculum and not due to deficits within the learner, it is essential that teachers make pedagogical changes regarding their teaching practice. It is only once the changes are made to pedagogy that students with exceptionalities will have their needs met in inclusive classrooms.

 COMMENTARY By Dr. Gabrielle Young

General Comments

Drake is a lively child who enjoys socializing with his peers and being part of the classroom. He is a peer helper who enjoys school and is compliant with adult requests. However, he experiences difficulty with following through on instructions, is disorganized, and has trouble starting tasks or completing tasks that require planning or long-term effort—all traits that are characteristic of students with attention deficit hyperactivity disorder (ADHD). Central nervous system stimulant medications were prescribed to help Drake control his impulsive and aggressive behaviour, but these medications decreased his appetite and made it difficult for him to sleep.

Connections to Theoretical Frameworks

Response to intervention (RTI) promotes the use of evidence-based teaching procedures for all students in the general education classroom, with increased levels of support for students who do not respond adequately to instruction. As part of the Primary Tier of the RTI model, Drake's teacher employs inclusive practices that enable him and his peers to be successful. In order to ensure Drake understands the tasks at hand, the teacher

makes eye contact with him when providing instructions. Drake's teacher provides preparatory cues to help prevent behaviour issues that may arise during transitions, and so that he may better attend to the question, the teacher lets Drake know when he will be called on for a response. This strategy is useful for students who show signs of anxiety when asked to speak in class. Classroom discussions are valuable for their ability to support the development of expressive and receptive language and the use of eye contact, proximity, and verbal cues can help ensure that classroom discussions are a milieu where all feel comfortable to participate.

Classroom distractions make it difficult for Drake to concentrate on independent work, and when engaged in group-work he often uses an outdoor voice. Drake and his classmates would benefit from the use of a classroom noise monitor, which can be used to help students visualize and monitor their own noise levels. Drake benefits from the predictability of routine as it helps him to better attend to the task at hand and helps to ensure he doesn't forget things. All students in the class, especially those with autism, can benefit from inclusive strategies such as the use

(continued)

of a visual schedule to highlight daily routines. Drake also benefited from breathing activities, which helped him to calm down and organize his thoughts prior to speaking.

Organization remains a challenge for Drake. In order to develop organizational skills, all students should be reminded of the material they will need for their morning routine and students should be scaffolded through the process of using an agenda to record their homework at the end of the day. Positive reinforcement, or a token system which can be used towards a class goal, can be used to motivate students to place colour-coded notebooks in their respective bins or places in their desk, and pencils and erasers in their pencil cases.

Drake's teacher employed strategic seating to help him remain on task. Drake was placed near a strong student who was able to monitor his behaviour and remind him to stay on task; this student changed throughout the year as he made new friends and gained common interests with others. In order to reduce verbal prompts, Drake was placed by a student who had the support of an educational assistant, as the presence of an adult helped him to focus and regulate his behaviour. In order to minimize adult support, students were paired while completing assignments. Students who had greater ability to support by redirecting were paired with students who needed more direction. This was an effective strategy as students were more willing to accept help from a classmate when they had the opportunity to help someone else on a task in which they excelled.

Strategies to Support Students with Learning Difficulties In alignment with a diagnosis of a specific learning disorder, Drake's intellectual potential was in the average range, but his academic performance was below grade level in all core subjects. In order to meet Drake's learning needs, his teacher effectively utilized components of UDL and DI in order to ensure that all students were fully included in the curriculum. Lessons and activities were designed with the learning needs of all students in mind and students were encouraged to work collaboratively in creating an end product that demonstrated their interests, strengths, and abilities. Project-based learning supports DI and motivates students by incorporating their interests and providing multiple means of engagement and expression. This strategy was effective for Drake who recognized that he was motivated to learn when he was interested in the topic and wasn't required to perform rote memory tasks. While the expectations may have been modified in regards to the assessment of Drake's process and product, through the use of DI, Drake was able to work on the same projects as his classmates, and have an end product he was proud to share.

As part of the Primary Tier of the RTI model, Drake's teacher employed evidence-based inclusive instructional approaches, such as the use of concrete examples and guiding questions. In math, students were given exemplars for sample questions and chunking was used to break down larger processes. Guiding questions and writing prompts were used to structure writing. Drake is a visual and kinesthetic learner, and like many students, Drake benefits from the use of a SMART Board and the use of manipulatives to help him to understand difficult concepts in math. He notes that the use of a laptop keeps him focused while writing and that using software programs have been effective in improving his reading and math skills.

Strategies to Support Students with Social Difficulties In alignment with a diagnosis of autism, Drake experiences difficulty socializing with his peers and at times may engage in repetitive and ritualistic behaviour. When provided with the opportunity to help another student with a developmental disability, or to assist the educational assistant, Drake took pride in being able to help his peers and has thrived since being provided with the opportunity to engage in the role of a helper. Drake needs to continue to be recognized for his strengths. In addition, Drake needs to be encouraged to build upon his interests and skills as a means to develop resiliency as he continues to face academic and social difficulties. Drake enjoys participating in organized sport; however, he does not have access to transportation for after-school extracurricular activities. As access to community programs may be limited, Drake should be encouraged to participate in intramural or extracurricular activities that may be held over the school lunch hour.

Drake can experience difficulty understanding and maintaining the boundaries of personal space. When engaged in unintentional conflict, Drake is quick to apologize or forgive. However, the class would benefit from employing a talking circle and taking a restorative approach to class conflict. By providing the class with the opportunity to discuss less than ideal interactions, and providing students with the opportunity to voice how disruptive or inappropriate behaviours make them feel, students can learn from their behaviour and be provided with strategies to employ when similar situations arise in the future.

Concluding Thoughts

Students with ADHD can be scattered, unorganized, and may continually speak out of turn.

Source: Used by permission of Gabrielle Young

However, it is important to remember that an educator's reactions to this behaviour can impact how other students view and treat the child. When Drake was centred out in front of the class, it embarrassed him and had a negative impact on his self-esteem. Additionally, the negative stigma towards Drake was recognized by educational staff and students. When constructive feedback is necessary, educators should relay this information to the child in a one-on-one setting, for as Drake noted, *"when I feel embarrassed I can't do anything in the classroom, I just want to hide."*

A student's self-esteem can be negatively impacted by their previous school experiences. It is important to listen to the child and remember that the child with the exceptionality can often tell us what works best for him or her. In order to promote an inclusive learning environment, students need to identify what is crucial for them to feel successful, and they need to be taught how to advocate for their learning needs.

Drake's profile is complex. In addition to his attention-related difficulties and his challenges with social interactions, Drake experiences involuntary motor tics such as body jerks and tense muscles and vocal tics such as yelling, humming, and echoing. In alignment with the Three-Block Model of UDL (Katz, 2012), Drake's teacher lays the groundwork for Block One by aligning beliefs and attitudes about diversity. As demonstrated in Drake's case profile, by modelling inclusive behaviour and the acceptance of students with exceptionalities, teachers can create classrooms that are communities of belonging for all.

Key Terms

attention deficit / hyperactivity disorder (ADHD) ADHD is one of the most common childhood disorders. Symptoms include difficulty staying focused and paying attention, difficulty controlling behaviour, and hyperactivity (over-activity).

autism spectrum disorder (ASD) ASD is a term used to describe a range of conditions with varying degrees of delay, typically associated with communication, social cues, intellect, and sensory processing. At one end of the spectrum is, which is a relatively mild degree of impairment, up to conditions such as Rett syndrome, fragile X syndrome, to PDD-NOS (Pervasive Developmental Disorder—Not Otherwise Specified).

Tourette syndrome Tourette syndrome (TS) is a neurological disorder characterized by repetitive, stereotyped, involuntary movements and vocalizations called tics.

Questions to Consider

1. What does this case study tell you about the importance of the teacher–student relationship? What strategies could a teacher use to facilitate a teacher–student relationship?

    _____

    _____

    _____

    _____

    _____

    _____

2. How could a classroom teacher create a classroom climate that is accepting of diversity, particularly for children with obvious exceptionalities? What particular activities could be planned for the very first day/week of school?

    _____

    _____

    _____

    _____

    _____

    _____

3. Why is it important to consider the student's voice when trying to answer his or her needs?

    _____

    _____

_____

_____

_____

_____

4. List all of the ways that the educational team and parents provided differentiated instruction to best meet Drake's needs.

_____

_____

_____

_____

_____

_____

5. What have you learned about the issue of multiple diagnostics?

_____

_____

_____

_____

_____

_____

Useful Websites

American Psychiatric Association: Specific Learning Disorder
www.dsm5.org/Documents/Specific%20Learning%20Disorder%20Fact%20Sheet.pdf

British Columbia Ministry of Education: Effective Transitions
www.bced.gov.bc.ca/specialed/landbdif/app16.htm

Reference

Katz, J. (2012). *Teaching to diversity: The three-block model of universal design for learning.* Winnipeg, MB: Portage & Main Press.

Chapter 11
Elvin Case Study

Dr. Jennifer Katz

Elvin's education is steeped in the culture of his community.
Source: Aboriginal Stock Images

TOPIC COVERAGE:

- Mild Intellectual Disability
- Respecting Diversity Program
- Mental Illness/Mental Health Supports
- Emotional/Behavioural Disorder
- Oppositional Defiant Disorder
- Attention Deficit/Hyperactivity Disorder
- Hearing Impairment
- Learning Profile

The student will:

- Analyze how this case study reflects **social inclusion** and **academic inclusion**

- Explain why UDL, and the team involved in this case, focus on Tier 1 interventions first

- Evaluate the advantages and potential pitfalls of a strengths based approach

Preamble

Elvin lives in a northern First Nations community with his mother, grandmother, and three siblings. Elvin was born with a hearing impairment. At age 3, he was assessed due to language delays, and determined to have a mild intellectual disability. Because he lives on a northern reserve where medical care is sparse and there is no audiology support, he did not receive a diagnosis regarding his hearing impairment or hearing aids until he entered the school system. The family experienced violence within the home when Elvin was 4 years old (and perhaps before). Since that time, Elvin has not been in contact with his father. Now in grade 8, he attends a local K–12 school that while under the umbrella of a public school division, operates with a significant level of independence. The student population is 90 percent First Nations, but the teaching staff are predominantly non-Aboriginal and from urban environments. Elvin entered school with little language. He has subsequently become reasonably proficient orally; however, he struggles with written language.

As you can see from the audiology report below, without hearing aids, Elvin's loss in both ears is between 40 and 60 dB. This means he can only hear sounds louder than 60 dB, and will miss almost all communication. With his hearing aids, Elvin is able to hear any sounds over 30 dB, thus allowing him to participate in the learning activities of the classroom.

Audiology Reports

Elvin's mother declined psychological testing, but level B tests (standardized tests completed by a resource teacher) indicated Elvin has a verbal IQ in the mild disability range (SS=68), and well below average verbal scores (SS=52) using the Kaufman Brief Intelligence Test II (K-BIT2), a level B cognitive abilities test. This test assesses students' ability to reason, problem solve, and draw analogies using both words and symbols. The verbal subtest of most cognitive abilities tests have been shown to be culturally biased, especially as Elvin is an English as a second language learner. However, the non-verbal subtest of the K-BIT uses symbols that are culturally neutral.

Consonant sounds range from 20 to 50 decibels (dB) and are higher pitched than vowels. As can be seen in the "speech banana" below (retrieved from www.firstyears.org/lib/banana.htm), most conversations take place between 40 and 60 dB.

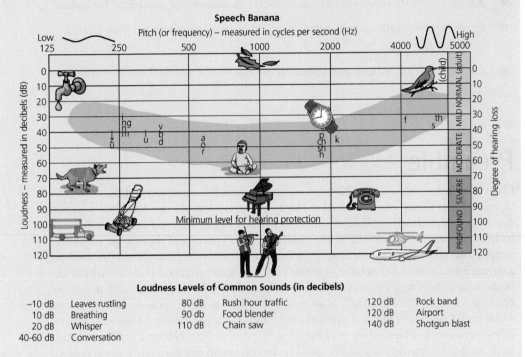

Figure 11.1 Speech Banana

Source: Retrieved from http://www.firstyears.org/lib/banana.htm

As a result, any loss over 40 dB results in students missing most of the discussion that takes place in classrooms.

Because Elvin's scores on the non-verbal subtest were higher than his verbal scores, the school believed the non-verbal test was a valid indicator of his abilities, and thus identified him as having a mild intellectual disability. However, as the score of 68 is borderline, the K-BIT is only a level B test, and both emotional and cultural factors may be influencing him, this label is questionable, and focus was placed on supporting his emotional needs and hearing impairment.

With hearing aids, Elvin has a mild loss to normal range of hearing; however, since he went so many years with them, he missed years of early language development. An additional problem is that in the northern regions, food is extremely expensive. Batteries need to be specially ordered and shipped in, and can cost upwards of

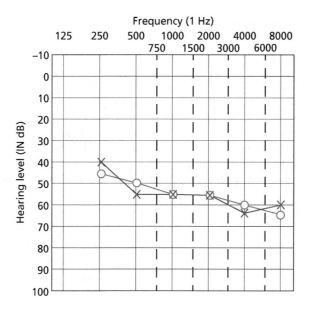

Figure 11.2 Unaided Audiology Report for Right and Left Ears

$100.00 for a small pack. Thus, maintenance of his hearing aids is often not prioritized, and Elvin goes significant periods of time where they are not working.

Elvin has also been diagnosed with attention deficit/hyperactivity disorder (ADHD) and oppositional defiant disorder (ODD; a form of emotional/behavioural disorder), in addition to his hearing impairment.

FAST FACTS ABOUT... HEARING IMPAIRMENT AND EMOTIONAL/BEHAVIOURAL DISORDER (EBD)

Hearing impairment

Characteristics

- partial or total inability to hear
- may occur in one or both ears
- can affect ability to learn language
- can be temporary or permanent

For more information see: Canadian Hearing Society at www.chs.ca

Emotional/behavioural disorder (EBD)

Characteristics

- severe behaviour problems
- strong underlying emotional causes
- some have life experiences that have threatened their personal safety
- their trust, hope, and sense of community have been damaged

For more information see: Manitoba Education at www.edu.gov.mb.ca/k12/specedu/bip/bkg_ebd.html

Initial Meeting

PARENT VOICE

A meeting was held with the parent in her home to try to reduce stress and build relationships. The meeting was informal—Elvin's mother was asked to share anything she thought the school team should know about him.

"I love my son. I love all my children, and I do the best I can. I work two jobs, and my mother looks after the kids a lot. Elvin is angry all the time. He yells and hurts the other kids. He won't listen to his grandmother. I see his spirit. I know it is a good thing. He is strong, fierce, he will not be beaten down like I was, and so many are here. I want everyone to see the truth of his gifts. He has a big heart, he carves and drums and has magic in him. He needs someone at the school to see his spirit.

I will tell you a story about Elvin. Last year I got really sick with pneumonia. I was sleeping all day. Elvin went and got a big piece of fishing net and attached it to a pole, like you use for catching butterflies or jumping fish. He sat in my room all day and all night. When grandmother asked him what he was doing, he said, 'I'm making sure she doesn't fly away.' Nobody at that school sees his magic."

RESOURCE TEACHER VOICE

"Elvin is a handful. We try to sit him near the front of the room so he can hear, but he gets angry because he thinks he is being punished. I try to explain it to him but he doesn't get it. The teachers complain that he never completes any of his work, even when it is modified for him. He just puts his head down on his desk and refuses to look at anyone or move. If a teacher or his peers get too close, he will swear, and sometimes hit them. His mother never answers my messages when I call home. I can't take all my time on him and neither can the classroom teachers so if his EA is not available, and she is only part time, he is left alone a lot. We need more support for him—here and from home."

Universal design for learning (UDL) is a pedagogy for inclusive education that allows educators to design learning environments, including the physical set-up of the classroom, the social interactions, and the curricular activities, to be accessible for diverse learners (Katz, 2012; Rose & Meyer, 2002). As special education has moved toward inclusive education, UDL has encouraged teachers to redesign programs for all their students, rather than making individual adaptations that single out students and lower expectations. Elvin's initial IEP reflected a special education approach (see Table 11.1). Note the individualized programming, with goals that focus on Elvin's behaviour, rather than on making the program work for him, and strategies that involve pull-out programming and behaviour modification.

Second Meeting

At the second meeting of the team, the district consultant and the school team recognized that Elvin's programming was very deficit-based and remedial. His mother made clear that Elvin's strengths were not being honoured. In the meeting, the team decided to take a UDL approach to programming for Elvin. This means they:

Table 11.1 Page from Initial Individual Educational Plan (IEP)

Goal	Strategies	Assessment
Elvin will be able to express his feelings in appropriate ways.	Counselling Positive behaviour intervention support (PBIS) reward system	Fewer incidents of aggression
Elvin will be able to complete assigned activities during class time.	Prompts to begin tasks Positive reinforcement for work completion Chunking of tasks EA support	Responds to prompts Increased completion rate
Elvin will interact positively with his peers and teachers.	Behaviour intervention plan (BIP) PBIS Counselling	Fewer incidents of aggression

1. Provided professional development for all of the teachers and clinicians involved. Staff learned about the Three-Block Model of UDL. The classroom teachers, resource teacher, PBIS (Positive Behaviour Intervention Support) consultant, guidance counsellor, educational assistant, and principal all participated.

2. Completed a class profile. They explored the strengths and challenges of the class as a community, and then created a plan to create an inclusive learning community, including both social and emotional programming and universally designed curricular units and assessment for all the students, rather than just for Elvin.

   a. The teacher agreed to implement social and emotional programming in the classes, including spirit buddies and the **Respecting Diversity program**. Staff also wanted to use the seven teachings and the medicine wheel to begin conversations about our values and beliefs.

   b. Many of the students, like Elvin, were visual and musical learners. As many of them hunt and fish, they also have connections to the land, nature, and learning by doing. The teachers decided to plan an integrated unit based around the fishing trade. They wanted students to engage in science, social studies, math, and English language arts (ELA) in relation to this theme. The team had a science and math teacher, and a humanities (social studies and ELA) teacher, and they agreed to teach some parts of the unit separately and some parts together.

   c. Staff wanted to implement First Nations programming with the whole class. An elder could lead the children through explorations of Cree culture, spiritual beliefs, and perspectives.

   d. An EA was assigned to the class, rather than specifically to Elvin, and she was asked to circulate and work with all students, so Elvin could interact with his peers without someone standing over him. The classroom teacher carefully chose three peers to be grouped with him, kids she knew he liked and would want to be with. Students were allowed to have phones, so if Elvin's hearing aids weren't working, they could talk by text.

e. The school requested an FM system, which will support many kids, and make Elvin less reliant on hearing aid batteries (though it's still better if he has them!).

RESOURCE TEACHER VOICE

"At first, we thought we needed to redo Elvin's IEP. We tweaked the goals/strategies, and added some academic goals, which we had never really thought to do before, as strange as that seems. It was all behavioural, and all about Elvin becoming obedient and doing what was asked of him."

The second IEP (Table 11.2) focused on strategies that involved all students. Note that the goals are the same, but the teachers have now recognized that rather than trying to address Elvin's behaviour, redesigning the environment is more likely to result in the outcomes they want, and many students will benefit.

Table 11.2 Page from Second Individual Educational Plan (IEP)

Goal	Strategies	Assessment
Elvin will be able to express his feelings in appropriate ways.	Class meetings Teach group work skills Sharing circles Songs, artwork	Elvin participates in circle, shares his thoughts and feelings. Elvin represents his feelings and beliefs through art and music.
Elvin will be able to complete assigned activities during class time.	Choice in formats Cooperative group work	Elvin contributes to class activities, plays a valued role.
Elvin will interact positively with his peers and teachers.	Seven teachings SEL programming Opportunities for success and leadership	Elvin begins to develop friendships, uses strategies to de-escalate.
Elvin will meet expectations in science and social studies.	Determine essential understandings, focus on them Alternative formats for process and product	Elvin is able to express curricular understandings using formats of his choosing.
Elvin will begin to use technological supports for literacy and numeracy—focus on understanding and expression.	Use of computers, smart board, calculator Read aloud software, voice to text	Elvin self-manages use of technology.

"Within a month of beginning the process, we were stunned to realize we didn't really need an IEP for Elvin. This was not because Elvin was magically cured! It's just that we realized all of our students needed the same supports. Yes, Elvin's needs were sometimes more intense/frequent, but other than the FM system, they really weren't unique. Many of our students have delays in basic skills and language development, have to learn to work collaboratively, and prefer non-written formats. Cree culture always emphasized visual and oral communication—so this fit with the community's way of life. That's not to say we didn't want our students to be literate—but visual and oral literacy, technological literacy, and other forms of communication are just as valuable as text based, written formats. When we took the time to invest in our students' social and emotional well-being, the climate in the classes changed. When we differentiated the instruction, our students experienced success in ways they never had before, including Elvin. He actually knew a lot about fishing, about the land, and about racism in Canadian history, unfortunately—his family were survivors of it. He was able to pass both social studies and science with these supports, but no modifications! We could see Elvin's anger reducing. We always blamed his home life, it never occurred to us that we were the source of a lot of his anger—he was frustrated, felt like he was dumb and couldn't be successful, and that nobody liked him."

The students created works of art depicting traditional and modern fishing practices, and the role of science and technology in them. They conducted studies of the pH of the water, counted fish stocks, and then used mathematical formulae to determine the likely population of each species. They looked at the geography of the North, waterways, settlement patterns, and our relation to the land and water. They created drum songs honouring the fish, and wrote letters to the minister with recommendations for sustainable management of our land. Elvin suggested the government "not pretend to be hearing impaired"!

The class "IEP" should have read:

Ink Drawing on Birch Bark titled "Eagles are major predators of fish in the wild."

Source: V. Budd/ Sam Parmar/ D. Monias

Table 11.3 Class IEP

Goal	Strategies	Assessment
Students will be able to express their feelings in appropriate ways.	Class meetings Teach group work skills Sharing circles Songs, artwork	Students participate in circle, share thoughts and feelings. Students represent their feelings and beliefs through art and music.
Students will be able to complete assigned activities during class time.	Choice in formats Cooperative group work	Students contribute to class activities, play a valued role.
Students will interact positively.	Seven teachings SEL programming Opportunities for success and leadership	Students develop friendships, use strategies to de-escalate.
Students will meet expectations in science and social studies.	Determine essential understandings, focus on them Alternative formats for process and product	Students are able to express curricular understandings using formats of their choosing.
Students will begin to use technological supports for literacy and numeracy—focus on understanding and expression.	Use of computers, smart board, calculator Read aloud software, voice to text	Students self-manage use of technology.

Classroom Teacher Voice

"We recently had a team meeting to review Elvin's progress… it was the first time his mother and grandmother came into school, answered their phone, or communicated at all in the three years he has been here. I was frustrated that they didn't seem to care. Now I realize that was not true—we just had such a negative perspective about Elvin. We tried to couch it in concern and care, but really, I never valued his strengths, it was all about his behaviour and what he couldn't do.

Now Elvin is a valued member of our school community. He is a gifted artist and has taught all of us to carve. He is usually happy, cooperative, and energetic—except when asked to write—but he is working on it. Now that Elvin has experienced success, he is more willing to try to work on his reading and writing. He has strategies and language for when he feels sad or angry, and more often than not asks for support to deal with them. His peers understand and value him, and they are able to support him in ways we couldn't. We still have room to go—but we have come a long, long way.

You have changed my teaching forever—I choose to heal, and I know how. Thank you."
I thank you. All the grandmothers thank you.
Megwetch."

Parent Voice

"I hate walking into schools. The smell of the cleaning fluid on the floor—I never wash my floors. I just vacuum, that's it. The sound of chairs and desks, the hallways and doors. What happens behind the doors. You have changed my family forever. Elvin comes home happy. We don't fight so much. His little brother wants to have the same teacher. My children and grandchildren won't be terrified when they walk into school. They will go to high school and maybe even university."

Summary of Elvin's Case Study

Elvin's community—professional and familial—came together to support his growth and well-being. They took the emphasis off of fixing Elvin, and put it on designing a learning environment where he and his classmates could be successful. They did not dumb down the curriculum, nor are they ignoring his challenges—they simply made the decision to first focus on his strengths, allow him to experience success, and have his peers see him as a valuable member of the learning community. Having done so, they may find his language skills now improve—because he will be interacting in natural ways with texts and peers, and will be engaged. On the other hand, they may decide to do some focused intervention for him around his reading/writing, and it is far more likely to be successful when he is willing, has trust in his teachers, and doesn't feel it is a punishment.

>>> COMMENTARY   By Dr. Nancy Hutchinson

General Comments

The case of Elvin provides an excellent example of the power of UDL, that is, of the impressive accomplishments that can result from us, as educators, focusing on how we can change the context to enable students to succeed. It is also an example of the importance of continuous monitoring when working individually with a student.

There are many lessons to be taken from this case. I will consider the importance of change that focuses on: (a) creating a positive social and emotional climate in the classroom; (b) taking an appreciative approach to every student and genuinely trying to understand why students might act in the way they do; (c) engaging students through their interests and beginning where students are; (d) encouraging students to take risks; (e) taking advantage of the context created by these first four changes to focus on academic differentiation; (f) monitoring to ensure effectiveness; and (g) celebrating the accomplishments of the community, as made up of students and their educators, families, and neighbourhoods.

To accomplish any of these goals with UDL, educators must embrace the belief that they are the ones who must change, not the students. Only when we accept responsibility for the context at school that contributes to students' actions in the

(continued)

classroom can we expect that students will do anything different. UDL offers a blueprint for acting on that belief.

Connections to Theoretical Frameworks

Creating a Positive Social and Emotional Climate in the Classroom In her book, *Teaching to Diversity*, Jennifer Katz (2012) describes UDL as an overarching concept with three main components. The fundamental component on which the other two rest is social and emotional learning. To enact this component we must create a caring and compassionate learning community where diversity is valued. We will know we have accomplished this when all our students express that they feel valued and act like they feel respected, and when this is also how students treat one another.

Students learn this classroom culture from us. There is considerable evidence to show that the quality of student–teacher relationships is central to school climate (Dalton, Hutchinson, & Dods, 2009). For many students, "being cared for is a precondition of caring about school" (Woolfolk, Hoy, & Weinstein, 2006, p. 210). Recent research suggests that this is especially true for exceptional students and students at risk for dropping out of school (Dods, 2013). In the case of Elvin, it is clear that the staff committed to making many and large changes beginning with learning about UDL and implementing the Respecting Diversity program.

Taking an Appreciative Approach and Understanding Why Students Act as They Do Appreciative inquiry focuses on using a positive approach to effect change (Whitney & Trosten-Bloom, 2010). Appreciation has to do with recognizing and affirming the positive in each individual—in emphasizing their present strengths and potentials. Inquiry is about asking questions in order to learn more. In this case, the teachers wisely recognized that they needed to know more about the all of the students, as well as knowing more about

Elvin. They used the students' knowledge of Cree culture and fishing as a basis for integrated units.

There are many possible reasons for students acting as they do in the classroom. Some students may not yet have learned the social skills we expect; for example, when Elvin has to sit near the front of the classroom he objects, and when the work is challenging he "just puts his head down." Sometimes, difficulties in executive functioning cause students to see situations differently than the way we see them. And we may think they are over-reacting, as when Elvin hits peers who come close to him, but such a reaction may have been adaptive when he experienced a real threat (e.g., when there was violence in the home). We can help Elvin and other students to see that such reactions are maladaptive when there is no threat. As teachers, we need to inquire, to ask questions, and to conscientiously look for the reasons for students' challenging behaviours in the classroom (Hutchinson, 2016), just as the teachers did in the case of Elvin.

Engaging Students through Their Interests and by Starting Where They Are We all know that interest guides our personal choices about how we use our time and energy. Elvin's teachers wisely understood that interest is also a powerful motivator for learning (Renninger, Hidi, & Krapp, 2014), and they chose to take advantage of their students' interest in fishing and in their Cree culture. One of the components of Katz's (2012) Three-Block Model of UDL is inclusive instructional practice, often called differentiated instruction. Basing instruction on students' interests begins with the teachers developing a profile of the students and then using this profile to adjust teaching for the class as a whole (such as inviting elders) and for individuals (such as grouping Elvin with students he wanted to be with). Often an accommodation made for one student (like an FM system) is essential for that student (Elvin) but helpful for many students in the classroom. Finding these kinds of accommodations, what Corno (2008) calls adaptive teaching, ensures effective teaching and learning in your classroom. Choosing topics that interest students (the "what" of teaching) and using approaches that enable students to be successful (the "how" of teaching) enable you to "start where they are," and like Elvin your students will reward you for such respectful teaching with academic accomplishments.

Encouraging Students to Take Risks Encouragement refers to giving someone courage or spurring them on to be the best they can be. Teachers who encourage expect the best of everyone, pay attention so they notice even small accomplishments by their students, smile and make eye contact, and remember how good it feels to be acknowledged (Hutchinson, 2016; Larivee, 2006). The revised IEP for Elvin focused on social-emotional goals for him, positive and encouraging strategies like class meetings and songs, and opportunities for leadership. With all of this encouragement, Elvin participated and so did his classmates, which meant taking risks; and the resource teacher observed that Elvin "didn't really need an IEP" any more.

Focusing on Academic Differentiation All of the approaches already described contributed to the teachers in Elvin's school focusing on academic differentiation. They realized that *"all of our students needed the same support,"* and that *"Cree culture always emphasized visual and oral communication—so this [adaptive way of teaching] fit with the community's way of life."* Positive classroom contexts that affirm the best in every student (*"he is a gifted artist"*) and engage students through their interests (*"an integrated unit based around the fishing trade"*) enable students to take risks and participate (Elvin and his classmates *"could talk by text"* if his batteries were not working). They found, like recent studies, that supportive learning environments enable students to make academic progress, which contributes to

student well-being and reduces the need to focus on behavioural issues (e.g., deLugt, 2015).

Monitoring to Ensure Effectiveness When Elvin's teachers first started working with him, they aimed to remediate a very challenging situation. Their first attempts were related to the Primary Tier of the response to intervention (RTI) model (Goodman, McIntosh, & Bohanon, n.d.) where teachers set clear goals and expected outcomes, give appropriate instruction, monitor the progress of the student, and rectify errors. His first IEP was a perfect example of this. It included (a) goals (e.g., Elvin will be able to express his feelings in appropriate ways); (b) strategies (e.g., positive reinforcement, counselling, and prompts to begin tasks); and (c) assessment periods (e.g., increased completion rate). It was during their second team meeting that his mother mentioned that her son's strengths were not being honoured. At that moment, the team members decided to take a UDL approach. They quickly realized that it was Elvin's strengths and not his challenges that were going to make all the difference for him.

Celebrating Accomplishments Together When inclusive education is working well, we all have a great deal to celebrate. Elvin feels valued by his teachers and peers and now is *"usually happy, cooperative, and energetic."* His teacher thanks him and celebrates her accomplishments by telling Elvin, *"You have changed my teaching forever."* One of the most uplifting parts of the case was the way Elvin's mother attributed changes in her son's life and her family's life to the change in the teachers' approach when she said, *"You have changed my family forever. Elvin comes home happy ... My children and grandchildren won't be terrified when they walk into school."* And she celebrated her genuine appreciation with the words: *"I thank you. All the grandmothers thank you."* The school staff couldn't ask for more affirmation of their commitment to fostering social and academic inclusion by embracing UDL!

Source: Used by permission of Nancy L Hutchinson

Key Terms

academic inclusion The purpose of including students with disabilities in the general education classroom is to increase academic achievement of all students.

Respecting Diversity (RD) program The Respecting Diversity (RD) program's emphasis is on the promotion of positive social and academic development among all children and youth. The program is most often implemented at the start of the school year or semester, and builds students' self-worth, belonging, respect for diverse others, and resiliency.

social inclusion The purpose of including students with disabilities in the general education classroom is to enhance the social-emotional intelligence of all students and encourage the development of social networks between those with and without disabilities.

Questions to Consider

1. What are the unique circumstances we must be aware of when discussing northern, First Nations schools? Would this case have been different in any way had it been set in an urban environment?

_____

_____

_____

_____

_____

_____

_____

2. How do the initial thoughts of Elvin's mother and teacher reflect cultural differences in educational philosophy and child development?

_____

_____

_____

_____

_____

_____

3. Do you agree with the resource teacher that "they didn't need an IEP" for Elvin? Why or why not?

_____

_____

_____

_____

_____

_____

_____

4. What do you notice about the changes in the first, second, and third IEPs? How does this reflect a shift in mindset?

    _____

    _____

    _____

    _____

    _____

    _____

5. Elvin has been identified as having an intellectual disability, ODD, and ADHD. How do you feel about these diagnoses? What role might his hearing impairment have played in this?

    _____

    _____

    _____

    _____

    _____

    _____

Useful Websites

First Nations, Métis & Inuit: Universal Design for Learning
https://sites.google.com/a/epsb.ca/fnmi-universal-design-for-learning

Three Block Model of UDL and the RD program
www.threeblockmodel.com

UDL: Safety and Diversity in the Classroom
www.udlresource.ca/?p=2677

CAST: Universal Design for Learning (American UDL)
www.cast.org

References

Corno, L. (2008). On teaching adaptively. *Educational Psychologist, 43*(3), 161–173.

Dalton, C., Hutchinson, N. L., & Dods, J. (2009). *Creating positive learning environments: A review of the literature*. Paper prepared for the MISA Professional Network, Kingston, ON.

deLugt, J. (2015, June). *Learning to read and thriving: The effect and affect of learning to read*. Paper presented at the annual meeting of the Canadian Society for the Study of Education, Ottawa, ON.

Dods, J. (2013). Enhancing understanding of the nature of supportive school-based relationships for youth who have experienced trauma. *Canadian Journal of Education, 36*(1). 71–95.

Goodman, S., McIntosh, K., & Bohanon, H. (n.d.). *Integrating academic and behavior supports within and RtI framework, Part 2: Universal supports*. Retrieved from http://www.rtinetwork.org/learn/behavior-supports/integrating-academic-and-behavior-supports-universal-supports

Hutchinson, N. L. (2016). *Inclusion of exceptional learners in Canadian schools: A practical handbook for teachers* (5th ed.). Toronto, ON: Pearson Canada.

Katz, J. (2012). *Teaching to diversity: The three-block model*. Winnipeg, MB: Portage & Main.

Larivee, B. (2006). *Authentic classroom management: Creating a learning community and building reflective practice* (2nd ed.). Boston, MA: Pearson Allyn & Bacon.

Renninger, K. A., Hidi, S., & Krapp, A. (1992/2014). *The role of interest in learning and development*. New York, NY: Psychology Press.

Rose, D. H., & Meyer, A. (2002). *Teaching every student in the digital age: Universal design for learning*. Alexandria, VA: ASCD.

Whitney, D. D., & Trosten-Bloom, A. (2010). *The power of appreciative inquiry: A practical guide to positive change* (2nd ed.). San Francisco, CA: Berrett-Kochler Pub.

Woolfolk Hoy, A., & Weinstein, C. S. (2006). Student and teacher perspectives on classroom management. In C. M. Evertson & C. S. Weinstein (Eds.), *Handbook of classroom management: Research, practice, and contemporary issues* (pp. 181–220). Mahwah, NJ: Erlbaum.

Chapter 12
Leon Case Study

Gabrielle Vienneau

Leon is learning to deal with his emotions.
Source: Tyler Olson/Fotolia

TOPIC COVERAGE:

Individual Educational Plan (IEP)

Gradual Entry

Applied Behaviour Analysis (ABA)

Autism Spectrum Disorder (ASD)

Non-Verbal Communication

Collaboration

Inclusive Leadership

The student will:

- State the importance of collaborating with the parents as soon as possible

- Describe the different steps that can be taken to encourage a gradual and positive transition from home to school

- Explain the leadership role of the principal in an inclusive school

- Explain the use of the Applied Behaviour Analysis program in an inclusive setting

- Identify the benefits when everyone participates together in the same classroom

Preamble

Leon is a 6-year-old who loves school. He has an **autism spectrum disorder (ASD)** characterized as Asperger syndrome.[1] He is part of a very likeable family made up of his two parents and his little brother Thomas, 4 years of age, who also has an ASD. Leon was only diagnosed a week before starting kindergarten, so he did not receive any early interventions. Leon has certain difficulties with social interactions and some moments of transition. He prefers individual activities and tends to avoid others' gaze. He has an excellent memory and an incredible thirst for learning. Leon is extremely intelligent and is interested in the following subjects: the solar system and planets, astronauts, science, constellations, and human anatomy and physiology. He is a very pleasant boy with whom it is a pleasure to learn and grow.

FAST FACTS ABOUT... AUTISM SPECTRUM DISORDER (ASD)

Autism spectrum disorder (ASD) and autism are disorders of brain development.

Characteristics

- difficulties with social interactions
- difficulties with verbal and non-verbal communication

- repetitive behaviours
- mild, moderate, severe, or profound cognitive delay
- sensory integration problems or sensory processing disorder

For more information see: Autism Speaks at www.autismspeaks.org/what-autism

---

[1] In the DSM-5, Asperger syndrome is referred to as an autism spectrum disorder.

Parent Voice

"Leon is the elder of my two boys. He is very intelligent and constantly having conversations with himself about different subjects that interest him, like space, the human body and scientific things. Sometimes he is hard to understand. When he's engaged and interested in a task or an idea, it can be hard to get his attention.

The year before Leon started kindergarten, I was very, very worried about him. He was a very stubborn five year-old boy who often had tantrums if he didn't get what he wanted or succeed in doing things his way. When he was three we started noticing that Leon had a few challenges on the social front. It was very hard for Leon to do group activities or follow children his own age, like at soccer or gymnastics. With one-on-one activities, Leon could do the activity and follow up to a certain point. So I was always afraid of how my eldest was going to adjust to school. I was afraid he was going to get himself expelled from school. I knew that my child was very intelligent, but my husband and I were aware that Leon couldn't follow a group.

In May last year, I enrolled Leon in French language sessions at l'École Bellefontaine, the school he was to attend the following September. We wanted to improve his comprehension of French before school started. It was a total failure. Leon was in a state of crisis all during the sessions, anxious and frustrated. He couldn't follow the group and had a number of social difficulties. He shared with us that he didn't want to go to the French sessions any more. That's when my vision of our future, especially academically, came crashing down. I remember feeling empty and discouraged because he wasn't going to like school or be able to succeed at school. I told myself that there was no way we were going to have this battle for 13 years of school. I can assure you that when my child decides that he doesn't like something it is very difficult to convince him otherwise.

In order to avoid this struggle with my child, not liking school, we decided to consult a psychologist to get some answers to our questions and to be able to better prepare our child to start school. We didn't think that Leon had an ASD because we didn't know the signs. With our second child it was obvious, because he was non-verbal and when he was two the specialists told us that he was autistic. It was really different with Leon. He had no obvious verbal or intellectual delay and we were concentrating on his brother, Thomas. We also communicated with Family and Early Childhood Services, which is a program of home visits and various family support services for parents who are concerned about their children. The program is voluntary, confidential and individualized. Ms. Charline, from Family and Early Childhood, came to our house once a week to make observations and try to help us to figure things out. In August last year, we were almost certain that Leon had Asperger syndrome, but we didn't know what was going to happen when he started school.

Over the summer, the school contacted me to tell me that Leon was going to have a full-time educational assistant, so I was happy. The École Bellefontaine team wanted to meet me for a conference. I attended, along with Leon's kindergarten teacher, the resource teacher, the psychologist who had been seeing Leon since May and Ms. Charline from Early Childhood Services. I was still very nervous for the first day of school, but this meeting was very beneficial in that it reassured me that they were going to work hard to help my son start school. I was also reassured that the staff of the school knew about his situation and that it wasn't going to be a surprise. After the first week of school, I knew things were going to work out.

I am sure that the various elements in place in Leon's classroom and the whole school helped ensure that starting school would be a success for him. Frequent communication from the teacher and the various interveners is greatly appreciated, and has been since the start of the school year. I also really appreciated that every time they communicated with me, they had a plan to suggest. They shared with us exactly what challenges Leon was facing, and they told us what they were going to try in order to overcome those challenges. Leon loves school and I'm so reassured.

He started gradually over several months, because at the beginning full days were just too much for Leon. I admit that it's a good thing I was only working part-time, because otherwise it wouldn't have been as easy and my stress level would have been higher. After the first full day of kindergarten, the school team met to suggest a plan to us. Leon would only go to school for a few hours a day so that he could slowly get used to one routine at a time, such as transitions. When he fully understood and mastered one aspect, the school team added more time. They added time week by week, until Leon was going full days in December. The school also had a detailed plan to add the bus in the morning and after school, and that made our lives easier. The first time Leon put in a full day at school, I remember clearly how he felt. He was so happy and proud of himself, and I was proud of him, too.

At the start of the year, Leon had a lot of tantrums at school. It was discouraging and made me feel bad. I was mentally prepared for the worst and seeing how he progressed made me feel better. Knowing how they were managed at school was very comforting to me. I saw so much progress in my child. All the systems set up to help Leon seem to help him and we use them a lot at home, as well, with both boys. For example, visual schedules, visual clocks, visual images, **social stories**, etc. These different strategies help Leon to orient himself in time, to know what to expect so he can prepare himself mentally and reduce his anxiety, etc.

Lately, Leon was invited to a classmate's birthday party. I went with him and saw a lot of progress. I liked how the other children interacted more with him and how Leon approached the others without me having to encourage him. Leon still has challenges, like when losing a game or not having enough time to finish a task, but now he reacts much differently than before he started school."

Classmate's Parent Voice

"I work at l'École Bellefontaine in administration. I've worked in education for a number of years. I also have two children who have had a chance to be part of inclusive classes in our school. My son Daniel is in Leon's kindergarten class. Inclusive education is part of daily life at our school. My child sees Leon as another child in his class, with his strengths and his challenges. He doesn't seem to find the situation abnormal, because Daniel has been with Leon since the first day of school. Like Leon, Daniel has strengths and challenges. My son doesn't talk about any major difficulties that Leon has, except when Leon has a tantrum, and that doesn't seem to do any harm to him personally or to his learning. Daniel doesn't identify Leon as being different because for him everybody is different.

Both of my children are in inclusive classes, and this experience is allowing them to develop certain skills—patience, empathy, comprehension of different situations, comprehension and appreciation of differences, a feeling of safety in a crisis situation, etc. The children in the class live in a peaceful, safe atmosphere. As a mother, I appreciate what inclusion is giving my children every day. These situations help with the development of a more whole person. In general, it's very positive. At their age I don't think they're aware of the situation. For them, it's normal. From what I've observed in the classroom, none of the students reacts when a situation is more difficult for Leon. They're used to it and very patient.

As Vice-Principal of the school, I see that in general, inclusive education is perceived positively, but the comfort level differs among staff members. The challenge is often collaboration among all the players because of the complexity of the case, since a number of interveners play important roles both in and out of school. The structure of the school is such that staff members and students feel safe. The atmosphere among staff is really positive and welcoming with respect to inclusive education. As a team, we want to value differences among all our students and differentiation is the key to success.

In Leon's case, the teacher and the resource teacher have communicated a great deal with the parents and have succeeded in winning the family's trust. With all their hard work, different strategies, trials and errors, they have succeeded in creating a positive inclusive education situation for Leon and his classmates."

Principal Voice

"As Principal of the school, I've had to adjust to the inclusive education movement. Our school has only been open for two years. When I applied for the principalship of a new school, I had an opportunity to present a vision that fit right into the inclusive education framework. My vision was really about learning cycles driven by differentiation. When we speak of differentiation, we recognize that there are differences among students, and this needs to be a fundamental value, a belief, and a way of thinking. I felt that I needed to get my staff to believe that each student is different, but also to see differences as richness. This is what we've created in our school and it's our shared discourse. This being said, once you believe in it, you have to set up conditions that create or respond to inclusive education. You can't just hope that you will attain inclusive education just by accepting all students into the classroom. It needs teamwork and collaboration to find the best solutions possible to lead each child to succeed at his or her full potential. Every child has potential; each one's potential is different. Some of them have exact diagnoses, from very complex to less so. However, what we know for sure is that each one deserves to be addressed and that all children have a right to their place in the classroom. However, to succeed in having inclusive education, the team must find the best solutions and the winning approaches for each child. Inclusion is a matter of belief, teamwork, planning, and collaboration. Beliefs are definitely at the crux of it. When people believe in inclusive education, it's much easier.

We can modify structures and interventions with various services to make sure that these students are well served. The essential aspect of inclusive education is to neither forget any child nor to exclude any child from the classroom. Our teaching model is based primarily on decompartmentalization. When you decompartmentalize, all of the students have a hand in the process. Inclusive education isn't only for students having difficulties; it's for all students, strong students, average students, and weak students. There are different ways to group students. Sometimes we give them choices and sometimes we choose for them. We reorganize all our students into small groups based on their challenges, strengths, interests, needs, etc. These are learning situations that are differentiated and planned to their needs. We want to make sure that all students have their place, and that we can meet each student's different needs.

We also want everyone to be able to experience success. We have to have high expectations of everyone.

When the school team believes in inclusion, I am convinced that everything else is possible. So it's essential to work on beliefs. On the other hand, beliefs don't make the job easy. We need people who are very flexible and highly skilled. They have to be able to incorporate different teaching strategies, and also adapt their classroom environment to meet the needs of all students. Obviously this doesn't happen alone. Staff needs to be trained, we need to discuss the process regularly, and continually maintain this discourse. It is important for staff to know that the child is at the centre of the decisions we make and that when we make decisions, it's always in the best interest of the student. When we're facing difficult situations, what always gets us back on the right track is this: Are we making the best decision for the student? It's important for parents to know that their child has his or her place at the school. Parents have high expectations of us, as we have of the children.

With Leon, we had various challenges when he arrived. We had to guarantee his safety and quickly create bonds so that we could advance slowly. There was also a language barrier because he neither spoke nor understood French. Inclusion wasn't an automatic process for this child. There absolutely had to be a teacher who was very committed, very engaged, very open, and who recognized that this child was like all the others, that he could learn but in his own way. It was important for the teacher to understand that this child would need differentiated structures and that we would have to be patient. Obviously, this has been a success.

A number of people were involved—the teacher, the educational assistant, but also the resource teacher, who was a specialist in the field. This was a crucial element in getting Leon into school, because it is important to know how to work with students who have an ASD. This resource person's experience was such that we were soon able to see incredible improvements in Leon in a short time. His parents noticed it as well. It's quite normal to try strategies and not see instant improvements, but you have to be patient. It would have been easy to exclude him, but Leon has made progress because of inclusion.

I think it's a success story. Inclusive education in the classroom is possible in 99.5 percent of cases. When it's properly planned, a student may leave the classroom occasionally to learn certain things. It is very important to not manage students based on their diagnoses, but on their needs. Leon needed to be included as quickly as possible, but gradually so that he would adapt well and experience as much success as possible. We didn't want to put him in a negative situation where he would experience failure and crises. The method we used with Leon, gradual school entry, allowed us to provide him with positive learning and adaptation situations."

Resource Teacher Voice

*"Ideally, Leon should have received early intervention services before he started school. Because he wasn't diagnosed before starting school, he wasn't able to benefit from the services of the regional autism centre. Usually this centre provides children with an ASD with different opportunities that prepare them for school and a multitude of basic skills that they acquire before starting school. For example, sitting in a group, stay seated, listening to the person who is talking, not making noise with their mouth, etc. These children arrive in school much more ready than Leon was. This centre uses **Applied Behaviour Analysis,** or **ABA,** the same as we do.*

Despite everything, we found ways to welcome Leon and to ensure that his transition from home to school was as positive as possible for Leon and his family. We started with a case conference with the persons concerned: the parent, who knows the child best, but also the people from the Early Childhood Services program who worked with Leon over the summer before he started school. At that time, we learned that Leon was being assessed by the psychologist at the hospital. I think that this conference was very important for getting to know Leon better: his strengths, his challenges, and to see where we were going with this child, and to target strategies to better welcome him on the first day of school. We offered the mother a social story and a tour of the school and playground. We found a way to make his transition easier.

However, Leon's first full day was very, very difficult for him and for us. After the first day, we changed our strategies, because we knew that for a student like Leon, success is very important. We chose the strategy of not only inclusive education but also gradual entry. This was an opportunity for us to get to know him better and to aim for successes instead of situations that were always negative for him. It is certain that Leon is very intelligent.

Leon's success today was made possible because of collaboration between the school and the home. We began with gradual entry, but when we saw an improvement or acquired behaviours we always intended to increase his time in school. That was always our goal. When we didn't increase the time the following week, it was because there was a challenge we wanted to work on. We wanted everything to be positive for him at that time. Inclusive education is not just in the classroom but everywhere else the students go—the bus, the cafeteria, etc.

The various challenges we faced with Leon were: sit in silence, respond to his first name, look at the person who is speaking (still a challenge), all transitions to a less structured environment (playground, cafeteria, music, physical education), put things away, put things away when he hasn't finished an activity, and language, because he didn't speak French. When faced with a challenge, collaboration was essential among all the players: assistant, teacher and resource teacher. When working on a challenge, normally, we need to know what function is served by the behaviour or the challenge created, the student's behaviour. For example, one of Leon's challenges was the playground. He would run away and he didn't want to come in when the bell rang. Our hypothesis was that he was looking for attention. Students with an ASD, 98 percent of the time, want attention, whether positive or negative. That's why we targeted "ignore" as a preventive behaviour in our behaviour reduction protocol.

School buses can be challenging social spaces.
Source: Vectorfusionart/Fotolia

When you run after him, that doesn't decrease the behaviour, it increases it. So it takes teamwork and observation [to determine] the function of his behaviour and to find winning strategies for this specific behaviour. For the playground, we prepared a modelling video and a social story, used the visual timer outside to give him a warning before going in, shared with him the number of minutes on the visual timer to make the situation predictable, and now we have a tangible reinforcement that gives him a five-minute reward at the end of the day. We also developed other social stories (react when he hears "no" or "stop") and did modelling with the help of other students in the class.

Autistic students need predictable, fixed routines and they have to know what's coming up. At the start of the year, we set up a visual schedule personalized for Leon. He follows the class schedule, but we also added schedules for getting dressed, depending on the season. Leon is responsible for following these schedules and putting the icons away when the activity is done. This schedule also helps Leon to know what is coming after recess.

The important thing is communication among all team members. When a challenge occurs, we don't change how we do things right away. On the one hand, we shouldn't be stopping a strategy too fast because we think the goal is achieved, but on the other hand we shouldn't be changing our strategies when they don't work because we know that with behaviour, when you put interventions in place things get worse before they get better. We can remove a strategy, like the visual schedule for getting dressed, only when no more encouragement is needed.

I'm convinced that inclusive education gives all students an equal chance to succeed, as much for Leon with his social challenges and his diagnosis as for the other students who have their own challenges but haven't been diagnosed. For Leon, inclusive education means being part of a group, but it also means giving him equal chances. From time to time he has to go out and do one-on-one activities in order to allow him to be included socially and to teach him socially acceptable behaviours. So yes, he is removed from the classroom for a few minutes a day, but this allows him to grow in a group setting."

Teacher Voice

"I've been teaching for four years and this is the first year that I've had a chance to work with a child with an ASD. When I learned that Leon was going to be in my class, I felt anxious. I had no experience of inclusive education with children having major difficulties. I had learned a lot at university and I'd read a number of books on various subjects, including autism. Theory is a great help right away, but the team around you, collaboration, communication, and **inclusive leadership** are essential to success with inclusive education.

Leon is an adorable child. He is a student with an incredible thirst for learning and shares this taste for learning with others. At the start of the year, he was only at school for a few hours a day. These few hours were filled with rich exchanges, mutual learnings, successes, and challenges. The first weeks are essential to developing a group dynamic based on valuing differences. We got to know ourselves and to know others with their strengths and challenges. Kindergarten is a crucial year when children learn to like school, to develop a taste for learning and, in our case, a taste for the French language. My job is to develop in my students basic social skills so that they can learn the hard and soft skills and good manners that they will need.

BEHAVIOUR REDUCTION PROTOCOL

Leon was only diagnosed in September, so he did not receive any specialized autism services before starting kindergarten. In order to allow him to experience success and prevent behaviour-related problems, a behaviour reduction protocol was put in place in September. He benefited from gradual entry stretching from September to mid-December and has been fully integrated since December. He takes the bus in the morning and evening without being accompanied, but he does have preferential seating. The behaviour reduction protocol was integrated into the current intervention plan when the latter was prepared.

Goals of the Behaviour Reduction Protocol

- Increase expected behaviours in and out of the classroom:
  - Stay seated in class when asked;
  - Remain silent (without making noise with his mouth and/or singing) when asked;
  - Come inside the school when the bell rings and/or when asked;
  - Get dressed independently (or with partial hand-on-hand encouragement).
- Reduce unexpected behaviours:
  - Prevent refusal (throwing himself on the ground or running away as a game);
  - Prevent tantrums (shouting and crying).

Specific Interventions

- ABA training to work on communication (social and French vocabulary as well as social skills);
- Proactive strategies;
- Reactive strategies.

First stage of intervention:

1. After speaking the direction once, say it again firmly with visual support;
2. Wait a few seconds (up to a maximum of 10 seconds, counting on the fingers) to see whether the student carries out the direction;
3. Show the visual support only;

4. Wait a few seconds (up to a maximum of 10 seconds, counting on the fingers) to see whether the student carries out the direction;
   - Ignore as much as possible unexpected behaviour from the student (try to eliminate surrounding sources of attention) and avoid speaking.
5. Reinforce socially and orally as soon as the student takes a step in the direction asked.

Second stage of intervention
(**not hindering** learning):

6. If the student still refuses to follow the direction AND his behaviour is not hindering others' learning (environment suitable for learning), sit the student on a chair or put him somewhere away from the others and set 2 minutes on the visual clock;
7. Try requests with high level of probability (e.g., Do what I'm doing, Do this, etc.) and reinforce when he carries them out;
8. Come back to the initial direction (hand-on-hand encouragement can be used at this stage).

Second stage of intervention
(**hindering** learning):

6. If the student still refuses to follow the direction AND his behaviour is hindering others' learning (he is shouting, crying, etc.), bring him into the quiet room using the approach in Non-Violent Intervention in a Crisis Situation (this must always involve two people; the assistant will be aided by the coach or the resource teacher);
7. The assistant enters the quiet room with the student and waits without speaking until the student calms down;
8. Try requests with high level of probability (e.g., Do what I'm doing, Do this, etc.) and reinforce when he carries them out;
9. Come back to the initial direction (e.g., If what set off the tantrum was not wanting to put things away, the student has to come back and put the things away when he leaves the quiet room).

When I welcomed Leon into my classroom, I had no idea what a positive effect this child was going to have on the other five-year-olds, and on me. Learning to live in community with one's peers and classmates is a life lesson. Welcoming students with their strengths, challenges, areas of interest, and learning styles makes it possible to value differences and to learn to love and respect each other without wanting to change others. Without meaning to, Leon succeeded in developing within our family, the kindergarten class, patience, respect, understanding of differences and empathy. My students enjoy helping each other and encouraging each other to do the right thing and to learn better. They celebrate everyone's successes and improvements. They appreciate the presence of each person in the classroom, even of those students with behavioural difficulties.

To welcome Leon to l'École Bellefontaine, a number of people had extremely important roles to play. School administrators were the primary players by implementing a vision and structure at the school that made inclusive education possible. They were the first contacts with the parents and the first to build a trusting relationship between the school and Leon's home. Then the resource teacher, who had fifteen years of experience with students who have an ASD, was the major key to success. Her collaboration with me, his teacher, was such an enriching experience. Leon has always been at the centre of our questions, our discussions, and our decisions. The educational assistant was an important asset. She is so patient with Leon and gives him time: time to think, time to act, time to decide between two choices. She is essential to the team, making everything positive and possible. The family has been exceptionally open and gave us their trust and their collaboration in order to maintain consistency between home and school.

The classroom was a place where each child in our class could grow, spread his or her wings and fly. It was no different for Leon. Sometimes he needed to get up and look at something that interested him and then come back to the group. Sometimes he needed to move or he might take a neurological break. To differentiate things learned in the classroom, I need to plan my instruction based on my students' needs. This year, Leon was a major reason why my teaching improved. I differentiated things not just for him but also for the others. Every day, I had to make sure that my planning was very detailed and included neurological breaks, times when we would move around while learning, times to work based on our needs, in differentiated activities, round-robin workstations, or clinical groups. The goal of this planning was to meet the needs of all my students and provide them not just with equal chances for success, but also with equitable interventions. When Leon had more difficult moments, he could take a walk and take deep breaths. So could the others in the class, for that matter. At the start of the year, Leon couldn't manage to calm himself down just by taking a walk, so he could go to the quiet room to let out his emotions. At the start of the year, he shouted and refused to go. Today, five weeks from summer vacation, he can walk calmly to the quiet room and in this lovely room he can shout and run about as much as he needs to.

The other students love to help Leon, even if just to encourage him to stay seated during assembly, or to invite him to play with them during free play, or to encourage him to do as they do by walking in the corridors. They are very patient. When Leon used to have tantrums in class, the others quickly learned to ignore him. We are constantly trying to develop independence in our students, and Leon is no exception.

This being said, inclusive education has its challenges and requires a lot of work. There are days when it is easier to get discouraged, but you just have to think about all the moments that make you smile, as well as to step back and think about the journey that each of your students is on, analyze their evolution, and concentrate on their successes. You have to see the challenges that come up as opportunities for improvement, and focus on the success of each of your students. Finally, the goal isn't to change students, but to adapt to them in order to discover their strengths, their challenges and their interests. For Leon, I plan my instruction with all these points in mind so that I can allow him to evolve as a learner."

Educational Assistant Voice

"Leon needs a full-time educational assistant to help him to concentrate and guide him through his day. Leon is a very intelligent child who adores school and loves to take the bus. We can use this to motivate him in tasks that he finds more difficult. Over time, we've gotten to know him and when we see Leon first thing in the morning, we can already tell what kind of a day it's going to be. So every day we have to adapt to him. Leon is a child who is passionate for knowledge and has a strong thirst to learn. That makes it much easier to motivate him. We also build on his specific areas of interest (solar system and planets, astronauts, letters and words, science, etc.). Here are a few examples of his challenges: listening, raising his hand to speak, asking permission to get up or to leave the classroom, finishing tasks, lining up, dressing and undressing quickly.

Teamwork between Leon's classroom teacher and me is essential to his success. I have to respect class routine and rules so I can model proper behaviour for Leon. I'm working very hard on developing his independence. So, gradually, I'm stepping back a little bit at certain moments of the day to encourage Leon to develop his independence.

It's a real team effort with the teacher and the resource teacher. We have to be in constant communication in order to exchange the various strengths and challenges found in the classroom. I have to trust my colleagues, and vice versa. It's important that everything be done in a way that respects those around us. The teacher and the resource teacher meet with me and the educational assistant who replaces me when I'm on a break and during my prep time at least once or twice a month to follow up on behaviours, strategies and curricula. I feel that it is important to plan these meetings in order to ensure follow-up and effective teamwork. I also find that the various social stories prepared for Leon are truly effective. We have around ten: for starting school, sharing, waiting his turn, entering the school when the bell rings, rules for the play structures, lining up to move around in the school and so on. I am so lucky to be part of Leon's life. He teaches me all sorts of things and I am very attached to this student."

Summary of Leon's Case Study

The different voices have shared how Leon's story is an example of a successful inclusive practice, and they consistently mention two important factors that are related to his success: collaboration and leadership. The first step in ensuring Leon's success was to facilitate the transition from home to school. As soon as Leon's parents learned that their son was diagnosed with an ASD, they immediately engaged with school personnel to share knowledge and help develop strategies. It proved to be profitable for everyone involved. Soon, the teacher had gained the trust of Leon's parents and together they were able to envision a year without too many obstacles. In most areas, it is common practice to have kindergarten students begin their school year progressively. In Leon's case, it just took him a bit more time to get to the point where he could successfully spend the entire day with his classmates. Along with progressive school entry, social stories and the ABA method proved to be worthwhile strategies.

Along with parents, teachers also need to learn to collaborate with each other. While it can still be a challenge for some, those who have a chance to work with team members, share ideas and talk about their experiences, find the road to inclusive education easier and beneficial for all those involved. This becomes an important strategy for school principals to develop among their staff.

In inclusive education, the principal has an important inclusive leadership role to play. Before attempting to work with teachers and parents, the principal in this story felt he himself needed to be convinced of the benefits of inclusion and understand how it was to be practiced. Here is a good example of how inclusive leadership led to positive changes for everyone involved. Not only were teachers willing to try, they succeeded by relying on practices they knew and transforming them to answer the needs of ALL students.

⟫⟫⟫ COMMENTARY   By Dr. Angela AuCoin

General Comments

Leon's teacher was only in her third year of teaching when she was told that her class in September would include a student who had an autism spectrum disorder (ASD). Although she was nervous at the thought of working with a child with an exceptionality about which she had received very little training, she approached the coming year with enthusiasm. Foremost, inclusive education is based on good educational practices for all students (Paré & Trépanier, 2015). Building on what she already knew, Leon's teacher began collaborating with his parents, the resource teacher, and their principal in order to plan effective strategies that would help Leon overcome barriers and succeed in his first year of school. She wanted the same for Leon as she did for all of her kindergarten students: to like school and develop a taste for learning.

The different voices in Leon's story explain how beneficial it was for him to progressively transition to a full day at school. They also talk about a few strategies that were developed specifically for him; these will be analyzed later using the response to intervention framework (see Chapter 3). The voices in this case also share how their overall approach helped Leon become part of the group by providing all students access to a variety of materials and instructional methods. Through inclusive practices, it is clear that Leon's success became everybody's success! The universal design for learning (UDL) model helps us present in more detail the different steps that were taken to make sure that Leon's success was celebrated by all members of his class.

Connections to Theoretical Frameworks

The basic concepts of the universal design for learning (UDL) framework reflect the changing face of society and thus, that of our schools. Educators understand that their instructional methods must be *flexible*, *equitable*, and *accessible* (Council for Exceptional Children, 2005) to all students every day of the year. Not only must students have access to the curriculum, they must also have access to learning. In other words, when students are given different tools, they must be taught how to use them. This promotes effective learning and self-sufficiency. When talking about Leon, his teacher reminds us that *"[w]e are constantly trying to develop independence in our students, and Leon is no exception."* For that reason, his educational assistant is often asked to step back and encourage him to work by himself. Although this is an important step in helping Leon become self-sufficient and thus a stronger learner, we also believe that more autonomy will help him make friends that much quicker.

Instructional methods also need to be flexible and equitable for all learners, and in this story, we have a few examples of how certain strategies were made available to all students even though they were mostly intended for Leon. *"Every day, I had to make sure that my planning was very detailed and included neurological breaks ... The goal of this planning was to meet the needs of all my students ..."* With time, the teacher's lesson plans became more and more differentiated based on everyone's learning needs. While planning different learning activities, his teacher made sure that Leon's specific areas of interests were presented among others. Planets and astronauts quickly became popular themes that were used throughout the year to keep Leon and also the other students interested. By broadening her capacity to deliver the curriculum (Council for Exceptional Children, 2005), today Leon's teacher is proud to tell us that her teaching skills have improved! This is a great feeling for any teacher but especially for one who is at the start of her career. While strategies such as these are enough to help most students, others such as Leon will require strategies that are specifically designed to help them overcome even more challenging

barriers. Together, let's look at how the different voices in Leon's story collaborated to specifically help him face his challenges.

Response to Intervention As we have seen in previous chapters, the response to intervention (RTI) model increases a student's chances for success by guiding teachers to evaluate and plan strategically for a diverse population of students (Whitten, Esteves, & Woodrow, 2012). According to this model, when a student needs intensive interventions to help him or her succeed, specific strategies must be developed, put in place, and evaluated on a regular basis. In Leon's story, three strategies proved to be very beneficial for him: his progressive entry to school, the social stories, and the Applied Behaviour Analysis (ABA) method.

The school principal reminds us that *"[i]t is very important to not manage students based on their diagnoses, but on their needs. Leon needed to be included as quickly as possible, but gradually so that he would adapt well and experience as much success as possible."* For this reason, the different voices in this story collaborated to make sure every step of the way was successful for Leon. With this in mind, the resource teacher reminds us, *"we always intended to increase his time in school. That was always our goal."* Time was added every week and even the first bus ride was meticulously planned. *"The first time Leon put in a full day at school ... [h]e was so happy and proud of himself, and I was proud of him, too"* beams his mother. While it is normal for kindergarten students to progressively increase their class time, members of the school team knew that Leon needed more time to adapt than did the others, and it proved to be successful.

Another important strategy that was developed only for Leon was his social stories. These are stories that were written by the teacher to help Leon develop and acquire a specific task or routine. Modelling

(continued)

videos were also created and used both at home and at school. The RTI model reminds all teachers of the importance of continuous evaluation. It was by evaluating Leon and knowing exactly where he was and what he needed that his teacher was able to dynamically engage in providing him with solutions tailored to his needs. Both of these are examples of strategies we would find in Tier 2 of the RTI pyramid.

While Leon was able to spend most of his time in class with the other students, every day he was removed from his classroom to receive training in the ABA method. We would invite Leon's teachers to see if this training could also be done in the regular classroom. Is it necessary for him to leave the classroom? Could we modify this Tier 3 intervention so that other students could also benefit from it?

When students with identified challenges are excluded or removed from the general classroom for long periods of time, we're teaching them that they must earn their way back into the classroom (Villa & Thousand, 2005). The staff at Leon's school understood this. From the beginning, it was clear to everyone that his learning was to take place in the regular classroom as quickly and as often as possible. As Kunc (2000) wrote, "when inclusive education is fully embraced, we abandon the idea that children have to become typical in order to contribute to the world" (p. 91). Leon's story exemplifies exactly what it means to belong because it is a right and not a privilege that must be earned. The school principal says it best when he states, *"It would have been easy to exclude him, but Leon has made progress because of inclusion"!*

Key Terms

applied behaviour analysis (ABA) ABA is a systematic approach to instruction which breaks tasks or skills into small, achievable steps. With frequent repetitions and corrective feedback, the learner slowly acquires the target skill.

autism spectrum disorder (ASD) ASD is a term used to describe a range of conditions with varying degrees of delay, typically associated with communication, intellect, and sensory processing. At one end of the spectrum is Asperger's syndrome, which is a relatively mild degree of impairment, up to conditions such as Rett syndrome, fragile X syndrome, to PDD-NOS (Pervasive Developmental Disorder—Not Otherwise Specified).

inclusive leadership In a broad sense, inclusive leadership has been defined by Ryan (2006) as a collective process of social influence aimed at a very definitive end: inclusion. Not only is the process inclusive, but the end goals of the process are geared towards including all students.

social stories Social stories are short stories written with words or pictures to address a social problem or task. These stories typically include actual names/pictures of the child and make reference to the student's environment.

Questions to Consider

1. In what ways can teachers benefit from knowing what a student with a disability likes to do at the end of the school day, on weekends, and on vacation?

    _____

    _____

    _____

    _____

    _____

    _____

2. How can teachers and resource teachers reach out to parents in the first year of schooling? What process should be put in place in order to facilitate the transition from home to school?

    _____

    _____

    _____

    _____

    _____

    _____

3. In this case, collaboration proved to be a key factor in its success. What does it mean to collaborate? How is collaboration different from cooperation? What role should an educational assistant play in this collaborative process?

    _____

    _____

    _____

    _____

    _____

    _____

4. Why is it important for the school principal to have a clear vision of what it means for a school to be inclusive? What can be done to help principals learn to be inclusive?

    _____

    _____

5. How should the Applied Behaviour Analysis program be practiced in an inclusive setting?

Useful Websites

Autism Speaks
www.autismspeaks.org/what-autism

Educate Autism: Using Social Stories
www.educateautism.com/social-stories.html

References

Council for Exceptional Children. (2005). *Universal design for learning. A guide for teachers and educational professionals.* New York, NY: Pearson.

Kunc, N. (2000). Rediscovering the right to belong. In R. A. Villa & J. S. Thousand (Eds.), *Restructuring for caring and effective education. Piecing the puzzle together* (2nd ed.) (pp. 77–92). Baltimore, MD: Paul H. Brooks.

Paré, M., & Trépanier, N. (2015). L'individualisation de l'enseignement pour les élèves intégrés en classe ordinaire. In N. Rousseau (Ed.), *La pédagogie de l'inclusion scolaire* (3rd ed.), (pp. 233–256). Québec, PQ: Presses de l'Université du Québec.

Ryan, J. (2006). *Inclusive leadership.* San Francisco, CA: Jossey Bass.

Villa, R. A., & Thousand, J. S. (2005). *Creating an inclusive school* (2nd ed.). Alexandria, VA: ASCD.

Whitten, E., Esteves, K. J., & Woodrow, A. (2012). *La réponse à l'intervention. Un modèle efficace de différenciation* (D. Demers, Trans.). Montréal, PQ: Chenelière Éducation.

Chapter 13
Review of Case Studies and Commentaries

Dr. Kim Calder Stegemann & Dr. Angela AuCoin

Inclusion means access, valuing, and opportunity for all students.
Source: Karelnoppe/Fotolia

TOPIC COVERAGE:

- Collaboration
- Representative Decision Making
- Redistribution of Access
- Process of Inclusion
- Recognition and Valuing

The student will:

- Identify common themes from the different case studies

- Describe how student needs, educational and community context, and family involvement impact the inclusion process

- Discuss how at least two case studies are examples of Waitoller and Artiles's (2013) framework of social justice (access, recognition, representation)

At the beginning of this text, we talked about the variability in both definition and implementation of inclusive education across Canadian educational jurisdictions. After reading the various case studies, you will see that there is no ONE way to provide inclusive educational opportunities for students, but rather a variety of approaches that are largely dependent upon the needs of the student. Family, community, culture, and school attributes also impact how inclusive education is operationalized. Therefore, it is difficult to find distinct similarities across the case studies.

In order to compare and contrast the case studies, we are using a framework by Waitoller and Artiles (2013), which is a three-dimensional conceptualization of justice. The three dimensions relate to access and participation, recognition and valuing, and opportunities for advancement of the non-dominant group. They state that "… inclusion should be the ongoing struggle towards a) the redistribution of access to and participation in quality opportunities to learn…; b) the recognition and valuing of all student differences as reflected in content, pedagogy, and assessment tools…; and c) the creation of more opportunities for non-dominant groups to advance claims of educational exclusion and their respective solutions" (Waitoller & Artiles, 2013, p. 322).* Waitoller and Artiles recommend that these tenets inform the work and decisions of educators at all levels.

We will first discuss the cases in term of the three components and then offer general comments, which will provide a summary of other key aspects of the cases. Following that, we summarize the significant commentaries that have been provided by Canadian experts in the field of inclusive education. Each commentator has been asked to respond to the case study in terms of universal design for learning (UDL) and response to intervention (RTI) frameworks, and we will take stock of these comments and also pull out other important concepts worth considering.

---

* From "A Decade of Professional Development Research for Inclusive Education: A Critical Review and Notes for a Research Program", Review of Educational Research by Federico R. Waitoller and Alfredo J. Artile. Copyright © 2013 by Sage Publications, Ltd. Used by permission of Sage Publications, Ltd.

Case Studies Reviewed in Terms of Waitoller and Artiles's Framework

The first of the three components relates to participation and access. You may have noticed that there is a difference in the nature of inclusive educational practices between the cases presented at the beginning versus the end of the text. For example, Wilson receives only some of his daily education in the general education classroom, and William and Jake transitioned from limited to full time in the classroom. Jennifer and Margaret and Vance, on the other hand, are examples of fully participating members of the classroom, and rarely if ever receive educational supports outside of the general education classroom setting. The reader should not interpret this to mean that Wilson's educational team has somehow failed at being inclusive educators, and that Jennifer, Margaret, and Vance are the happy recipients of stellar inclusive educational efforts. Rather, the cases demonstrate the process of increasing the inclusive educational experiences as the students were able to manage the general education classroom. Wilson's story is also an example of providing quality social and educational opportunities outside of the classroom, as he transitioned from a special-needs summer camp to the same one attended by his brother. A similar opportunity was offered to Leon when he was permitted to gradually transition from home to school full time.

There are some educators in Canada who staunchly believe that inclusive education means that *every* child should be educated within the general education classroom, *every day, all the time*. Our experience, and that of the individual voices presented in this text, leads us to believe that a "one-size-fits-all" approach to education is neither desirable nor appropriate. Individualizing education to optimize the learning experience for every student entails making adjustments and responding appropriately, given student needs, parental wishes, and the school and community cultural contexts. While the diversity in educational approaches across Canadian jurisdictions can mean an inconsistency in approach and vision, it can also allow learning contexts to reflect and respond to student and community needs. Though we should always focus on trying to have the student included in the general education classroom, we believe that inclusive education should be rooted in student need and not a mechanistic approach. Ultimately, *any* student who requires some additional assistance, for whatever reason, should have access to those supports, whether that be inside or outside of the classroom. As we know with RTI, most supports are easily provided within the classroom; others are available outside of the classroom, such as in the Gabrielle case where she and her educational assistant needed to travel to the city to receive additional education about new technologies.

The second component of the conceptual framework proposed by Waitoller and Artiles (2013) relates to genuine respect for all types of diversity, as represented in curriculum, pedagogy, and assessment. Our case studies offer different examples of recognition and value, especially in pedagogy. For example, Margaret and Vance's teachers use their FM microphone technology with their entire classrooms. It proved to be a very useful tool not only for the brother and sister that needed it most, but for everyone involved. In Drake and Elvin's cases, the methods used by their teachers reflected great respect. By listening to both Drake and Elvin, their teachers created a space where their "curriculum was not dumbed down," but where their strengths were used and celebrated throughout the school year. Elvin was an artist and by encouraging all students in his classroom to use art, they provided him with the opportunity to excel.

The third component required for social justice is a shared role in problem solving and decision making. Margaret, Vance, and Leon's parents were collaborating with the school as soon as they were aware of their children's diagnostics. Together, they were able to provide structure and solutions to support the students' needs. William's case demonstrates how a young adult begins to assume increasing control over his work, home, and leisure environments, making decisions about how he wishes to live his life and spend his time. Gabrielle's story shows us how a child, and later a teenager, can advocate for themselves, clearly articulating what types of supports or accommodations are needed in order to succeed. As a member of an Aboriginal community, it was important for Elvin's community to participate in his schooling. This participation benefited Elvin in a number of ways: his teachers were better able to understand his cultural needs and provided a more welcoming place for his mother to be understood.

Common Themes

Let's now turn to common themes that have emerged through the various case studies. We will address these common themes first through groups of case studies, and then across the entire set of cases. Wilson, Gabrielle, and William are students with complex medical and educational needs. Indeed, both Wilson and William have a number of diagnoses which require specialized medical and psychological interventions. Gabrielle has a rare form of cerebral palsy that was largely misunderstood early on by members of her educational team. Both Wilson and William had difficulty adjusting to the general education context without the provision of additional support and also required opportunities to decompress in alternate settings. Gabrielle, on the other hand, was eager to be included as much as possible in all of the general education classroom activities. The barriers to participation that Gabrielle experienced seemed, in part, to be distal, and attributable to the environment rather than her own interests or needs. It could be argued that with more understanding and support, Gabrielle could have participated far more in the general education classroom.

Jake, Elvin, and Jennifer have stories that could inspire any novice teacher. The stories of Jake and Elvin, in particular, show us how important it is for students with exceptionalities to develop social networks in and outside of school. This is not always an easy task, however, and as Jake's mother indicates, parental efforts in this regard are critical. You will also notice, however, how the educators create the conditions within the general education classroom to facilitate not just the acceptance of exceptionalities, but the genuine care and regard for all members of the classroom. Jennifer, with a significant visual impairment, was able to academically and socially participate in all general education activities, even physical education. Instructional, environmental, and assessment accommodations were required so that she could safely navigate around the school, achieve academic success, and conserve her

Technology provides access and opportunities to learn, grow, and shine.

Source: Elypse/Fotolia

physical energy. Her case study was a good reminder of the emotional and physical energy that is required by students who have physical challenges. Producing written work can be a Herculean task (even with the use of assistive technologies) for students like Jennifer and Gabrielle, which is often overlooked by parents and educators.

Drake, Margaret and Vance, and Leon are another group of stories that highlight many key aspects of successful educational experiences for children with unique learning needs. In these three cases, the parents, educators, and administrators were keenly aware of the need to address the social and emotional aspects of the children's lives, in addition to the academic needs. Self-esteem, personal agency, and a sense of accomplishment were important components of the educational experience for these students. Teacher empathy and understanding were very important to Drake. He noted that, *"I feel successful when I get a good grade. When teachers are nice to me and I can make friends, I feel good. I like going to school now. The teachers understand me better!"* Self-advocacy is also apparent in these and other cases in this text, such as Jennifer's story. Developing these skills in students with unique learning needs is essential in both the short and long term. It is also apparent in these cases, as others, that collaborative teamwork is vital, and this may involve expertise of others in the wider community.

It is also notable that technology played an important role for these students, and in particular for Drake, Margaret, and Vance. Technology that is not available, or does not work properly, is frustrating for teachers and students alike. When these supports function properly, they permit full access to, and mastery of, the curriculum. In the case of Margaret and Vance, the FM system was even beneficial for other students within the classroom.

The principal and vice-principal in Leon's case highlight other key ingredients for successful inclusion. Both individuals point out the importance of having a *belief* and *commitment* to including all children in the general education stream. As the principal said, *"Beliefs are definitely at the crux of it."* These administers also acknowledge that not all staff members have the same levels of experience to enact inclusive education, nor do they all have similar belief systems. In these instances, it is prudent to *gradually* develop the necessary capacity within the school, in the same way that Leon made a gradual entry to public school. Ultimately, these administrators kept their vision

Collaboration is essential to successful inclusion.
Source: Rawpixel.com/Fotolia

for inclusive education, while they worked on developing the necessary skills, attitudes, and conditions that would enable success for all—students, staff, and parents. This brings us back to the beginning of the text when we introduced the UNESCO definition of inclusive education—that being a *"process"* (and not a destination) of responding to the diverse learning needs of students, through a common vision and conviction to social justice and equity.

Summary of Commentaries

The Canadian experts who have provided commentaries for the various case studies have highlighted the importance of the UDL and RTI frameworks. Through their comments we have also identified several key themes and we will discuss those below. Note that in most cases the comments or suggestions are relevant to ALL teaching and learning environments, not just those that include children and youth with unique learning needs.

PARENTS AS FIERCE ADVOCATES

Parents' involvement and advocacy is absolutely essential for all children and youth, but even more so for children with special learning needs. Wilson, William, and Gabrielle's parents often had to go "above and beyond" to access services for their children. Recall that Wilson's parents sought assistance for at-home or community supports, William's parents purchased a house with living space for their son, and Gabrielle's mother made regular trips to the city to get specialized guidance on assistive technologies.

Other parents had to leave their "comfort zone" in a different way. Vance and Margaret's mother, a teacher, knew the school well. While most times, **collaboration** with her children's teachers was easy, on a few occasions she felt she needed to plead in favour of her children's well-being. We can imagine how difficult this must have been for her, considering she needed to work alongside these same teachers. In a different but nonetheless stressful situation, Elvin's mother needed to be strong when she attended her son's team meeting being led by a group of predominately non-Aboriginal teachers.

While we would like to think that schools can provide everything that is required for a child's education, it "takes a village," as some of our commentators have noted. Parents should advocate for UDL to be carried out in all school and community settings. They can also work with their children's schools to ensure that different levels of support are provided (RTI) and that movement occurs between the tiers. Let us not forget that parents can be inclusive education's best promoters and supporters!

TEAMWORK

Collaboration between staff within and outside of the school is also viewed as an essential component for successful inclusive education. Jake's case study is a very good example of the cooperation and coordinated efforts between all members of his support team. Each teacher in his high school adjusted instruction and collaborated with the ABA lead to ensure that they were all "on the same page." Leon's family and school staff also worked closely to ensure his successful inclusion in the general education classroom. When he eventually spent the entire day at school, everybody felt compelled to celebrate his achievement because, in some way, they had all helped to make it happen.

In Elvin's story, we see that by working with Elvin's mother, his teachers realized that their interventions were mostly based on his weaknesses instead of on his strengths. His mother's opinion was, therefore, an important component in her son's success. In a similar way, by facilitating communication between their children's specialists and the school, Vance and Margaret's parents allowed for them to reduce barriers more quickly and efficiently.

These examples illustrate that RTI is far more successful and seamless when all members of the school team and the students' parents work towards the same goal. When inclusion is rooted in values of acceptance, respect, and teamwork, every accomplishment becomes an event worth celebrating.

THE POWER OF RELATIONSHIPS

Jake's case is a wonderful example of peers supporting peers. Every parent wants his or her child to have friends. This does not always materialize for all children, particularly if they have communication challenges, which is the case with Wilson. Although he has very limited expressive language, he shares a love of music and movement, both universal languages. These alternate channels of expression provide an avenue for peers to connect. Drake also enjoys socializing and being part of the classroom, but encounters some difficulties when it comes to interacting with his peers. While he is currently given small tasks to improve his social skills, Drake and his classmates would benefit from receiving support when it comes to managing class conflict. An example would be to engage the students in a talking circle where everyone could share how he or she feels and learn from the situations that arise in class. In Elvin's case, we are reminded to focus on using a positive approach when initiating change. We should never forget to question and continuously look for reasons that could explain a student's behaviour, especially when behaviours are challenging and repetitious. Friendships and social acceptance are important factors in every student's life. Teachers need to make sure that they do their best to foster a class culture where everyone is accepted and respected.

CULTURE

It is implicit in most of the commentaries that culture has an impact on the educational experience. Elvin is a perfect example of an initial mismatch in approaches, but how this acknowledgment put both UDL and RTI in a culturally responsive light. When his teachers decided to use their students' interest in the Cree culture to teach their courses, everyone responded favourably. Not only did Elvin and his classmates feel respected, they now had the confidence needed to take risks and engage more fully in their learning process.

Culture was dealt with a bit differently in Leon's story since his first day at school was spent in a classroom where the spoken language was different from the one he was accustomed to speaking at home. With one of his parents being francophone, Leon had the right to be taught in French. When Leon attended French language sessions to better prepare him for the start of his academic year, his parents noticed his social difficulties. Culture is an important part of schooling; one that is, or should be, part of the regular curriculum. When students feel acknowledged and respected for "who" they are, they are more likely to feel more confident and secure.

MULTIPLE BASIC STRATEGIES

UDL can be simple or complex. The commentators of Margaret and Vance, Drake, Jake, and Jennifer's stories show us that it is most important that these adjustments are made continually and to greater and lesser degrees, depending upon the student and task. Some strategies rely on advanced technologies, while others have become routine in many schools. In Vance and Margaret's case study, the FM system played an important role in their learning experience, but their teachers were also able to use it as a significant tool with all students in their classrooms.

The same can be said for the Tier 1 strategies that were used with Drake. While most students probably never noticed that their teacher was giving cues to help Drake deal with anxiety or his ability to respond to instructions; together, the teacher and student team managed to reduce multiple barriers. And these same strategies were probably also being used with other students.

FLUIDITY BETWEEN TIERS

RTI is a framework that should encourage a fluid movement between tiers and the different types of supports that are required by all students, not just those with a special label or diagnosis. Leon, Jake, and William's cases exemplify this flexibility. In Leon's case, even though his teachers feel he still needs to leave the classroom for a few minutes each day, he spends the rest of the time included with his classmates where his teachers incorporate both Tier 1 and Tier 2 strategies. William was able to move from a contained specialized setting to a general education classroom where his interests could be piqued. In many ways, he thrived in the robust high school setting, having the necessary structure and supports. As he transitioned into adult life, this fluidity of movement between levels of supports continued, but to a lesser degree.

As you read at the beginning of this section, the comments represented here are relevant to ALL teaching and learning environments. This reinforces the idea that inclusive education is NOT merely the merging of general and special education, but a completely new way of conceptualizing our classrooms so that barriers are reduced for each and every student. While the commentators were able to pinpoint specific strategies that were used for specific students, they all stated the importance of providing universal strategies for everyone. This gives each student the confidence they need to flourish both in the classroom and out.

Chapter Summary

The journey towards inclusive education is, indeed, a process and not a destination. The case studies that we have presented in this text illustrate the complex and multidimensional nature of creating inclusive educational experiences for all students, and in particular those who have unique or exceptional learning needs. It may be desirable for some to have a cookie-cutter template that can be applied for all students in the hopes of ensuring consistent, effective, and streamlined approaches to education. However, teaching is as much an art as a science, and the nature of the human condition is too complex to suggest that one approach or method is suitable for all students, not to mention their families, local community, and the needs and abilities of educators and administrators.

As educators, we are tasked with providing the best possible education for our students, which means constantly reviewing our practice and questioning the status quo. It also means that we must work collaboratively with parents, external agencies, and school personnel in order to provide quality education for ALL students. Our hope is that the reader will understand the complex dynamics involved in successful inclusion of children and youth with exceptional learning needs, and also use this knowledge and compassion to champion inclusion within your own educational and community contexts. It has, no doubt, become evident that the "process of inclusion is far more complex than simply placing students with disabilities in general education classrooms" (Ornelles, Cook, & Jenkins, 2007, p. 153).[†] Rather, as Norwich (2008) reminds us, moving towards more inclusive practices sometimes means "hard choices and no easy solutions" (p. 4).[‡] But the rewards are worth it: by bringing everyone's strengths together, the journey can be amazing for all students.

[†] From Middle School General Education Teachers' Perspectives on Including Students with Learning Disabilities by Cecily Ornelles, Lyssandra Cook and Amelia Jenkins from Journal of Learning Disabilities: A Multidisciplinary Journal 14(3):145-154, Published by Sagamore Publishing LLC, © 2007.

[‡] From Dilemmas of Difference, Inclusion and Disability: International Perspectives and Future Directions by Brahm Norwich, Published by Routledge Publishers, © 2007.

Key Term

collaboration Collaboration is a process where individual contributions are valued and combined to achieve a shared goal.

Questions to Consider

1. Now that you have read the various case studies and commentaries, how would you define inclusive education? Has your definition (and accompanying beliefs and attitudes) changed? If so, in what ways?

_____

_____

_____

_____

_____

_____

2. What social benefits of including students with exceptional learning needs in the general education classroom were evident in the cases that you read? What conditions are necessary to capitalize on these potential benefits?

_____

_____

_____

_____

_____

_____

3. What do you hope inclusive education will look like in your classroom? What challenges do you anticipate as a novice teacher while providing an inclusive educational environment for your students?

_____

_____

_____

_____

_____

_____

4. What future steps will you take in order to develop your inclusive education skill set? What resources can you access to help in your journey?

_____

_____

_____

_____

_____

_____

Useful Websites

Canadian Teachers' Federation on Diversity and Human Rights
www.ctf-fce.ca/en/Pages/Issues/Diversity-and-Human-Rights.aspx

New Brunswick Inclusive Education, Policy 322
www2.gnb.ca/content/dam/gnb/Departments/ed/pdf/K12/policies-politiques/e/322A.pdf

References

Norwich, B. (2008). *Dilemmas of difference, inclusion and disability: International perspectives and future directions*. New York, NY: Routledge.

Ornelles, C., Cook, L., & Jenkins, A. (2007). Middle school general education teachers' perspectives on including students with learning disabilities. *Learning Disabilities, 14*(3), 145–154.

Waitoller, F. R., & Artiles, A. J. (2013). A decade of professional development research for inclusive education: A critical review and notes for a research program. *Review of Educational Research, 83*(3), 319–356.

Chapter 14
Future Directions in Inclusive Education

Dr. Kim Calder Stegemann & Dr. Angela AuCoin

Human rights and social justice are at the heart of educational inclusion.
Source: wwwebmeister/Fotolia

TOPIC COVERAGE:

- Capacity Building
- Ethic of Care
- Collective Self-Efficacy
- Inclusion/ Exclusion
- Public Policy
- Needs-based Funding

The student will:

- Describe the impact of current legislative and policy changes that impact inclusive education

- Identify "cutting edge" practices in education that support the philosophy of inclusive education

- Describe a minimum of five ways that initial teacher education and in-service professional development could be improved to increase the capacity of educators to provide effective inclusive educational practices within the public school system

- Consider alternate frameworks for conceptualizing inclusive education that could reform public education

The field of inclusive and special education continues to change and evolve. Even since beginning to write this text, we have noted shifts within our respective provinces, not to mention globally, as educators and administrators grapple with practices and policies that will reduce barriers and enhance the educational experience for all students. In this chapter we look ahead, as well as highlight where change is occurring (or needs to occur) within public education. We begin by identifying noteworthy changes in legislation of public policy which will have a direct impact on inclusive education. Next we point out interesting developments in inclusive education both globally and within Canada. Though some of these advancements relate directly to teacher education, we include a separate section that addresses the needs related to initial teacher education and in-service professional development. We also briefly discuss the changes in the *Diagnostic and Statistical Manual of Mental Disorders* (DSM) (American Psychiatric Association, 2013), which has had a significant impact on diagnoses of psychological disorders. We end this chapter by identifying significant trends in the conceptualization of inclusive education and how this is in contrast to the efforts to merge general and special education.

Legislation and Public Policy

One significant change seen in educational policy is the notion that inclusion is about more than students with exceptional learning needs. Instead, it is being broadly identified in policy as about student diversity in general (Loreman, Forlin, Chambers, Sharma, & Deppeler, 2014). Indeed, the province of Ontario has an entire series of documents about creating inclusive spaces for students in order to respect differences in ability, gender, culture, language, sexual orientation, race, etc. (The reader is encouraged to examine such documents as "Realizing the promise of diversity: Ontario's equity and inclusive education strategy" (Ontario Ministry of Education, 2009); "Special education transformation" (Bennett & Wynne, 2006); and "Equity and inclusive education: Going deeper" (Council of Ontario Directors of Education, 2014).) There are benefits and disadvantages of this shift in focus. One clear advantage is that a broad-base attention to equity and human rights issues provides more political and economic energy to improve public education. A disadvantage is that particular attention to unique individual needs, particularly when dealing with a disability or if serious medical issues are involved, may become lost.

Another important change in public policy is the proliferation of charter schools and accountability. Though charter schools allow parents more choice in placement and programming for their children, some would contend that they are market-driven and foster a climate of competition (Waitoller & Thorius, 2015). Closely related to this trend is the focus on standards and accountability. In and of itself, striving for excellence and outstanding achievement for all students is not negative; however, it can inadvertently lead to increased rates of **exclusion**. As Anderson and Boyle (2015) note, in a climate of rampant standardized testing as a means of accountability, teachers and educational jurisdictions are forced to exclude any students who may decrease the overall test results.

A more positive change in educational policy is a movement towards needs-based funding. The focus of this initiative is on the needs and not the deficits of the child. Rather than pathologizing student functioning for the purposes of funding appropriate services (categorizing), funding of supports is based on functional need. Jurisdictions that base support services on labels and categorization tend also to have more segregated educational settings (Anderson & Boyle, 2015). Though this is a subtle distinction (funding based on need versus a label), it sends the message that students are individual human beings and not categories. With changes in funding policies, there is a similar impetus to reduce the number of segregated settings within school districts (Kurth, Morningstar, & Kozleski, 2014). Segregated settings reflect the belief that for some, inclusion is still about a *"place"* instead of a *process*.

Across Canada, response to intervention (RTI) is becoming policy in many jurisdictions. As we have seen, the RTI framework has been designed to address the needs of those students who continue to experience barriers to the curriculum despite universal design for learning (UDL) applications. Although RTI is considered functional and serves as a helpful guide to planning, instruction, and intervention, we would be remiss if we did not mention the emerging misuse of this approach. In some jurisdictions, it has become a standardized and rigid format, which is contrary to its original intentions. For example, Björn, Aro, Koponen, and Fuchs (2016) point to a practice in the state of Tennessee that specifies that special education teachers are not involved as support services until after a student is unsuccessful at Tier 3. In this case, the roles and division of labour between general and special education teachers is sharply divided, supposedly using an RTI framework.

Noteworthy Practices

One innovative practice and expanding area of research is in co-teaching models of delivering public education. In co-teaching practices, general and special educators plan and teach together as a team, jointly determining how best to structure lessons and activities that will engage all students in the class, regardless of ability. If

Innovation is lead by diversity and creativity.
Source: 123RF

embedded in an RTI framework, the educators continually problem solve and adjust instruction to best meet individual needs (Björn et al., 2016).

Another noteworthy practice is happening in our high schools. If the organizational structure of these schools makes it more challenging for teachers to be inclusive, it isn't stopping some principals from getting together to plan creative and effective inclusive strategies. For example, in the province of New Brunswick, high school principals have been meeting on a regular basis to organize ways in which they can help their teachers reduce barriers for ALL students. These administrators are far from being alone when they question whether some form of segregated setting is more beneficial for students with learning disabilities or behaviour challenges (Chmiliar, 2009; Friesen, Hickey, & Krauth, 2010; Krull, Wilbert, & Hennemann, 2014; McLeskey & Waldron, 2011; Mowat, 2010); more and more of them are open to the idea of offering alternative possibilities. Some students, who previously spent their entire day in a segregated setting, can now choose to have a course or two per week in an inclusive classroom where part of their individualized plans are being taught using differentiated instruction. This way, these principals are making sure that inclusive education is not a *one-size-fits-all* approach, but rather one that is tailored to meet the needs of ALL students.

Teacher Education and Professional Development

There is no question that classroom teachers are one of the key determinants of student success (OECD, 2014), and this is even more imperative in inclusive educational settings (Avramidis & Norwich, 2002; Forlin, Earle, Loreman, & Sharma, 2011). The positive attitudes of teachers, as well as principals and other school staff, towards diversity and belonging are crucial to the success of inclusive education. A strong sense of self-efficacy about addressing the needs of diverse learners is also a contributing factor (Pratt, 2005; Tschannen-Moran, Woolfolk Hoy, & Hoy, 1998). Further, a collective efficacy (Schmitz & Schwarzer, 2002; Urton, Wilbert, & Hennemann, 2014), where all members of the educational team have common beliefs and actions about including all students, regardless of differences, in the general education classroom, is necessary. Moreover, we must counter the myth of the "normal child" (Hasinoff & Mandzuk, 2015, p. 21), and the idea that anyone who does not fit in this category must be dealt with elsewhere until they are fixed and able to re-join the *regular* classroom.

The question, however, is how to develop the attitudes and sense of **collective self-efficacy** that is required of these educators? The task is extremely challenging, given the growing diversity of public school student bodies. Many would say that teacher education programs fail to prepare new teachers for this complex task (Bergeron & St-Vincent, 2011; Eva & Walker, 2010; McCrimmon, 2015; Porter & AuCoin, 2012; Silverman, 2010). In order to rectify this situation, some university teacher education programs are ensuring that at least one course is offered in special education or addressing diverse learners (McCrimmon, 2015). Given that the number of years of training is positively related to positive attitudes towards inclusion (Avramidis, & Kalyva, 2007), it may seem logical to extend initial teacher education programs. However, there continue to be universities that offer post-degree teacher education in compressed 12-month formats, which puts into question the possibility of developing positive attitudes towards diversity and inclusive education.

If teacher education programs cannot or will not be extended, perhaps the focus should be on the way that diversity is taught at the university. Some institutions have embedded issues of disability and diversity within philosophy or methods courses, but with limited success. Indeed, one of the most effective ways of changing attitudes is through direct exposure and reflective practice (LePage et al., 2010; Sharma, Forlin, & Loreman, 2008). The pedagogy of these courses must include critical analysis of the structures and practices that perpetuate racism and marginalization of groups of learners who are different from the dominant majority (Waitoller & Thorius, 2015). Teacher candidates must view themselves as agents of change and be willing to question the status quo. Some take this even further by suggesting that educators become "cultural vigilantes" (Corbett & Slee, 2000, p. 134) who are political activists "seeking school communities of equality and human diversity" (Danforth & Naraian, 2015, p. 72).

It is also very evident that teacher education programs (both pre- and in-service) must focus on skill development in collaborative problem solving (Waitoller & Artiles, 2013). In particular, teachers must learn how to effectively navigate collective problem solving with individuals who may be from distinctly different fields (e.g., physiotherapists). Teacher education programs and professional development initiatives must clearly demonstrate how to overcome interpersonal difficulties (Waitoller & Artiles, 2013).

Changes to the Diagnostic and Statistical Manual of Mental Disorders (DSM-5)

The *Diagnostic and Statistical Manual of Mental Disorders* (DSM) (American Psychiatric Association, 2013) is the standard classification system of mental disorders used by mental health and other health professionals, including psychiatrists and other physicians, psychologists, social workers, nurses, occupational and rehabilitation therapists, and counsellors, in Canada and the United States. School psychologists or behavioural consultants who do assessments of children and youth in educational settings also rely on the DSM (referred to as the DSM-5 because it is in its fifth edition) for diagnosis of some conditions such as intellectual disabilities, specific learning disorder (for impairments in reading, writing, or mathematics), and conduct disorder. Typically, a physician, psychiatrist, or registered psychologist is responsible for making diagnoses related to autism spectrum disorder, bi-polar disorder, attention deficit/hyperactivity disorder, and anxiety disorders (such as phobias, mutism, and social anxiety). The DSM-5 consists of three major components: the diagnostic classification, the diagnostic criteria sets, and the descriptive text.

While changes to this type of classification system may seem out of the realm of the classroom teacher, a great deal can often hinge on these diagnoses. For example, in some provinces and territories, children and youth must have a DSM label in order to receive funding or specialized supports (both in the school and in the home/community). A change in criteria can mean that a child becomes ineligible for supports that were once provided. In these cases, it may be imperative for the teacher and school staff to lobby or advocate for services on behalf of the child and family.

Conceptualizing Inclusion within Public Education

Conceptions of what constitutes an inclusive education is not as simple as counting the number of students who have special learning needs who are sitting in general education classrooms. Waitoller and Artiles (2013) state that exclusion is a

Participation, recognition and valuing, and opportunities for advancement.
Source: M.studio/Fotolia

multifaceted and complex interaction of multiple factors (fields such as education, psychology, health care; family dynamics; students). Our conceptual understanding of inclusion must also represent this multifaceted nature of humans, accounting for dimensions such as gender, ability, culture, and socio-economic status. It is a messy business because ideas must be situated within different social contexts. Therefore, a new understanding cannot be based on simplistic formulae, frameworks, or policies.

Until now, most educators have viewed inclusion as a step beyond mainstreaming or integration, but within what is typically considered standard public education. New trends are emerging which challenge us to consider education in a totally new light. Rather than modifying what currently exists and attempting to mesh general and special education, we need a totally new conceptualization (Loreman et al., 2014). As Slee (2004) suggests, this means looking at the deep structure of education and schooling, and starting anew. That means that we must identify the underlying concepts which should guide our practice as inclusive educators and which can be applied to any cultural or educational setting, in order to move towards a "transnational theorizing of inclusive education" (Danforth & Naraian, 2015, p. 72).

Danforth and Naraian (2015) propose four tenets to guide this rebuilding process. First, we must hold a commitment to democracy where there is equality among all individuals. Second, we must have a focus on interpersonal relationships with an **ethic of care** (as Nel Noddings would espouse). Third, we are called to be political activists who expose and change structures that perpetuate inequity. Fourth, our activism must be situated within our respective communities.

We must continually ask ourselves how we can do better (Graham & Slee, 2008). As we have stressed throughout this text, this is a process and not an outcome or destination!

Chapter Summary

In this chapter we have examined some future directions in the field of inclusive education. Undoubtedly, legislation and educational policies at provincial and school district levels will impact how inclusive education is operationalized and funded. Teachers are central to student success, and it is incumbent upon all initial and in-service teacher education programs to ensure that teacher preparation is comprehensive and addresses attitudinal and skill dimensions. Finally, the way that educators and the wider public conceive of education must change and reflect 21st century teaching and learning. In Nancy Hutchinson's words (see Chapter 11), "we will know we have accomplished [a community where diversity is valued] when all our students express that they feel valued and act like they feel respected, and when this is also how students treat one another."

Key Terms

collective self-efficacy This term compliments and builds on the concept of self-efficacy; instead of having to depend on one's own determination and resiliency to succeed, people choose to work together and speak with a collective voice to solve certain problems.

ethic of care This is a political theory that places the phenomenon of care at the centre of ethical reflection, guiding individuals and organizations to prioritize human relationships.

exclusion Exclusion is when individuals who are part of a disadvantaged or marginalized group are denied access to certain rights, opportunities, and resources that are normally available to others who are part of a majority group.

Questions to Consider

1. Of the legislative and policy changes noted in this chapter, which do you feel are most important in terms of advancing equity in public education? What changes at a provincial/territorial or school district level have you observed within your jurisdiction that support the move towards more inclusive educational practices?

_____

_____

_____

_____

_____

_____

2. Educational innovation is everywhere! What approaches, techniques, or practices have you observed that reduce barriers and enhance equitable participation for all students within the classroom?

_____

_____

_____

_____

_____

_____

3. Some universities in Canada offer post-degree teacher education that can be completed within a 12-month period. What are the drawbacks to shortened teacher education programs in terms of teacher knowledge, skill, and efficacy for inclusive educational practices? How can these be resolved without lengthening initial teacher preparation?

_____

_____

_____

_____

_____

4. How could teacher education programs model UDL and RTI in course work and field experiences?

_____

_____

_____

_____

_____

5. If you could create a totally new education system, what would it look like? Challenge yourself to not simply replicate current practices, such as special and general education, but to actually build something new. On what philosophy would you base this new education system?

_____

_____

_____

_____

_____

_____

Useful Websites

American Psychiatric Association—DSM
www.psychiatry.org/psychiatrists/practice/dsm

Inclusive Education Canada
www.inclusiveeducation.ca

Inclusion International
http://inclusion-international.org

International Journal of Inclusive Education
www.tandfonline.com/toc/tied20/current#.VqYmI3I0z4g

References

American Psychiatric Association. (2013). *Diagnostic and statistical manual of mental disorders* (5th ed.). Arlington, VA: American Psychiatric Publishing.

Anderson, J., & Boyle, C. (2015). Inclusive education in Australia: Rhetoric, reality and the road ahead. *Support for Learning, 30*(1), 4–22.

Avramidis, E., & Kalyva, E. (2007). The influence of teaching experience and professional development on Greek teachers' attitudes towards inclusion. *European Journal of Special Needs Education, 22*(4), 367–389.

Avramidis, E., & Norwich, B. (2002). Teachers' attitudes toward integration/inclusion: A review of the literature. *European Journal of Special Needs Education, 17*, 129–147.

Bennett, S., & Wynne, K. (2006). *Special education transformation: The report of the co-chair with the recommendations of the Working Table on Special Education.* Ottawa, ON: Ministry of Education.

Bergeron, G., & St-Vincent, L.-A. (2011). L'intégration scolaire au Québec: Regard exploratoire sur les défis de la formation à l'enseignement au primaire et préscolaire. *Éducation et Francophonie, 39*(2), 272–295.

Björn, P. M., Aro, M., Koponen, T. K., & Fuchs, L. (2016). The many faces of special education within RTI frameworks in the United States and Finland. *Learning Disabilities Quarterly, 39*(1), 58–66.

Chmiliar, L. (2009). Perspectives on inclusion: Students with LD, their parents, and their teachers. *Exceptionality Education International, 19*(1), 72–88.

Corbett, J., & Slee, R. (2000). An international conversation on inclusive education. In F. Armstrong, D. Armstrong and L. Barton (Eds.), *Inclusive education: Policy, contexts and comparative perspectives* (pp. 133–146). London, UK: David Fulton.

Council of Ontario Directors of Education. (2014). *Equity and inclusive education: Going deeper. A tool to support Ontario school boards in the implementation of equitable and inclusive education.* Retrieved from http://www.bced.gov.bc.ca/diversity/diversity_framework.pdf

Danforth, S., & Naraian, S. (2015). This new field of inclusive education: Beginning a dialogue on conceptual foundations. *Intellectual and Developmental Disabilities, 53*(1), 70–85.

Eva, A. L., & Walker, B. (2010). Leveling the playing field: Preparing teachers for equitable instruction in diverse, inclusive classrooms. *AILACTE Journal, 7*, 15–32.

Forlin, C., Earle, C., Loreman, T., & Sharma, U. (2011). The Sentiments, Attitudes, and Concerns about Inclusive Education – Revised (SACIE-R) scale for measuring pre-service teachers' perceptions about inclusion. *Exceptionality Education International, 21*(3), 50–65.

Friesen, J., Hickey, R., & Krauth, B. (2010). Disabled peers and academic achievement. *Education Finance and Policy, 5*(3), 317–348.

Graham, L. J., & Slee, R. (2008). An illusory interiority: Interrogating the discourse/s of inclusion. *Educational Philosophy and Theory, 40* (2), doi: 10.1111/j.1469-5812.2007.00331.x

Hasinoff, S., & Mandzuk, D. (2015). *Case studies in educational foundations: Canadian perspectives.* Don Mills, ON: Oxford University Press.

Krull, J., Wilbert, J., & Hennemann, T. (2014). The social and emotional situation of first graders with classroom behavior problems and classroom learning difficulties in inclusive classes. *Learning Disabilities: A Contemporary Journal, 12*(2), 169–190.

Kurth, J. A., Morningstar, M. E., & Kozleski, E. B. (2014). The persistence of highly restrictive special education placements for students with low-incidence disabilities. *Research and Practice for Person with Severe Disabilities, 39*(3), 227–239.

LePage, P., Courey, S., Fearn, E. J., Benson, V., Cook, E., Hartmann, L., & Nielsen, S. (2010). Curriculum recommendations for inclusive teacher education. *International Journal of Whole Schooling, 6*(2), 19–45.

Loreman, T., Forlin, C., Chambers, D., Sharma, U., & Deppeler, J. (2014). Conceptualising and measuring inclusive education. In *Measuring inclusive education: International perspectives on inclusive education, Vol. 3* (pp. 3–17). Bingley, UK: Emerald Group Publishing Ltd.

McCrimmon, A. W. (2015). Inclusive education in Canada: Issues in teacher preparation. *Intervention in School and Clinic, 50*(4), 234–237.

McLeskey, J., & Waldron, N. L. (2011). Educational programs for elementary students with learning disabilities: Can they be both effective and inclusive? *Learning Disabilities Practice, 26*(1), 48–57.

Mowat, J. G. (2010). Inclusion of pupils perceived as experiencing social and emotional behavioral difficulties (SEBD): Affordances and constraints. *International Journal of Inclusive Education, 14*(6), 631–648.

Organization for Economic Cooperation and Development (OECD) (2014). *Education at a glance 2014: Highlights.* Retrieved from http://dx.doi.org/10.1787/eag_highlights-2014-en

Ontario Ministry of Education. (2009). *Realizing the promise of diversity: Ontario's equity and inclusive education strategy.* Retrieved from http://www.edu.gov.on.ca.

Porter, G. L., & AuCoin, A. (2012). *Strengthening inclusion, strengthening schools.* Fredericton, NB: Department of Education and Early Childhood Development. Retrieved from http://www.gnb.ca/legis/business/currentsession/57/57-2/LegDocs/2/en/StrengtheningInclusion-e.pdf

Pratt, D. D. (2005). *Five perspectives on teaching in adult and higher education.* Malabar, FL: Krieger.

Schmitz, G. S., & Schwarzer, R. (2002). Individuelle und kollektive Selbstwirksamkeitserwartung von Lehrern. *Zeitschrift für Pädagogik, 44,* 28–53.

Sharma, U., Forlin, C., & Loreman, T. (2008). Impact of training on pre-service teachers' attitudes and concerns about inclusive education and sentiments about persons with disabilities. *Disability and Society, 23*(7), 773–785.

Silverman, S. K. (2010). What is diversity? An inquiry into preservice teacher beliefs. *American Educational Research Journal, 47*(2), 292–329.

Slee, R. (2004). Inclusive education: A framework for school reform. In V. Heung and M. Ainscow (Eds.), *Inclusive education: A framework for reform* (pp. 29–66). Hong Kong: Hong Kong Institute of Education.

Tschannen-Moran, M., Woolfolk Hoy, A., & Hoy, W. K. (1998). Teacher efficacy: Its meaning and measure. *Review of Educational Research, 68*(2), 202–248.

Urton, K., Wilbert, J., & Hennemann, T. (2014). Attitudes toward inclusion and self-efficacy of principals and teachers. *Learning Disabilities: A Contemporary Journal, 12*(2), 151–168.

Waitoller, F. R., & Artiles, A. J. (2013). A decade of professional development research for inclusive education: A critical review and notes for a research program. *Review of Educational Research, 83*(3), 319–356.

Waitoller, F. R. & Thorius, K. K. (2015). Playing hopscotch in inclusive education reform: examining promises and limitations of policy and practice in the US. *Support for Learning, 30*(1), 23–41.

Index

Note: Page numbers followed by "*f*", "*n*" or "*t*" indicate figure, note, or table, respectively.